INTERNATIONAL LINE DANCE FAVORITES

Judy Dygdon & Tony Conger

Illustrations by Tony Conger

With music by
Scooter Lee

Published by
Sigma Press, 1 South Oak Lane, Wilmslow, Cheshire, SK9 6AR, England.

British Library Cataloguing in Publication Data
A CIP record for this book is available from the British Library.

ISBN: 1-85058-696-9

Typesetting and Design: Sigma Press, Wilmslow, Cheshire.

Cover Design: The Agency, Wilmslow

Illustrations: Tony Conger

Printed by: MFP Design & Print

Music Copyright: We are pleased to acknowledge copyright in the five songs featured on the CD accompanying this book. All songs are by Scooter Lee (Lowery Music BMI/BMG); licensed from Southbound/Southern Tracks Records UK Ltd

Hi, Dancers!

Many times I have been asked why I don't put out a book of dances. After careful thought I came to the conclusion that I am a singer, writer and entertainer - not a dancer or an instructor. I felt I did not have the kind of knowledge or background to take on such a task.

I have also been asked in the past to promote other books by instructors but I just didn't feel there were any out there to lend my name to. Then this one came along and let me tell you, it's a dandy! The research that went into this book is incredible. The energy that went into putting it together and tearing it apart just to put it back together again to make it better was the same energy I put into writing and recording a album. At last, I have something to shout about!

For years we have needed a collection of some of the World's most popular dances. Though I am not a dancer myself, I have come to love those who are. I see many of the dances in this fabulous book done every night all over the world. It really is worthy of its title – *International Line Dance Favorites* is the essential line dance book for dancers wherever they dance!

Wherever you do your dancing and whatever your experience, here's your chance to learn some old dances and some new ones - and some that will live forever. Enjoy reading the history that is attached to line dancing and finally understand what all those words and steps mean. We want this wonderful sport to last for years and this book will make a difference for those who dance and those who want to dance. I have added a CD of some of my favorite songs so you can practice some of these dances and you know - practice does make perfect!

I'll see you somewhere on the dance floor!

Cheers

Scooter

Scooter Lee

Dances A-Z

Contents

LEVEL II DANCES

LEVEL III DANCES

LEVEL IV DANCES

The Free CD from Scooter Lee

At the back of this book there's a **Free CD** of great songs by Scooter Lee.
The tracks have been selected for a range of tempos,
expressed in Beats per Minute (bpm):
Old Friend: 100bpm
Can't Help It: 118bpm
Don't Walk Away: 158bpm
Moving On Up: 184bpm
Honey Hush: 128bpm

Introduction to
International Line Dance Favorites

Shortly after our second line dance book, *UK Line Dance Favourites*, was released in March of 1998, it became apparent to us that most of the dances it described, known to be favorites in the UK, were in fact favorites world-wide. For that reason, we decided to do something a bit unusual in publishing. We rearranged *UK Line Dance Favourites*, removing just a few dances and replacing them with dances whose popularity seems to be quite enduring. That was how this book was born. We feel we now can offer our readers instruction in today's most loved line dances. And, just like our first book, this one comes with a free CD, this time by Scooter Lee, *Linedancer Magazine's* International Solo Artist of the Year. We hope that having a CD handy will make it easier for you to practice these dances before you take them out to your local dance hall.

We have used a format in this book identical to the one we used in our first book, *Country and Western Line Dancing: Step-By-Step Instructions for Cowboys and Cowgirls*. If you used our first book to learn some dances, you will find this book very easy to use. If you haven't used our first book, please be sure to read carefully the chapters that precede the dances. They tell you what you need to know in order to follow our dance descriptions.

The terminology we use to describe dances is the same in this book as it was in our first. Choreographers are, by definition, creative people, however and some step combinations and foot placement locations are new to this book. If you come across a term with which you are not familiar, remember to check its definition in the Glossary included at the end of this book. Also, please review the foot placement chart included in "What You Need To Know About Your Feet" before you begin to work with the step descriptions.

If you are brand new to Country and Western line dancing, we recommend that you begin your instruction through our first book, and then follow up with this book. Both books will take you through their dances in a carefully graded fashion. However, the dances in this book were chosen because they are currently "hot", while the dances in our first book were chosen because they have become the "classics" of line dancing. Also, dances in our first book were chosen to provide our readers with a solid background in the different types of line dances (drill, contra, circle, etc.) that there are.

Lately, many line dances have been choreographed to non-country music. In the history of line dancing, this is not really an unusual event. There have been other periods (e.g., early days of rock and roll, the disco era) during which line dancing was done to non-country music. There is a style in which a dance is done that distinguishes a country-western line dance from any other type. You can read more about

this in "About Country-Western Dance Style". We alert you to dances that are choreographed to non-country music in the "About this Dance" section which introduces each dance. Dances done to non-country music include New Jack Swing, Strokin', and Electric Reel!

When we describe a dance, we suggest music to which that dance is particularly well suited. Because the music that is best for dancing is not always best for practicing a dance you do not yet know well, we offer different suggestions for music to which you might practice the dance. While you can practice a dance to any song of appropriate rhythm, for each dance we offer two suggestions for practice music – one from the Scooter Lee CD which is included with this book and one from the CD which is included with our first book. Scooter Lee's CD contains some slow and fast music: most of our practice recommendations are for slower tempo music, but you might want to try some of the dances to the faster music once you know them well.

Dancing is an important part of our lives and we continue to learn more about the technique and artistry of it with each passing year. Our line dancing has been active and we are always polishing up our partner round dances, two-stepping, and other lead and follow dances. The people who have taught us about dance have helped to shape our instructional style and our books and we are grateful for what they have given us. We would particularly like to acknowledge Cheryl and Norman Schnepf and Bob and Faith Brown for teaching us line and pattern dances, Cal and Kathy Walker (competition C/W dancers) who coach our two step and swing, and Monika Olejnik (a competition ballroom dancer) who is teaching us ballroom dance. (And for those of you who remember our story from Book 1: Yes, Tony can now Mambo and Rumba and Samba and Tango and more.)

We chose to include 52 dances in this book for a particular reason: tackling only one a week will give you a very sizeable repertoire in just one year! Also, the cows are back – sometimes to illustrate a tricky move, other times to help you smile as you work your way through the dances. Happy Dancing!

A Brief History of Country-Western Dancing

These days, as country-western dancing is gaining popularity across the world, it is not uncommon to hear people ask, "Where did this come from?" We are surprised to find that some people assume country-western dancing *started* with the release of an early 1980s movie, *Urban Cowboy*, or that it was a brainstorm of dancers who had tired of "disco". Neither frequently made assumption is warranted, as country-western dancing has been around, as a folk dancing form, for some considerable time.

Most cultures have some form of folk, or social, non-professionalized dance in their histories (e.g., English round and square dances which date back to Medieval times, German schottisches, Mexican fandangoes and danzas, and African juba dancing). Dance historians tell us that folk dancing blossoms in areas that are "cut-off" from professionalized dance. Given the geographic distances involved, and the speed with which information traveled, it is difficult to imagine an area more "cut-off" than the American West in the middle 1800s. It seems conditions were right for the development of a new folk dancing style, and the beginnings of country-western dancing, as we know it today, were formed.

The look of country-western dancing reminds many of other, older, folk dance forms. This, too, is not surprising when one considers the population of the American

West during this time. People from a wide variety of cultures (European – especially English, German, Irish, French, Spanish; North American – Mexican and Native American; and African), each with different folk dance histories, went into this mix. Country-western dancing, which looks a little bit like many, but not exactly like any, other folk dance style, is what came out.

In its early days, and continuing today, the country-western dance tradition is made up of four forms:

1. The line dances (drill, spoke, and contra), in which people dance singly, mostly in one place on the dance floor, executing identical, planned moves.

2. The round dances, in which people dance with partners around the floor, executing identical, planned moves.

3. The square dances, in which people dance in formations of 4 couples, executing identical moves chosen by a "caller";

4. The partnered "free style" dances of two step, polka, waltz and later, cha-cha and swing.

Country-western dancing is certainly enjoying a revival of interest these days. Many of the dances being done are old; more are very new. Line and round dances are being choreographed by dancers in the United States and in several other countries. Country-western dancing has certainly achieved trend status. The reasons for the trend are not entirely clear. Perhaps country-western dancing appeals to many because of the music to which it is danced. Perhaps it is popular because country-western dancing has now been professionalized: You can take lessons in it and there are competitions for dancers and choreographers (You can even read books about it!). Perhaps many people prefer country-western dancing because you can dance even if you don't have a partner. Whatever the reasons for the trend, country-western dancing was not born with the trend, and it will not die when the trend has run its course.

If you would like to learn more about the history of Country-Western dancing, we suggest you consult the following books:
Dance Across Texas by Betty Casey (University of Texas Press, 1985)
Kicker Dancin' Texas Style by Shirley Rushing and Patrick McMillan (Hunter Textbooks, 1988)

Before you Start to Dance

What you Need to Know about Music

Dances are choreographed to match the rhythm, or beats, in a piece of music. Before you try to learn dances, you must be able to hear the rhythm in music. You probably are already able to do that, but, if you are not, spending some time listening to music and trying to tap out its rhythm will be time well invested in your dancing future. Our dance descriptions are written in terms of the beats of music which a set of steps should match. It is the beats which signal you to move.

Some hints: the rhythm is usually expressed by a percussion instrument – a drum, for example. You will be able to detect repeating patterns of four evenly spaced beats (4/4 time, or variants of it) and repeating patterns of three evenly spaced beats (3/4 or waltz time). There are also patterns in which half beats are pronounced as in country cha-cha rhythms. In contrast to the *one, two, three, four*, of 4/4 time, in cha-cha patterns, you should be able to hear a percussion instrument on beats *one, two, three, and, four*.

Any dance can be done to many pieces of music of similar rhythm. In addition to rhythm, music varies in tempo, or speed (often described in "beats per minute" or "bpm"). Because it is easier to learn a dance doing it slowly, but more challenging to do a dance you know well, quickly, we suggest music for praticing and music for dancing. (When you first try a dance to faster music, you may find it easier if you take smaller steps). Our dancing music suggestions identify songs with which that dance works well, or for which it is particularly popular. Do not feel limited by our suggestions. Pay attention to the rhythm of each dance and enjoy trying it to other songs.

Most of the dances in this book will fit any music in 4/4 rhythm (or variants of 4/4 rhythm). However, 4/4 rhythm music varies in tempo (the speed with which the music is played) and the mood of the melody. In each dance description, we make suggestions for songs you might enjoy for each dance. We also present the rhythm line for the tempo to which the dance is most typically done. Keep in mind that you are always free to try a dance to any song of compatible rhythm. Some dances fit cha-cha rhythms better than basic 4/4 rhythms and two of the dances in this book are waltzes (3/4 rhythms). We point this out in our introductory material accompanying each dance.

Because much of the music you will hear when you dance these dances has four beats per measure, we have chosen to present steps in clusters of four. We believe this helps the dancer organize and remember the movements in a dance. Sometimes we deviate from this "cluster of four" rule. When we do that it is because we believe that, for a particular dance, an alternative organization will be better at helping you remember the steps.

What you Need to Know about Country-Western Dance Floor Etiquette

In country-western dance halls, line dancing, in which people typically dance singly and do not travel across much of the floor, is often accompanied by stationary or "slot" couples' dances (like swing) and couples' dances (pattern, two-step and polka) which move around the floor. In order to allow room for all three of these forms of country dancing, a few simple rules must be followed. Line dancing, unless otherwise dictated by house rules, is done in the center of the dance floor, allowing room for traveling couples' dances on the outside perimeter and "slot" couples' dances just inside the ring of dancers traveling the perimeter.

When you do line dancing, it is important to remember that part of the beauty of these dances is the regularity of the lines. When you join a dance on the floor, make sure you are: facing the same direction as the other dancers, positioned squarely behind the person in front of you, and that you continue a straight line with the people next to you. Often two or more different line dances will take place in the center of a dance floor. When this happens, each group must allow room for the pattern of the others.

If you are at a club with a disc jockey, the DJ may make suggestions for a dance to

Moove over, please

accompany the next song. If you know that dance, join in. Dances typically begin facing the bandstand and with the onset of lyrics. It pays to know your dance music, as your feet must be ready to move at the same time that the lyrics begin. Sometimes, someone very familiar with the song will "cue" the others on when to begin a dance, often by counting down "six, seven, eight". When you do any of the dances in this book, assume that the pattern should begin with the lyrics. We alert you to the rare dances for which this is not the case in the "About this dance" section of the dance descriptions.

What you Need to Know about Country-Western Dance Style

In traditional country-western dancing, foot movements (with the attached legs) are primary. Hip movements (rocks, bumps, swivels) and hand claps or boot slaps also come into play. Generally, the arms and hands (except when needed for a clap or slap) should be placed out of the way. For a woman, one hand can hold the other behind the back or one or both hands can be placed on the belt in front. Women are allowed some stylistic leeway in the use of arms and hands, but C&W dancin ain't no ballet! A man should put his hands on his belt or hook the thumbs in the belt or front pockets. This will help maintain that slightly detached air. "Cowboys" do not flail or dangle their arms — even when doing spins or turns. When you do not use your arms for momentum, spins and turns are much more challenging to do. This adds some legitimacy to those claims of the athletic skill required by country-western dancing!

Country-western line dances are done in one of several configurations on the dance floor. The most common configuration is what is known as parallel or drill lines. This means that each dancer positions him/herself on the dance floor so that the dancer is directly behind another dancer and directly alongside another dancer. Viewed from above, the dance floor should look like a perfect grid.

In taking your position on the dance floor for a drill line dance, look for a vacancy in the "grid", being sure to have space around you so that you are able to execute the moves of the dance without crowding anyone else. Remember also that on many country-western dance floors, some

Arm Position

𝒜 la seconde   A la belt

". . . Line Dancin' ain't no ballet! . . ."

dancers may choose to do partner pattern or freestyle dances instead of the line dance. These dancers use the outside of the dance floor and circle around it as they dance. When you choose your position in a line dance, make sure to leave that outside circle clear. When reading the dance descriptions in this book, you should assume that they are intended to be done in parallel, or drill, lines unless we tell you otherwise in the "About This Dance" section before each dance.

Some dances are designed to be done with dancers arranged in a circular pattern on the floor. Sometimes this arrangement is called "spoke line" to differentiate it from "parallel or drill lines". To dance in spoke lines, a small number of dancers form a circle in the center of the floor, with lines of other dancers forming behind each of the people in the original circle. An aerial view would reveal a pattern that looked liked the hub and spokes of a big wheel. In this type of circle formation, dancers face the backs of other dancers. Unlike line dances, some circle dances progress around the dance floor.

Some circle dances get a bit fancy. Instead of all dancers facing the center of the dance floor, circles alternate between facing the center and facing the outside of the dance floor. In this type of circle formation, dancers will be face-to-face with other dancers (at least until the music starts and one circle goes counter-clockwise and the other goes clockwise). When a circle formation is more appropriate, or an alternative, for a dance in this book, we inform you of that in the "About this dance" section.

Finally, some dances are designed to be done in contra lines. Contra lines are like drill lines in that dancers are arranged on the floor in sets of parallel lines. However, in drill line formation the dancers all face the same direction, while in contra line formation dancers are arranged so that pairs of lines face each other. In other words, there are two lines of dancers across from each other. The most interesting feature of contra dances is that, on the appropriate beats, the dancers pass between one another, ultimately turning to again face one another.

There are two different contra line formations: partner and staggered. These formations are shown in the diagram. The upper set of footprints depicts dancers standing in "partner contra lines" − lines in which dancers are directly opposite one another. Some contra dances have dancers in one line standing opposite an empty space between the dancers in

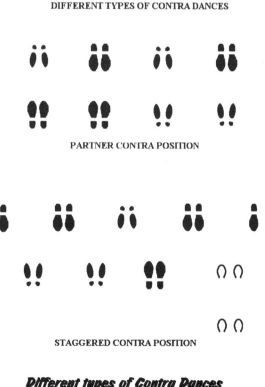

DIFFERENT TYPES OF CONTRA DANCES

PARTNER CONTRA POSITION

STAGGERED CONTRA POSITION

Different types of Contra Dances

the other line, or in "staggered contra lines". The lower set of footprints depicts dancers in "staggered contra lines". When you are doing a contra dance, whether in partnered or staggered lines, you should be about arm's length away from the line opposite you. This is generally referred to as "slapping distance" apart.

A word of warning: when you are first learning a contra dance, do not try to copy what the person across from you is doing, especially on the vines or other movements to the side! You will end up going in the wrong direction with an inevitable crash. If you are unsure of your footwork, copy a person to either side of you.

What you Need to Know about your Feet

The dance descriptions in this book will tell you *where* and *how* to place *what-part* of your foot. Please read the following before attempting to follow the dance descriptions.

What: Foot Parts

In the dance descriptions, you will sometimes see us refer to the toe, heel, instep and ball of the foot. When "toe", "heel", "instep" or "ball" is mentioned in the step line, it is important for styling that you execute the move using the part mentioned. When an instruction is given for "foot", you may do the motion as it is most comfortable for you.

How: Foot Orientations

Parallel: Indicates that one foot is held in essentially the same direction as the other foot. "Parallel" for you should be your comfortable standing position.

Turned Out: Indicates that the toe of one foot points diagonally away from the other. When the right foot is "turned out", its toe points diagonally right. When the left foot is "turned out", its toe points diagonally left.

Turned In: Indicates that the toe of one foot points diagonally toward the other foot. When the right foot is "turned in", its toe points diagonally left. When the left foot is "turned in", its toe points diagonally right.

TURNED IN   PARALLEL   TURNED OUT

Positions of Right Foot

When it is important for styling, we use *parallel*, *turned out*, and *turned in* to tell you how to hold your foot when making a particular move. We do not often tell you how to hold your foot. If no particular instruction is given, assume that the parallel orientation works best.

Where: Foot Locations

Home: Home describes a position in which your feet are directly under your body and are parallel to one another. For example, when you are instructed to move your right foot "home", you are to return it to a comfortable standing position under your right hip. When used in combinations, "home" refers to your location just before the combination began. ("Home" is sometimes used to refer to your starting position on the dance floor, but that definition will not be used in this book.)

Place: Sometimes you will be told to execute a foot action without changing the foot's location. In these cases, you will be told to do the action "in place". For example, if you are told to "step right foot in place" you are to put weight on your right foot, wherever it was after your preceding move.

Several other locations need to be defined before we can begin. We find that these other locations are best defined by the following diagram. This diagram provides you with the names of the locations to which your feet will be directed in step descriptions.

LOCATIONS FOR FOOT PLACEMENTS

Locations for foot placements

What you Need to Know about this Book's Organization

Country-western line dances are sequences of steps that form a pattern. Line dancing is done by repeating the pattern for the duration of a piece of music. The patterns range from those that consist of only a few, relatively simple steps, to very lengthy arrangements of intricate moves. As in anything else, if you are just beginning to learn line dancing, you will be more successful more quickly if you begin with the easier dances and move to the more difficult. For this reason we have organized the dance descriptions in this book according to their complexity. Within each category, the dances that appear early generally are made up of fewer and less complicated steps, or are designed to be done more slowly, than the dances that appear later. We have assigned a difficulty rating (from I to IV) to each of the dances in this book to communicate our judgment of its difficulty. The dances are presented, within each dance category, in ascending order of difficulty.

If you are new to dancing, we recommend that you try to learn the dances in the order in which they appear as mastering the earlier dances will prepare you to learn the later dances more easily. Preceding the step by step description for each dance is detailed instruction in how to do the steps and combinations that are used for the first time in that particular dance.

If you are not new to dancing, you may wish to learn these dances as they appeal to you. If you try to learn these dances in an order different from the sequence we have used, please remember to check the Glossary for detailed instruction on any step or combination that is new to you.

Many of the steps, or individual foot movements, that make up dances are used so frequently and in so many dances that they have special names. Also, individual steps can often be grouped into combinations, or sequences of steps that frequently recur and are used in a variety of dances. In other words, individual *steps* are put together in *combinations. Combinations* are put together in different ways to form dances. If you can learn to see dances, not as sequences of many steps, but as patterns of a few combinations, you will find dances easier to learn, and easier to remember. Ultimately, this ability should make it easier for you to learn new dances simply by watching someone do them.

We use great care in deciding on names for steps and combinations. When names are commonly used among country western dance choreographers and teachers, we make sure to use them. Often, steps and combinations are known by several different names, even within the country western line dance world. In these cases, we make sure to tell you all the names that we know a move to have. And, because country western line dancing is dancing, after all, we tell you about the names a particular move might have in other dance worlds like ballet, jazz, or ballroom. In other words, we have tried to prepare you to recognize a move by any name. Some of the books which we have found to be particularly useful for terminology are:

Jazz Dance Class: Beginning Through Advanced by Gus Giordano (Princeton Book Company, 1992)

The Language of Ballet: A Dictionary by Thalia Mara (Princeton Book Company, 1987)

Modern Ballroom Dancing by Victor Silvester (Trafalgar Square Publishing, 1993)

NTA Teaching Manual by the National Teachers Association for Country Western Dance (1994)

Understanding the Dance Pages

New Concepts, Steps, and Combinations

We open our presentation of each dance with detailed descriptions of the new steps, combinations, and other dance concepts found in that dance. The terms we use to identify individual foot movements and combinations are consistent with those recommended by the National Teachers' Association for Country Western Dance (NTA) and the British Western Dance Association (BWDA). Some terms used by country-western dance choreographers and teachers are not yet part of NTA's vocabulary: we have also included those terms. If you are learning the dances in order, you will be instructed in steps and combinations as you need them. If you prefer to learn dances in an order different from the one we have chosen, remember that you can always refer to the Glossary for detailed information on steps, combinations and dance concepts.

The Dance

Of course, most of the dance pages are devoted to the choreography: the step by step descriptions. However, other useful information is also provided. Before the step descriptions, we provide some basic information about the dance: difficulty level, choreographer, number of directions the dance faces, and the number of beats in the dance pattern. You will also find suggested music for practicing and dancing. In particular, note the references to the **free CD** which accompanies which accompanies this book and the free CD which accompanies Book 1. After the step descriptions, we have included three other tools we believe will be useful to you:

The Variations: Part of the fun of line dancing for many people is the challenge of mastering the specific steps and combinations. If you are one of these people, we attempt to add to your challenge and to your fun. Following several dance descriptions, we suggest "variations" for you to try after you have mastered the basic dance. A variation might be a new way to do a combination, perhaps by adding a turn, or a replacement set of more difficult steps. It isn't necessary for you to try the variations, but they are there for you to explore.

The Rhythm Line: The "rhythm line" summarizes the dancer's foot and hand movements with the rhythm and tempo of the music. Dance music tempo roughly can be categorized as slow, medium, medium/fast, and fast. In preparing rhythm lines we have chosen 90, 120, 150, 180 beats per minute to represent slow, medium, medium/fast, and fast tempos, respectively. For each dance, we display the beats and movements under a timeline which represents the tempo to which the dance is most often done.

The Cues: We also include a tool we call "cues". In this section we offer a "cue" or reminder for every step of the dance. Most often, these are simple, one syllable words. While you cannot learn a dance from the cues alone, once you have reviewed the steps of a dance, saying the cues to yourself as you practice should help you remember the steps. Also, the cues can be useful for a dance instructor to call aloud as a class practices a new dance.

Step Descriptions

We should like to explain a little about the format we have chosen for the presentation of each dance's steps. Under the heading "**Beat – Description**" you will see levels of information that look something like the following:

Beats	Description	
	Boot Hook And Swivels	<—— Section Line
1-4	Left boot hook combination	<—— Combination Line
	1 Touch **left** heel forward	<—— Step Line
	2 Hook **left** left across **right** leg	<—— Step Line
	3 Touch **left** heel forward	<—— Step Line
	4 Step **left** foot next to **right** foot	<—— Step Line
5	Swivel heels to left	<—— Step Line
6	Swivel heels to center	<—— Step Line

The Section Lines: We have included "section" labels to help you remember portions of the dance. Many dances can be easily divided into sections of similar movements. The "section" labels will not tell you in detail what to do, but they will help you remember what kinds of movements are coming next in the dance.

The Combination Lines: In contrast to the section label, "Combination Name" will tell you what to do and, once you have some experience in dancing, the combination name is probably all you will need to look at in order to execute the appropriate sequence of movements. You can tell when you are looking at a combination name because it is always preceded by a range of beats (for example, 1- 4, as above; 1 - &; 1 - 2; etc.). Combinations always consist of more than one movement so they are always associated with more than one point in time.

The Step Lines: If you are new to dancing, or when you encounter a combination name that is new to you, you will need to check the third level of information provided. This information is inset under the combination name and gives you step by step information on how to do a particular sequence of movements.

Dances also include a variety of specific steps that are not included in combinations. In these cases, the step lines appear as lines 5 and 6 appear in the sample above. Note that these lines are not inset.

In a step line, we adhere to a strict format for describing foot movements: action, foot, location. The first term you see will tell you what kind of movement or action is to be done. The second term tells you what foot is to do the movement. The third expression tells you the location where the foot will be placed.

In the individual step instructions, we always boldface "right", "left", and "both" when they are used to identify feet, so that you quickly can determine which foot is to move. We have tried to minimize confusion between feet and directions by showing the foot in boldface (for example, **left** foot) but showing directions in regular font (for example, turn left).

Most of the time, only one foot action is required for each beat of the dance pattern. Sometimes, two foot movements are required for a single beat of music. When this is the case, we connect the two instructions with "and". When you see this, know that you are to execute both movement simultaneously. To minimize confusion, we have adopted the following rule for beats involving two movements: we describe the first movement in our "Action, Foot, Location" format. If the second movement is done with the same foot as the first, the second movement is described by "Action, Location". If the second movement is done with a different foot from the first movement, it is described by "Action, Foot, Location".

When a body or hand motion, as opposed to a foot motion, is required for a particular beat of music, we put the direction at the end of the step line, separated from the rest of the step line by a comma.

By the way, don't be alarmed if the terms used in the sample (boot hook, touch, swivel, etc.) don't make sense to you now. In this book, you will be given clear instructions on how to make every movement as it is needed for a dance.

Level I

Birchwood Stroll

About this dance: U.S. Country-western Line Dancing has gained popularity all around the world. In fact, many dances have been choreographed by dancers outside the U.S. John and Janette Sandham, the choreographers of Birchwood Stroll, live in Britain. They choreographed Birchwood Stroll in 1993 when they taught line dancing at Fort San Antone near Blackpool, England. The dance is also known as San Antone and it remains a favorite around the world. We like the idea that the first dance in this book has its roots in Blackpool, England, a town that is known as a center for dance of a variety of styles.

New Concepts, Steps and Combinations

New Concepts

Hand Move- ments	Many dances include arm and hand movements as part of the pattern. Hand and arm movements may accompany foot movements or they may be the only activity choreographed for a sequence of beats. Commonly used arm and hand movements will be defined under "new steps" as they are introduced.
Turn	Indicates that the orientation of your body (direction or wall that you face) will change. There are different kinds of turns (pivot, military turn, etc.) and each will be defined as needed. Instructions to turn will specify a direction and amount of turn. Sometimes, dancers become confused with the direction specified for a turn. To turn left means to turn counterclockwise. One way to ensure that you are turning in the prescribed direction is to think of your shoulders. In a turn to the *left*, you will turn toward your left shoulder. Your *left shoulder will move backwards*, while your right shoulder moves forward. Similarly, in a turn to the *right*, you will turn toward your right shoulder. Your *right* shoulder will move backwards, while your left shoulder moves forward. The amount of turn may be given as fractions of a full circle ($\frac{1}{8}$, $\frac{1}{4}$, $\frac{1}{2}$, etc.) or in degrees (90 degrees, 180 degrees, etc.)

New Steps

Clap	Instructs you to clap your hands together, once, on the designated musical beat.
Kick	Instructs you to kick the specified foot about halfway between the floor and knee-height. Kicks are most often done forward, but the direction of the kick will be specified in the step instruction. In country-western dancing, kicks are done with the toes pointing up, as if to shake *something* off the boot.
Pivot	Instructs you to turn. The amount of the turn will be specified ($\frac{1}{4}$ or 90 degrees, $\frac{1}{2}$ or 180 degrees, etc.) as will the direction of the turn (right or left). Pivots are usually done on the ball of the designated foot (or

feet); however, on occasion a pivot is done on the heel of one foot and the ball of the other. Pivots are easier, if you "prepare" your pivoting foot by slightly pointing it in the direction of the turn before you step down to pivot.

For example, "pivot on **left** foot $\frac{1}{4}$ turn left" instructs you to turn 90 degrees left while your weight is supported by your left foot. You would begin this move by pointing your left foot diagonally left. The move is completed by pivoting the rest of the $\frac{1}{4}$ turn on the ball of your left foot.

If a pivot is done on both feet, pay attention to the subsequent step because, at the end of the turn, you will need to prepare for that move by supporting your weight on the leg opposite the leg that will move next. Consider, for example, a pivot on both feet in the following sequence of steps.:

1 Step **right** foot forward
2 Step **left** foot forward
3 Pivot on **both** feet $\frac{1}{4}$ turn right
4 Step **left** foot forward

In this sequence, the turn on beat 3 would be executed by supporting the weight of the body over both feet. During this turn the feet maintain their positions on the floor that were indicated last: The right foot maintains its position from beat 1 and the left foot maintains its position from beat 2. However, when the turn is completed, most of the weight of the body should be supported by the right foot so that the left foot can move easily on beat 4.

Step

Instructs you to position your foot at the identified location and to transfer all or most of your weight to that foot. The amount of weight transferred usually depends on the sequence of steps.

For example, "step **right** foot forward" instructs you to position your right foot ahead of your left (as though you were walking forward), with your weight supported on your right foot, leaving your left foot ready to move next.

Stomp

Instructs you to bring the identified foot down with force and with a weight transfer to the stomping foot. This will make a noise and, as with scuffs, stomp sounds are often used to accentuate the beats of the music. A "stomp" differs from a "stomp-up" in that in a "stomp" the stomping foot bears weight, but in a "stomp-up", it does not.

For example, "stomp **right** foot next to **left** foot" instructs you to bring your right foot down with force next to your left. Your right foot supports all or most of your weight after the stomp.

Stomp-up

Instructs you to bring the identified foot down with force, but without a weight transfer to the stomping foot. This will make a noise and, as with scuffs, stomp sounds are often used to accentuate the beats of the music. A "stomp" differs from a "stomp-up" in that in a "stomp" the stomping foot bears weight, but in a "stomp-up", it does not.

For example, "stomp-up **right** foot next to **left** foot" instructs you to bring your right foot down with force next to your left. Your left foot supports your weight during and after the stomp.

New Combinations

Heel Split   Instructs you to move your heels apart and then bring them back together in two beats of music. A heel split will begin from a position in which your feet are together and your weight is supported by both feet. On beat "1", move your heels apart. To execute this move, have your weight on the balls of your feet and move your right heel to the right and your left heel to the left. On beat "2", move your heels back together. Heel splits are also called: "butterflies", "buttermilks", "pigeon toes", and "scissors".

Vine   Instructs you to make a three step sideways movement to three beats of music. A vine will be described as either a right vine or left vine, indicating the direction of movement and the foot that moves first. On the first beat, the designated foot will move to the side. On the second beat, the other foot is crossed behind the first before it steps down. On the third beat, the foot that was first to move, moves again to the side.

For example, "right vine" instructs you to: step your right foot to the right, step your left foot behind your right, then step your right foot to the right.

When vines are used in 4/4 time music, a fourth, "finishing move" for the foot that is free to move after the vine is often specified with the vine. For example, you will see directions like "right vine with left scuff" or "left vine with right touch".

If the movement of a vine is not directly to the side, the direction of movement will be specified (for example, left vine diagonally back).

Vines are also referred to as "grapevines". Other dance descriptions may use "vine" or "grapevine" to describe combinations other than the one described above. That is, combinations that begin with a step other than the side step or combinations that include more than one cross step are called vines. To avoid confusion, we use other labels to refer to these less common vines (see, for example, "weave").

The Dance

Difficulty Level: I   **Choreographers:** John and Janette Sandham

Dance Faces: four directions   **Pattern Length:** 28 Beats

Suggested Music:

For practicing – "Don't Walk Away" by Scooter Lee (Track 3 on **Free CD**), "I'm So Miserable Without You" originally recorded by Billy Ray Cyrus (Track 7 on CD included with Book 1.)

For dancing – "San Antonio Stroll" by Tanya Tucker; "Achy Breaky Heart" by Billy Ray Cyrus, "This Is Where The Cowboy Rides Away" by George Strait; "Walk On" by Reba McEntyre, "Ribbon of Highway" by Scooter Lee

Beats	Description
	Heel Splits
1 - 2	Heel Split
	1 Move heels apart
	2 Return heels to center
3 - 4	Heel Split
	3 Move heels apart
	4 Return heels to center
	Walk Forward, Kick and Clap
5	Step **right** foot forward
6	Step **left** foot forward
7	Step **right** foot forward
8	Kick **left** foot forward and clap
	Walk Back and Stomp
9	Step **left** foot back
10	Step **right** foot back
11	Step **left** foot back
12	Stomp-up **right** foot next to **left** foot
	Vines with Kicks and Claps
13-16	Right vine with left kick and clap
	13 Step **right** foot to right side
	14 Step **left** foot behind **right** foot
	15 Step **right** foot to right side
	16 Kick **left** foot across **right** leg and clap
17-20	Left vine with right kick and clap
	17 Step **left** foot to left side
	18 Step **right** foot behind **left** foot
	19 Step **left** foot to left side
	20 Kick **right** foot across **left** leg and clap

Steps and Kicks and Claps

21	Step **right** foot to right side (step only slightly to right side)
22	Kick **left** foot across **right** leg and clap
23	Step **left** foot left side (step only slightly to left side)
24	Kick **right** foot across **left** leg and clap

Vine and Turn

25-28   Right vine with ¼ turn right and left stomp
          25   Step **right** foot to right side
          26   Step **left** foot behind **right** foot
          27   Step **right** foot to right side and pivot ¼ turn right
          28   Stomp **left** foot next to **right** foot

Repeat Pattern

Rhythm Line:

```
secs      .....1.....2.....3.....4.....5.....6.....7.....8.....9....10
120bpm    1  2  3  4  1  2  3  4  1  2  3  4  1  2  3  4  1  2  3  4
foot      B  B  B  B  R  L  R  L  L  R  L  R  R  L  R  L  L  R  L  R
other                       c                       c              c
                        (clap)

Secs      ....11....12....13....14....15....16....17....18....19....20
120bpm    1  2  3  4  1  2  3  4  1  2  3  4  1  2  3  4  1  2  3  4
Foot      R  L  L  R  R  L  R  L  repeat pattern
Other        c     c
```

Cues:

split / close / split / close
right / left / right / kick
back / back / back / stomp

right / behind / right / kick
left / behind / left / kick
right / kick / left / kick
right / behind / turn / stomp

Copperhead Road

About this dance: This dance has been around for some time and is also known as "Kentucky Jug". Like "Thunderfoot" in our first book, it is also a favorite when the band (or disc jockey) plays "Copperhead Road" by Steve Earle. On beats 9 and 10, the scoots and hitches (or scoots and kicks) may at first feel and look awkward, but with a small scoot (and some practice), a smoother look can be obtained.

New Concepts, Steps and Combinations

New Steps

Hitch
Instructs you to bend your knee and raise your leg. During a hitch, the thigh of the hitching leg should be almost parallel to the floor. The feet are almost always parallel to each other although, on occasion, a hitch across or to the side may be specified.

Hook
Instructs you to bend your knee, raise your leg, and cross it in front of or behind the weighted leg. The leg to be hooked and whether it crosses in front of or behind the weighted leg will be specified in the step description. The hooked leg crosses the weighted leg slightly below knee level with the shin nearly parallel to the floor. The foot of the hooked leg should be turned out. This movement is done in one beat of music. On occasion, a step description will instruct you to hook your leg to the side. In a hook to the side, the hooked leg will angle out to the side and the toe will point down.

For example, "hook **right** leg across **left** leg" instructs you to bend the knee of your right leg, lifting it off the floor, and to cross your right leg in front of your left leg. Your right foot should be turned out.

Scoot
Instructs you to make one movement in one beat of music. On a scoot, the weight of your body is supported by the identified foot and you take a small jump or hop in the indicated direction. This movement is subtle: you neither move very far nor come high off the floor.

Slap
Instructs you to slap your foot (or other identified body part). The instruction will identify the slapping hand and the body part. The left hand always slaps the left side of the designated parts and the right hand slaps the right side.

Touch
Instructs you to position your foot at the identified location without a weight transfer. Many dancers execute a touch by touching only with the toe of the boot.

For example, "touch **right** foot next to **left** foot" instructs you to bring your right foot next to your left and lightly touch the floor, leaving your right foot ready to move next.

AN EARLIER VERSION OF COPPERHEAD ROAD

The Dance

Difficulty Level: I   **Choreographer:** Steve Smith
Dance Faces: four directions   **Pattern Length:** 24 Beats
Suggested Music:

For practicing – "Can't Help It" by Scooter Lee (Track 2 on **Free CD**), "I Wanna Go Too Far" originally recorded by Trisha Yearwood (Track 4 on CD included with Book 1.)

For dancing – "Copperhead Road" by Steve Earle, "We Won't Dance" by Vince Gill, "Bubba Shot The Jukebox" by Mark Chestnutt, "Sticks and Stones" by Tracy Lawrence.

Beats	Description
	Touch and Step
1	Touch **right** heel forward
2	Step **right** foot next to **left** foot
3	Touch **left** toe behind **right** foot
4	Step **left** foot next to **right** foot
	Touch and Vine with Turn
5	Touch **right** toe behind **left** foot
6 - 8	Right vine with ¼ turn right
6	Step **right** foot to right side
7	Step **left** foot behind **right** foot
8	Step **right** foot to right side and pivot ¼ turn right
	Scoots
9	Hitch **left** foot and scoot **right** foot to left side
10	Hitch **left** foot and scoot **right** foot to left side
	Vines with Heel Slaps
11-14	Left vine with right hook and slap
11	Step **left** foot to left side
12	Step **right** foot behind **left** foot
13	Step **left** foot to left side
14	Hook **right** leg behind **left** leg and slap heel with left hand
15-18	Right vine with left hook and slap
15	Step **right** foot to right side
16	Step **left** foot behind **right** foot
17	Step **right** foot to right side
18	Hook **left** leg behind **right** leg and slap heel with right hand
	Walk Back with Scoot and Stomps
19	Step **left** foot back
20	Step **right** foot back
21	Step **left** foot forward
22	Hitch **right** leg and scoot **left** foot forward
23	Step **right** foot next to **left** foot
24	Stomp **left** foot in place

Repeat Pattern

Variation

One variation we learned involves a more complicated kick and scoot pattern in place of the hitch and scoot pattern on beats 9 and 10. That pattern also had a stomp on beat 23.

9   Kick **left** foot diagonally forward and scoot **right** foot forward
10   Kick **left** foot diagonally forward and scoot **right** foot forward

23   Stomp **right** foot next to **left** foot

Rhythm Line:

```
secs      .....1.....2.....3.....4.....5.....6.....7.....8.....9....10
120bpm    1  2  3  4  1  2  3  4  1  2  3  4  1  2  3  4  1  2  3  4
foot      R  R  L  L  R  R  L  R  B  B  L  R  L  R  R  L  R  L  L  R
other                                              s              s
                                             (slap)
secs      ....11....12....13....14....15....16....17....18....19....20
120bpm    1  2  3  4  1  2  3  4  1  2  3  4  1  2  3  4  1  2  3  4
foot      L  B  R  L  repeat pattern
other
```

Cues:

heel / together / toe / together
toe / right / behind / turn
scoot / scoot

left / behind / left / hook
right / behind / right / hook
back / back / left / scoot
step / stomp

Cowboy Macarena

About this dance: If you have been line dancing for any length of time, you probably have danced the Macarena (Macarena is described in our first book). And, if you have done the Macarena for any length of time, you have possibly tired of it. Well, Cowboy Macarena is a new and refreshing variation of that dance. Its pattern length is the same, but its hand movements are more reminiscent of the Wild West! They are a pantomime of a cowboy lassoing his quarry, drawing pistols, shooting, and holstering his weapons. We think you'll enjoy it.

George tells us that he choreographed these moves because he (too) had gotten a little tired of the Macarena. It was taught for the first time at his dance hall, "Bootscooter's" in Waterford, Pennsylvania on December 31, 1996. It has spread quickly to most places where line dancing is done. We saw a description of the dance on the internet, did it once at a local dance establishment, and there was an immediate demand for us to teach it!

New Concepts, Steps and Combinations

New Concepts

Latin-　　　"Latin-" is used as a prefix with a variety of steps and instructs you to sway your hips in the direction of the moving foot. Unlike the bump, which is sharp and pronounced, this sway is a fluid movement of the hips from one location to the next.

　　　　　　For example, "Latin-step **left** foot to left side" instructs you to step to the left, swaying your left hip to the left as you take the step.

New Steps

Jump　　　Instructs you to jump in the specified direction, lifting off from and landing on both feet. Jumps are done to one beat of music.

New Combinations

Hip Roll　　Instructs you to move your hips around your body in a specified number of beats. The direction (clockwise or counter-clockwise), extent of rotation (half-circle or full circle) and the starting position of the hips (e.g. left diagonal back) will be specified in the dance description. The hip roll is a continuous movement over the specified beats of music. The hips begin a hip roll by moving out from under the body in the direction specified and remain out from under the body until they reach the roll's end position. As with a hip bump, hip rolls are generally easier to execute if the weight is supported by both feet and the knees are bent slightly. Unlike the hip bump, which is completed at a single point in time, the hip roll will take more than one beat of music to complete.

For example, "beats 1-4   Full hip roll, counter-clockwise (begin left hip diagonally back)" instructs you to move your hips to the left diagonal back position (if they are not already there), push them to the right, then diagonally forward, and next, keeping the hips pushed out, circle them left and back until they reach their starting position.

Paddle Turn

Instructs you to make a turn while you alternate weight from your "anchor" foot (the foot in the direction of the turn) to your "paddle" foot. In a paddle turn you will make a series of small turns in order to complete a $\frac{1}{4}$, $\frac{1}{2}$, $\frac{3}{4}$ or full turn. Each small turn will involve stepping the "anchor" foot in place but toward the direction of the turn and stepping the "paddling" foot in the direction of the turn, about shoulder width from the anchor foot. The paddle turn has the look of a boat going around in a circle as it is paddled with one oar. The number of beats it will take to execute the turn, the total amount of the turn and the direction of the paddle turn will be specified in the dance description.

For example, "beats 1-4 $\frac{1}{4}$ Paddle turn to the left" instructs you to: on beat "1", step your left foot in place and pointed diagonally left, on beat "2", step your right foot parallel to your left foot about shoulder width apart (completing a $\frac{1}{8}$ turn to the left), on beat "3", step your left foot in place and diagonally left, and on beat "4", step your right foot parallel to your left about shoulder width apart (completing another $\frac{1}{8}$ turn to the left).

The Dance

Difficulty Level: I   **Choreographer:** George De Virgilio
Dance Faces: four directions   **Pattern Length:** 16 Beats
Suggested Music:

For practicing – "Honey Hush" by Scooter Lee (Track 5 on **Free CD**), "Talk Some" originally recorded by Billy Ray Cyrus (Track 3 on CD included with Book 1.)

For dancing – "Macarena" by Los Del Rio, "Country Macarena" by Groove Grass Boyz.

Beats	Description
	Lasso
1	Latin-step **left** foot in place; extend left arm forward (as though holding reins) and circle right arm counterclockwise above head (as though holding lasso)
2	Latin-step **right** foot in place; keep left arm forward (as though holding reins) and circle right arm counterclockwise above head (as though holding lasso)
3	Latin-step **left** foot in place; keep left arm forward (as though holding reins) and circle right arm counterclockwise above head (as though holding lasso)
4	Latin-step **right** foot in place; keep left arm forward (as though holding reins) and extend right arm forward (as though throwing the lasso)

Draw your Guns and Shoot

5　　　　Latin-step **left** foot in place and place right hand (shaped like pistol) on right hip

6　　　　Latin-step **right** foot in place and place left hand (shaped like pistol) on left hip

7　　　　Latin-step **left** foot in place and hold right hand out and in front of you at chest height, shooting the pistol (hand shaped like pistol)

8　　　　Latin-step **right** foot in place and hold left hand out and in front of you at chest height, shooting the pistol (hand shaped like pistol)

Blow out the Smoke and Holster your Guns

9　　　　Latin-step **left** foot in place and hold right hand (shaped like pistol) near mouth, blowing "smoke" away from "pistol"

10　　　Latin-step **right** foot in place and hold left hand (shaped like pistol) near mouth, blowing "smoke" away from "pistol"

11　　　Latin-step **left** foot in place and place right hand (shaped like pistol) on right hip

12　　　Latin-step **right** foot in place and place left hand (shaped like pistol) on left hip

Hip Rolls and Turn

13-14　　Full hip roll, counter clockwise (begin hips forward)

15　　　Half hip roll, counter clockwise (begin hips forward)

16　　　Jump, landing $\frac{1}{4}$ turn to left, and clap

Repeat Pattern

Variations:

Some dancers replace the hip rolls and jump with three Latin-steps in place (left, right, left) followed by a $\frac{1}{4}$ turn left while jumping forward and clapping. Others retain the original *salsa* look by doing a Latin-paddle turn on beats 13-16:

13-16　　$\frac{1}{4}$ Latin-paddle turn to the left

　　　　13　Latin-step **left** foot *(turned out)* in place, "pistols" remain on hips

　　　　14　Latin-step **right** foot next to **left** foot, "pistols" remain on hips

　　　　15　Latin-step **left** foot *(turned out)* in place, "pistols" remain on hips

　　　　16　Latin-step **right** foot next to **left** foot, "pistols" remain on hips

Rhythm Line:

```
secs    .....1.....2.....3.....4.....5.....6.....7.....8.....9....10
120bpm  1 2 3 4 1 2 3 4 1 2 3 4 1 2 3 4 1 2 3 4
foot    L R L R L R L R L R L R . . . B repeat pattern
other   h h h h h h h h h h h h h — hip — c
        (hand movements-right, left, ...)   (hip roll)(clap)
```

Cues:

rope / rope / rope / rope
holster / holster / shoot / shoot
smoke / smoke / holster / holster
hip/ roll / roll / jump

Ain't Goin' Down

About this dance: This is a relatively simple dance incorporating aspects of the "Freeze". However, it is often done to a fast tempo, making it a little more challenging. This dance illustrates a vexing problem in the country-western dance world. Recently, we came across another dance by this name, but it has entirely different steps. We are aware of many entirely different dances by the same name.

New Concepts, Steps and Combinations

New Steps

Brush

Instructs you to move the specified foot by gently dragging the ball of the foot across the floor. Brushes are most often done forward but the direction will be specified in the dance description. This movement is much like a "scuff" except that in a "scuff" the heel comes in contact with the floor (and makes considerable noise) whereas in a "brush", the ball of the foot is in contact with the floor (and produces much less noise). The brush involves no weight transfer.

For example, "brush **left** foot forward" instructs you to gently push the ball of the left foot forward across the floor. In "brush **left** foot forward" the right foot supports your weight during and after the brush.

Hold

This one is easy. "Hold" instructs you to maintain your position, or do nothing, for the designated beats of music.

Swivel toes

Instructs you to turn one or both toes in the direction specified (i.e., left, right or center). Movement is executed by supporting the weight on the heels of both feet and turning the toes approximately 45 degrees in the direction indicated. While your feet move in this step, your body continues to face forward. Note that a "swivel" is different from a "twist" in which your body would be allowed to move with your feet. Note, also, that toe swivels differ from heel swivels in which you move your heels while supporting your weight on your toes.

For example, "swivel toes to left"

THE "HOLD"

instructs you to put your body weight over the heels of both feet and turn your toes to the left. Note that when you complete this move, your toes will be pointed to the left. "Swivel toes to center" instructs you to return your toes to their starting position under your body.

New Combinations

Toe Fan   Instructs you to make two swivel movements of the identified foot in two beats of music. On "1", the toe swivels away from the stationary foot. On "2", the toe swivels to center.

For example, "right toe fan" instructs you, on "1", to swivel your right toe to the right, and on "2", to swivel your right toe to center.

The Dance

Difficulty Level: I

Dance Faces: four directions

Suggested Music:

Choreographer: Unknown

Pattern Length: 24 Beats

For practicing – "Don't Walk Away" by Scooter Lee (Track 3 on **Free CD**). "South's Gonna Do It" originally recorded by Charlie Daniels Band (Track 6 on CD included with Book 1.)

For dancing – "Ain't Goin' Down 'Til The Sun Comes Up" by Garth Brooks.

Beats	Description
	Toe Fans and Turn
1 - 2	Left toe fan
	1 Swivel **left** toe to left
	2 Swivel **left** toe to center
3 - 4	Left toe fan
	3 Swivel **left** toe to left
	4 Swivel **left** toe to center
5	Swivel **right** toe to right
6	Hold
7	Pivot on **right** foot ¼ turn right and step **left** foot across **right** foot as turn is completed
8	Hold
	Vines and Brushes
9 -12	Right vine with left brush
	9 Step **right** foot to right side
	10 Step **left** foot behind **right** foot
	11 Step **right** foot to right side
	12 Brush **left** foot forward

13-16	Left vine with right brush
	13 Step **left** foot to left side
	14 Step **right** foot behind **left** foot
	15 Step **left** foot to left side
	16 Brush **right** foot forward

Walk Back and Forward with Stomps

17	Step **right** foot back
18	Step **left** foot back
19	Step **right** foot back
20	Touch **left** toe back

21	Step **left** foot forward
22	Hitch **right** leg
23	Stomp **right** foot next to **left** foot
24	Stomp **left** foot in place

Repeat Pattern

Rhythm Line:

```
secs     .....1.....2.....3.....4.....5.....6.....7.....8.....9....10
180 bpm  1 2 3 4 1 2 3 4 1 2 3 4 1 2 3 4 1 2 3 4 1 2 3 4 1 2 3 4 1 2
foot     L L L L R . B . R L R L L R L R R L R L L L R R L  repeat pattern
other
```

Cues:

left toe / center / toe / center
right toe / hold / turn / hold
right / behind / right / brush
left / behind / left / brush

back / back / back / touch
left / hitch / stomp / stomp

Cowboy Cha-Cha

About this dance: Like Waltz Across Texas in our first book, Cowboy Cha-Cha is one of a few line dances that can also be done as a partner dance. Another very popular partner dance is sometimes called Cowboy Cha-Cha and sometimes called Travelling Cowboy Cha-Cha. That one is not a line dance, but an eighty-beat (100 step) round dance, in which pairs move around the perimeter of the dance floor.

New Concepts, Steps and Combinations

New Concepts

Half-beat   Most dance steps are choreographed to match full beats of music. On occasion, steps are choreographed also for half-beats. Moving on half versus full beats makes a big difference in the overall look of a dance. In this book, when a dance requires a movement on a half-beat, that half-beat is labelled with the symbol "&" placed between full beats: "&" should be read as "and".

New Steps

Rock   Instructs you to move your body in the direction specified, over the foot that is in that location. The instruction, "rock", refers to movement of the body, and not the feet. If the dancer needs to move the foot in order to execute the body movement, the term "rock-step" is used. A rock is easier to execute if the knees are bent slightly.
For example, "rock forward on **right** foot" instructs you to move, or lean, your body forward, over your right foot.

Rock-step   Instructs you to step in the direction specified but, unlike a simple "step", it requires you to lean your body in the direction of the step. If the dancer does not need to move the foot in order to execute the body movement, the term "rock" is used. A rock-step is easier to execute if the knees are bent slightly.
For example, "rock-step **left** foot back" instructs you to step back on your left foot and lean your body slightly back, over your left foot, as you take this step.

New Combinations

Cha-Cha   Instructs you to take three small steps to two beats of music. The foot which leads the combination, as well as the direction (right, left, forward, back, in place, etc.), will be specified in the dance description.
For example, "right cha-cha forward" instructs you to: On "1", step forward on your right foot; On "&", step forward on your left foot; On "2", step forward on your right foot.

A cha-cha is much like a shuffle: both have three steps to a two beat, syncopated rhythm. However, in a cha-cha forward or back the three steps are all the same size, whereas, in a shuffle forward or back the second step is shorter than the first and third. Because there is no travelling in a "shuffle in place" or "cha-cha in place", the "in place" versions of these combinations look identical.

The Dance

Difficulty Level: I   **Choreographer:** Unknown

Dance Faces: four directions   **Pattern Length:** 16 Beats

Suggested Music:

For practicing – "Can't Help It" by Scooter Lee (Track 2 on **Free CD**)."Gulf of Mexico" originally recorded by Clint Black (Track 12 on CD included with Book 1.)

For dancing – "Shadows In The Night" by Scooter Lee, "Traces" by Scooter Lee, "Gulf of Mexico" by Clint Black; "Neon Moon" by Brooks and Dunn.

Beats	Description
	Rocks and Cha-Cha
1	Rock-step **left** foot forward
2	Rock back on **right** foot
3 - 4	Left cha-cha in place
	3 Step **left** foot next to **right** foot
	& Step **right** foot in place
	4 Step **left** foot in place
	Rocks and Cha-Chas with Turns
5	Rock-step **right** foot back
6	Rock forward on **left** foot
7 - 8	Right cha-cha with ½ turn right
	7 Step **right** foot next to **left** foot and pivot ¼ turn right
	& Step **left** foot next to **right** foot and pivot ¼ turn right
	8 Step **right** foot next to **left** foot
9	Rock-step **left** foot back
10	Rock forward on **right** foot
11-12	Left cha-cha with ½ turn left
	11 Step **left** foot next to **right** foot and pivot ¼ turn left
	& Step **right** foot next to **left** foot and pivot ¼ turn left
	12 Step **left** foot next to **right** foot
	Rocks and Cha-Cha
13	Rock-step **right** foot back
14	Rock forward on **left** foot and pivot ¼ turn left
15-16	Right cha-cha in place
	15 Step **right** foot next to **left** foot
	& Step **left** foot in place
	16 Step **right** foot in place

Repeat Pattern

Rhythm Line:

```
secs    .....1.....2.....3.....4.....5.....6.....7.....8.....9....10
90bpm    1   2   3 & 4   1   2   3 & 4   1   2   3 & 4   1   2   3
foot     L   R   L R L   R   L   R L R   L   R   L R L   R   L   R


secs    ....11....12....13....14....15....16....17....18....19....20
90bpm    & 4   1   2   3   4   1   2   3   4   1   2   3   4   1   2
foot     L R   repeat pattern
```

Cues:

rock forward / back / cha - cha - cha
rock back / forward / turn - turn - cha
rock back / forward / turn - turn - cha
rock back / turn / cha - cha - cha

Strokin'

About this dance: This dance seems to have been around for a long time, and in other than country-western dance halls. This, we believe, is the most popular version of Strokin' and is always done when the DJ plays "Strokin'" by Clarence Carter. We have seen dances named "Strokin" that are quite different from this one. Oh, well, different strokes for different folks.

New Concepts, Steps and Combinations

New Concepts

Slow
Instructs you to perform the designated step over two beats of music rather than one. For example, "slow touch **right** heel forward" instructs you to use two beats of music to touch your right heel to the floor. Initially, the slow move may feel clumsy and seem difficult to do. Most steps are choreographed to match one beat of music. Although not used in this book, a step done to one beat of music is often called a "quick" step. It is in contrast to the name "quick" that steps done to two beats of music are called "slow". Steps done on half-beats of music are often called "syncopated".

New Steps

Bump
Gives you an instruction for hip movement independent of foot movement. Bump instructs you to move your hips, once, on the designated musical beat. The hip that moves out (right or left) and the direction of the bump (e.g., forward, backward) will be specified in the dance description. In a bump, your weight is supported by both feet. Bumps generally are easier to execute if the knees are bent slightly.
For example, "bump **right** hip to the right" instructs you to move your right hip to the right on the beat of music.
The expression "Bump **both** hips forward" is sometimes called a "pelvic thrust".

Draw
Instructs you to slide the identified foot for a designated number of beats. The action is continuous, but slow. This move produces a look of the foot being pulled from one position to the next. At the conclusion of a draw, most or all of the body weight is supported by the drawn foot. A draw is similar in movement to a slide: they differ only in that a slide is completed in one beat of music. Note that a draw is different from a draw-up. In a draw, the sliding foot bears weight; in a draw-up, it does not.
For example, "beats 1-3 Draw **left** foot next to **right** foot" specifies a three beat draw of the left foot. On beat "1", you would begin to slide your left foot toward your right, and you would continue this motion through beat "2". On beat "3", the draw is completed with most or all of your weight transferred to your left foot.

Draw-up
Instructs you to slide the identified foot for a designated number of beats. The action is continuous, but slow. This move produces a look

of the foot being pulled from one position to the next. When a draw-up is completed, the drawn foot is touching the floor but bears no weight. A draw-up is similar in movement to a slide-up: they differ only in that a slide-up is completed in one beat of music. Note that a draw is different from a draw-up. In a draw, the sliding foot bears weight; in a draw-up, it does not.

For example, "beats 1-3 Draw-up **left** foot next to **right** foot" specifies a three beat draw-up of the left foot. On beat "1", you would begin to slide your left foot toward your right, and you would continue this motion through beat "2". On beat "3", the draw is completed with the left foot touching the floor next to the right foot.

Shimmy
Describes an upper body movement in which the shoulders alternately are moved forward and backward in syncopated rhythm (i.e. on beats and half-beats).

For example, "beats 1-4 Shimmy shoulders" tells you to: on beat "1", move your right shoulder forward (left goes back), on "&4" move your left shoulder forward; on beat "2", move your right shoulder forward, on "&" move left shoulder forward, and so on.

Dance descriptions may call for shimmies with or without foot movements. Some individuals, particularly men, inadvertently do hip wiggles instead of shimmies, and these hip movements may interfere with foot movements. Thus, alternatives to shimmies, which do not interfere with foot movements, may be offered as "variations".

Slide
Instructs you to move the designated foot while keeping it lightly in contact with the floor. This move produces a look of the foot being pulled from one position to the next. When a slide is completed, all or most of the weight is on the sliding foot. Note that a slide is different from a slide-up. In a slide, the sliding foot bears weight; in a slide-up, it does not.

For example, "slide **right** foot next to **left** foot" instructs you to move your right foot from its last position to a position next to your left foot, keeping your right foot lightly in contact with the floor. As you finish the move, put all or most of your weight on the right foot.

New Combinations

Military Turn
Instructs you to make a 180 degree ($\frac{1}{2}$) turn in two beats of music. The direction of the turn (right or left) will always be specified. On beat one, the foot opposite the direction of the turn steps forward. On beat two, the body makes a half turn in the direction specified, pivoting on the balls of both feet. A "military turn" includes only one instruction for a change of foot location: at the close of a military turn the dancer will be standing with one foot in front of the other with weight supported by both feet and either foot is ready to move next.

For example, "military turn to the left" instructs you to, on beat "1", step forward on your right foot and, on beat "2", pivot $\frac{1}{2}$ turn left on the balls of both feet. At the close of a "military turn to the left" the dancer will be standing with feet separated and with the right foot behind the left.

The Dance

Difficulty Level: I   **Choreographer:** Unknown

Dance Faces: one direction   **Pattern Length:** 28 Beats

Suggested Music:

For practicing – "Honey Hush" by Scooter Lee (Track 5 on **Free CD**). "Talk Some" originally recorded by Billy Ray Cyrus (Track 3 on CD included with Book 1.)

For dancing – "Strokin'" by Clarence Carter.

Beats	Description
	Rock Steps
1	Rock-step **right** foot across **left** foot
2	Rock back on **left** foot
3	Rock-step **right** foot behind **left** foot
4	Rock forward on **left** foot
5	Rock-step **right** foot across **left** foot
6	Rock back on **left** foot
7	Rock-step **right** foot behind **left** foot
8	Rock forward on **left** foot
	Turns
9-10	Military turn to the left
9	Step **right** foot forward
10	Pivot on **both** feet ½ turn left
11-12	Military turn to the left
11	Step **right** foot forward
12	Pivot on **both** feet ½ turn left
13	Step **right** foot forward
14	Pivot on **both** feet ¼ turn left
	Slides and Draws with Shimmies and Claps
15	Slide **left** foot next to **right** foot
16	Stomp-up **right** foot and clap
17-18	Slow-step **right** foot to right side (bending knees, step as far to the right as you can)
19-20	Draw-up **left** foot next to **right** foot while shimmying shoulders and clap on beat 20
21-22	Slow-step **left** foot to left side (bending knees, step as far to the left as you can)
23-24	Draw **right** foot next to **left** foot while shimmying shoulders and clap on beat 24

| 25-26 | Slow-step **left** foot to left side (bending knees, step as far to the left as you can) |
| 27-28 | Draw-up **right** foot next to **left** foot while shimmying shoulders and clap on beat 28 |

Repeat Pattern

Variations

On beats 19-20, 23-24, and 27-28, some dancers (especially men) prefer to do forward hip bumps (pelvic thrusts) instead of shimmies. For example:

| 19-20 | Draw-up **left** foot next to **right** foot and, on beat 20, bump **both** hips forward and clap |

Rhythm Line:

```
secs     .... 1.....2.....3.....4.....5.....6.....7.....8.....9....10
120bpm   1  2  3  4  1  2  3  4  1  2  3  4  1  2  3  4  1  2  3  4
foot     R  L  R  L  R  L  R  L  R  B  R  B  R  B  L  R  - R-  - L-
other                                                  c        - sc
                                                     (clap)  (shimmy and clap)

secs     ....11....12....13....14....15....16....17....18....19....20
120bpm   1  2  3  4  1  2  3  4  1  2  3  4  1  2  3  4  1  2  3  4
foot     - L-   - R-   - L-   - R-   repeat pattern
other          - s c  - s c
```

Cues:

rock right / back/ behind/ forward
rock right / back/ behind/ forward
step/ turn/ step/ turn

step/ turn/ slide/ stomp
slow/ right/ draw/ left
slow/ left/ draw/ right
slow/ left/ draw/ right

Haych Haych

About this dance: Haych Haych was choreographed by Rob Fowler. Rob is from London, England and is one of a small group of choreographers who excel at writing line dances for individual dancers as well as partner line and round dances. He won UK Line dancer Magazine's UK Choreographer and UK Instructor of the Year awards for 1997.

New Concepts, Steps and Combinations

New Combinations

Shuffle   Instructs you to make three steps, in a specified order, to two beats of music. The direction of the shuffle (forward, backward, or to the side) and the foot that begins, or leads, the shuffle, will be specified in the dance description. On the first beat of music in a shuffle, the leading foot steps in the direction specified. On the half beat, the following foot steps next to the heel of the leading foot. On the second beat of music, the leading foot again steps in the specified direction. In a shuffle, feet are gently dragged or barely lifted from position to position.

For example, "right shuffle forward" instructs you to step forward on your right foot, step your left foot next to your right foot, and step forward on your right foot, to a rhythm of "one-and-two".

A shuffle is different from a cha-cha. Like a shuffle, the cha-cha includes three steps to two beats of music; however, in a shuffle forward or back, the second step does not move beyond the lead foot while in a cha cha the three steps are equally long. Sometimes a shuffle is called a triple step.

The Dance

Difficulty Level: I   **Choreographer:** Rob Fowler

Dance Faces: four directions   **Pattern Length:** 24 beats

Suggested Music:

For practicing – "Honey Hush" by Scooter Lee (Track 5 on your *Free CD*, "I'm So Miserable Without You" originally recorded by Billy Ray Cyrus (Track 7 on CD included with Book 1).

For dancing – "Honey Hush" by Scooter Lee

Beats	Description
	Rock an "X"
1	Rock-step **right** foot diagonally forward
2	Rock back on **left** foot
&	Step **right** foot next to **left** foot
3	Rock-step **left** foot diagonally back
4	Rock forward on **right** foot
&	Touch **left** foot next to **right** foot
5	Rock-step **left** foot diagonally forward
6	Rock back on **right** foot
&	Step **left** foot next to **right** foot
7	Rock-step **right** foot diagonally back
8	Rock forward on **left** foot
	Pelvic Thrusts
9	Stomp **right foot** forward and bump **both** hips forward
&	Bump **both** hips back
10	Bump **both** hips forward
&	Bump **both** hips back
11	Bump **both** hips forward
&	Bump **both** hips back
12	Bump **both** hips forward
	Turns and Shuffles
13-14	Military turn to the right
	13 Step **left** foot forward
	14 Pivot on **both** feet ½ turn right
15-16	Left shuffle forward with ½ turn right
	15 Step **left** foot forward
	& Pivot on **left** foot ½ turn right and step **right** foot next to **left** foot (as turn is completed)
	16 Step **left** foot back

17	Step **right** foot back
18	Rock forward on **left** foot
19-20	Right shuffle forward

    19   Step **right** foot forward
    &   Step **left** foot next to **right** foot
    20   Step **right** foot forward

21-22	Military turn to the right

    21   Step **left** foot forward
    22   Pivot on **both** feet ½ turn right

23-24	Left shuffle to side with ¼ turn right

    23   Pivot on **right** foot ¼ turn right and step **left** foot to left side (as turn is completed)
    &   Step **right** foot next to **left** foot
    24   Step **left** foot to left side

Repeat Pattern

Rhythm Line:

```
secs      .......1.......2.......3.......4.......5.......6.......7....
120bpm    1   2 & 3   4 & 1   2 & 3   4   1 & 2 & 3 & 4   1   2   3
foot      R   L R L   R L L   R L R   L   R . . . . .     L   B   L
other                                     b b b b b b b
                                          (hip bumps)

secs      ...8.......9......10......11......12......13......14......15
120bpm    & 4   1   2   3 & 4   1   2   3 & 4   repeat pattern
foot      B L   R   L   R L R   L   B   B R L
```

Cues:

forward / back - and - back / forward - close
forward / back - and - back / forward

forward bump - and - bump - and - bump - and - bump
left / turn / left - turn - back

back / forward / right - and - right
left / turn / turn - and - side

Twist-em

About this dance: Jo Thompson's name appears as a choreographer for several of our dances. On this dance, she recommends that you do the "twist" anyway you want on the first 8 beats. She suggests a Supremes singing group style for the forearm swings.

Jo Thompson, the choreographer of Twist-Em, grew up with country-western dancing. In her family, square and round dancing were routine. She has been teaching line and partner dancing for 16 years and is a 1997 Feather Award nominee for best female Country Western teacher. She is also UK Linedancer Magazine's "International Instructor of the Year" for 1997.

New Concepts, Steps and Combinations

New Concepts

Face   Instructs you to change, temporarily, the orientation of your body. Face is used with foot directions to add body styling, but it does not change your reference point or wall. "Face" is different from "turn" in that "face" directs body orientation only for the beat(s) on which it appears, "turn" results in a permanent change of body orientation and a new reference point or wall.

New Steps

Twist   Instructs you to turn your body without lifting your feet from the floor. The direction of the twist will be specified. Generally, twists are rather small moves and "twist right" or "twist left" instructs you to move about 45 degrees in the specified direction. Occasionally, a bigger movement will be required. In these cases, the dance description will contain more precise information, such as "twist $\frac{1}{4}$ turn right". Often, after a series of twists, "twist center" will instruct you to return your body to a forward facing position. Twists are easier to execute if the knees are bent slightly and the weight is over the balls of the feet, not the heels.

For example, "twist left" instructs you to turn your body diagonally left by supporting your weight on the balls of your feet and moving your heels to the right.

The Dance

Difficulty Level: I   **Choreographer:** Jo Thompson

Dance Faces: four directions   **Pattern Length:** 32 Beats

Suggested Music:

For practicing – "Don't Walk Away" by Scooter Lee (Track 3 on **Free CD**), "I Wanna Go Too Far" – originally recorded by Trisha Yearwood (Track 4 on the CD with Book 1).

For dancing – "The Twist" by Ronnie McDowell, "Twistin' The Night Away" by Scooter Lee.

Beats	Description
	Twists
1	Twist right
2	Twist left
3	Twist right
4	Twist left
5	Twist right
6	Twist left
7	Twist right
8	Twist left
	Steps and Kicks
9	Step **right** foot to right side
10	Kick **left** foot across **right** leg
11	Step **left** foot to left side
12	Kick **right** foot across **left** leg
13	Step **right** foot to right side
14	Kick **left** foot across **right** leg
15	Step **left** foot to left side
16	Kick **right** foot across **left** leg
	Side Steps and Forearm Swings
	(On forearm swings, upper arms are at sides, elbows are bent with forearms forward, parallel to the floor, hands lightly closed)
17	Step **right** foot to right side, face diagonally right and swing forearms to right
18	Step **left** foot next to **right** foot, face forward and swing forearms to center
19	Step **right** foot to right side, face diagonally right and swing forearms to right
20	Jump forward and clap, face forward

21	Step **left** foot to left side, face diagonally left and swing forearms to left
22	Step **right** foot next to **left** foot, face forward and swing forearms to center
23	Step **left** foot next to **right** foot, face diagonally left and swing forearms to left
24	Jump forward and clap, face forward

Turns, Holds and Scoots

25	Stomp **right** foot to right side and pivot $\frac{1}{4}$ turn right
26	Hold
27	Pivot on **right** foot $\frac{1}{2}$ turn left and stomp **left** foot forward (as turn is completed)
28	Hold
29	Scoot **both** feet forward, landing with feet together
30	Scoot **both** feet forward
31	Clap
32	Clap

Repeat Pattern

Variation:

29	Stomp **right** foot forward
30	Stomp **left** foot next to **right** foot

Rhythm Line:

```
secs      .....1.....2.....3.....4.....5.....6.....7.....8.....9....10
120bpm    1  2  3  4  1  2  3  4  1  2  3  4  1  2  3  4  1  2  3  4
foot      .  .  .  .  .  .  .  .  R  L  L  R  R  L  L  R  R  L  R  B
other     t  t  t  t  t  t  t  t                                   c
          (twist)                                            (clap)


secs      ....11....12....13....14....15....16....17....18....19....20
120bpm    1  2  3  4  1  2  3  4  1  2  3  4  1  2  3  4  1  2  3  4
foot      L  R  L  B  R  .  B  .  B  B  .  .  Repeat pattern
other        .  c                 c  c
```

Cues:

twist right / left / right / left
twist right / left / right / left
side / kick / side / kick
side / kick / side / kick

right / together / right / jump
Left / together / left / jump
turn / hold / turn / hold
scoot / scoot / clap / clap

Rita's Waltz

About this dance: This is another dance choreographed by Jo Thompson. She created it in 1997 for her mother, Rita. Like Waltz Across Texas in our first book, Rita's Waltz can be danced by individual dancers or partnered dancers in parallel/drill lines so it is very good at getting everyone out on the dance floor. When done as a line dance, Jo suggests holding hands with the dancer on either side of you, letting go at the turn, and rejoining hands after it.

New Concepts, Steps and Combinations

New Concepts

Waltz Rhythm

Waltzes are done to music played in 3/4 rhythm. Waltz music is counted 1 - 2 - 3, 1 - 2 - 3 with a stress on the "1". In country western dancing, waltz dance steps are traditionally counted in two groups of three beats (1 - 2 - 3, 4 - 5 - 6). With some exceptions, your feet will alternate left - right - left, right - left - right, making it easy to remember which foot moves next: The one different from the one you just moved!

In dancing a waltz, it is important to remember that these dances are distinguished not only by the type of music to which the dance is done, but by the style with which the steps are taken. Waltzing is characterized by a subtle accent or emphasis placed on the step to the first beat of each three beat sequence. The accent involves a "fall" on the first beat, followed by a "rise" on beats 2 and 3. In line dancing, the look of falling and rising is acheived by making the first step in each three step unit relatively long, while the second and third steps in each three step unit are relatively short, and/or taken on the toes of the feet.

New Combinations

Spiral

Instructs you to make a three step movement to three beats of music. Spirals also involve facing specific directions on each step. A spiral will be described as either a right spiral or left spiral, indicating the foot that moves first. On the first beat, the designated foot will step across the other as you face diagonally in the direction of movement. On the second beat, the other foot steps to the side (this is usually a small step) and you face diagonally in the other direction. On the third beat, facing the same direction as on the second beat, the foot that was first to move steps in place.

For example, "left spiral" instructs you to: 1) step your left foot across your right foot as you face diagonally right, 2) step your right foot to the right side and face diagonally left, 3) step your left foot in place and continue to face diagonally left.

Spirals often appear in a series, alternating left and right (or right and left). In such a series of movements it is easy to see the s-shaped motion underlying the name.

Spirals are different from twinkles in that in a spiral, the three steps are taken in different locations on the floor but in a twinkle all three steps are taken at the same point on the floor. Both a spiral and a twinkle involve a change in the orientation of your body, but in spirals the change is always small and temporary while in twinkles the change is more variable.

The Dance

Difficulty Level: I   **Choreographer:** Jo Thompson

Dance Faces: 4 walls   **Pattern Length:** 24 Beats

Suggested Music:

For practicing – "Old Friend" by Scooter Lee (Track 1 on your **Free CD**), "You Got Me Over A Heartache Tonight" originally recorded by Dolly Parton (Track 10 on CD included with Book 1)

For dancing – "The Christmas Card" by Scooter Lee, "Tucson Too Soon" by Tracy Byrd, and "Fields of Forever" by Rick Tippe

Beats	Description
	Forward and Back
1	Step **left** foot forward
2	Step **right** foot next to **left** foot
3	Step **left** foot in place
4	Step **right** foot back
5	Step **left** foot next to **right** foot
6	Step **right** foot in place
7	Step **left** foot forward
8	Step **right** foot next to **left** foot
9	Step **left** foot in place
10	Step **right** foot back
11	Step **left** foot next to **right** foot
12	Step **right** foot in place
	Spirals and Turns
13-15	Left spiral
13	Step **left** foot across **right** foot (face diagonally right)
14	Step **right** foot to right side (face diagonally left)
15	Step **left** foot in place (face diagonally left)

16-18	Right spiral
	16 Step **right** foot across **left** foot (face diagonally left)
	17 Step **left** foot to left side (face diagonally right)
	18 Step **right** foot in place (face diagonally right)
19-21	Left spiral
	19 Step **left** foot across **right** foot (face diagonally right)
	20 Step **right** foot to right side (face diagonally left)
	21 Step **left** foot in place (face diagonally left)
22	Step **right** foot across **left** foot (face forward)
23	Pivot on **right** foot 1/4 turn right and step **left** foot back (as turn is completed)
24	Pivot on **left** foot ½ turn right and step **right** foot forward (as turn is completed)

Repeat Pattern

Rhythm Line:

```
secs      .....1.....2.....3.....4.....5.....6.....7.....8.....9....10
90bpm      1    2    3    1    2    3    1    2    3    1    2    3    1    2    3
foot       L    R    L    R    L    R    L    R    L    R    L    R    L    R    L

secs      ....11....12....13....14....15....16....17....18....19....20
90bpm      1    2    3    1    2    3    1    2    3    repeat pattern
foot       R    L    R    L    R    L    R    B    B
```

Cues:

left / together / place
back / together / place
left / together / place
back / together / place

across / side / place
across / side / place
across / side / place
across / turn / turn

Armadillo

New Concepts, Steps and Combinations

New Steps

Scuff

Instructs you to bring your heel in contact with the floor while you move your foot forward. This will make a noise and that is important in country-western dancing. Scuff sounds are often chosen to accentuate the rhythmic beats in the music to which the dance is done. The scuff involves no weight transfer.

For example, "scuff **left** foot" instructs you to push or scrape your left heel against the floor. In "scuff **left** foot" the right foot supports your weight during and after the scuff.

New Combinations

Charleston Kick

Instructs you to make four movements to four beats of music. The foot that begins (leads) the combination is specified. On beat "1", the lead foot steps forward. On "2", the following foot kicks forward. On "3", the following foot steps back, and, on "4", the lead foot touches back. (On occasion, a movement other than a touch will be specified for beat "4".)

For example, "Right Charleston kick" instructs you to: on "1", step your right foot forward; on "2", kick your left foot forward; on "3", step back on your left foot; and on "4", touch your right toe back.

For a very advanced "Charleston" look, swivel your heels alternately out and in to a syncopated rhythm. (We have never seen this done on a country-western dance floor.)

The Dance

Difficulty Level: I   **Choreographer:** Unknown

Dance Faces: one direction   **Pattern Length:** 32 Beats

Suggested Music:

For practicing — "Honey Hush" by Scooter Lee (Track 5 on **Free CD**), "I'm So Miserable Without You" originally recorded by Billy Ray Cyrus (Track 7 on CD included with Book 1.)

For dancing — "Holed Up In Some Honky Tonk" by Dean Dillon, "Janie's Gone Fishin" by Kim Hill, "Chitlin Time" by Kentucky Headhunters.

Beats	Description
	Toe Fans and Kicks
1 - 2	Right toe fan
	1 Swivel **right** toe to right
	2 Swivel **right** toe to center
3	Kick **right** foot forward
4	Touch **right** foot next to **left** foot
5 - 6	Right toe fan
	5 Swivel **right** toe to right
	6 Swivel **right** toe to center
7	Kick **right** foot forward
8	Step **right** foot next to **left** foot
	Charleston
9	Touch **left** toe back
10-13	Left Charleston kick
	10 Step **left** foot forward
	11 Kick **right** foot forward
	12 Step **right** foot back
	13 Touch **left** toe back
14	Step **left** foot next to **right** foot
15	Stomp-up **right** foot in place
16	Stomp-up **right** foot in place
	Vines and Turns
17-20	Right vine with ¼ turn and left scuff
	17 Step **right** foot to right side
	18 Step **left** foot behind **right** foot
	19 Step **right** foot to right side
	20 Pivot on **right** foot ¼ turn left and scuff **left** foot
21-24	Left vine with ¼ turn and right scuff
	21 Step **left** foot to left side
	22 Step **right** foot behind **left** foot
	23 Step **left** foot to left side
	24 Pivot on **left** foot ¼ turn left and scuff **right** foot

25-28   Right vine with ¼ turn and left scuff
        25   Step **right** foot to right side
        26   Step **left** foot behind **right** foot
        27   Step **right** foot to right side
        28   Pivot on **right** foot ¼ turn left and scuff **left** foot

29-32   Left vine with ¼ turn and right stomp-up
        29   Step **left** foot to left side
        30   Step **right** foot behind **left** foot
        31   Step **left** foot to left side
        32   Pivot on **left** foot ¼ turn left and stomp-up **right** foot next to **left**
               foot

Repeat Pattern

Rhythm Line:

```
secs    .....1.....2.....3.....4.....5.....6.....7.....8.....9....10
120bpm  1  2  3  4  1  2  3  4  1  2  3  4  1  2  3  4  1  2  3  4
foot    R  R  R  R  R  R  R  R  L  L  R  R  L  L  R  R  R  L  R  B
other
```

```
secs    ....11....12....13....14....15....16....17....18....19....20
120bpm  1  2  3  4  1  2  3  4  1  2  3  4  1  2  3  4  1  2  3  4
foot    L  R  L  B  R  L  R  B  L  R  L  B  repeat pattern
other
```

Cues:

right toe / center / kick / touch
right toe / center / kick / together
toe back
left / kick / right / back
left / stomp / stomp

right / behind / right / turn
left / behind / left / turn
right / behind / right / turn
left / behind / left / turn

For more dance books
— see the back of this book!

Judy & Tony's classic book & CD package "Country & Western Line Dancing: Step-by-Step Instructions for Cowgirls and Cowboys" is an essential companion for all line dancers!

At the back of this book, you'll find our full list of high-quality publications covering all styles of modern dancing!

Level II

The J Walk

New Concepts, Steps and Combinations

New Steps

Bend knee	Instructs you to bend the knee of the identified leg to a degree that is comfortable for you. Unless otherwise specified in a step description or combination definition, the direction to "bend knee" should be executed without lifting the heel off the ground. This will result in a subtle lowering of the body to the side of the bending knee. The direction to which the bent knee should point will be specified, as in "Bend **right** knee forward".
Hitch-hike	Instructs you to bend the designated arm at the elbow and move the hand over the shoulder of that arm. The hand is held with the fingers folded and the thumb perpendicular to the palm.
Straighten knee	Instructs you to return a leg that has been bent to its normal standing position.

The Dance

Difficulty Level: II   **Choreographer:** Sue Lipscomb

Dance Faces: four directions   **Pattern Length:** 32 Beats

Suggested Music:

For practicing – "Can't Help It" by Scooter Lee (Track 2 on **Free CD**), "Talk Some" originally recorded by Billy Ray Cyrus (Track # 3 on CD included with Book 1)

For dancing – "Walking to Jerusalem" by Tracy Byrd.

Beats	Description
	Heel Rocks and Cha-Chas
1	Rock-step **right** heel forward
2	Rock back on **left** foot
3 - 4	Right cha-cha in place
	3 Step **right** foot next to **left** foot
	& Step **left** foot in place
	4 Step **right** foot in place
5	Rock-step **left** heel forward
6	Rock back on **right** foot
7 - 8	Left cha-cha in place
	7 Step **left** foot next to **right** foot
	& Step **right** foot in place
	8 Step **left** foot in place
	Turn, Stomps and Knees
9	Step **right** foot forward
10	Pivot on **both** feet ¼ turn left

11	Stomp **right** foot next to **left** foot
12	Stomp **left** foot next to **right** foot
13	Bend **right** knee forward
14	Hold
15	Straighten **right** knee and bend **left** knee forward
16	Hold

Turn and Hitch-Hike

17	Step **right** foot forward
18	Step **left** foot forward
19-20	Military turn to the left
	19 Step **right** foot forward
	20 Pivot on **both** feet ½ turn left

21	Step **left** foot back and hitch-hike right hand over right shoulder
22	Step **right** foot back and hitch-hike right hand over right shoulder
23	Step **left** foot back and hitch-hike right hand over right shoulder
24	Touch **right** foot next to **left** foot and hitch-hike right hand over right shoulder

Touches, Crosses and Turn

25	Touch **right** toe to right side
26	Step **right** foot across **left** foot
27	Touch **left** toe to left side
28	Step **left** foot across **right** foot

29	Touch **right** toe to right side
30	Step **right** foot across **left** foot
31	Pivot on **both** feet ½ turn left
32	Clap

Repeat Pattern

Rhythm Line:

```
secs     .....1.....2.....3.....4.....5.....6.....7.....8.....9....10
120bpm   1  2  3 & 4  1  2  3 & 4  1  2  3  4  1  2  3  4  1  2  3  4
foot     R  L  RLR   L  R  LRL   R  B  R  L  R  .  B  .  R  L  R  B
other

secs     ....11....12....13....14....15....16....17....18....19....20
120bpm   1  2  3  4  1  2  3  4  1  2  3  4  1  2  3  4  1  2  3  4
foot     L  R  L  R  R  R  L  L  L  R  R  B  .  repeat pattern
other    h  h  h  h                    c
         (hitch hike)                  (clap)
```

Cues:

rock forward / back / cha-cha-cha
rock forward / back / cha-cha-cha
right / turn / stomp / stomp
knee / hold / knee / hold

right / left / right / turn
back / back / back / touch
side / cross / side / cross
side / cross / turn / clap

Dean Express

About this dance: Glenn and Maureen choreographed this dance for "My Baby Thinks She's A Train" at the request of the Dean Brothers. Glenn and Maureen started country-western dancing in 1990 and now teach as well as run their dance club "Amigos" in Harrogate, North Yorkshire, England. Remember that on beats 28 and 34 your hitching leg stays in the air.

New Concepts, Steps and Combinations

New Steps

Flick   Instructs you to kick the identified foot backward. In a flick, the toe points down.

The Dance

Difficulty Level: II   **Choreographers:** Glenn Robinson and Maureen Parker

Dance Faces: four directions   **Pattern Length:** 38 Beats

Suggested Music:

For practicing – "Don't Walk Away" by Scooter Lee (Track 3 on **Free CD**), "I Wanna Go Too Far" originally recorded by Trisha Yearwood (Track 4 on CD included with Book 1.) Keep in mind the "Whoo Whoo's" might not fit this music!

For dancing – "My Baby Thinks She's a Train" by The Dean Brothers.

Beats	Description
	Steps and Kicks
1	Step **right** foot forward
2	Step **left** foot forward
3	Step **right** foot forward
4	Kick **left** foot forward and clap
5	Step **left** foot back
6	Step **right** foot back
7	Step **left** foot back
8	Flick **right** foot back and clap

Charleston Kick and Stomps

9-12   Right Charleston kick with claps and flick
         9   Step **right** foot forward
         10   Kick **left** foot forward and clap
         11   Step **left** foot back
         12   Flick **right** foot back and clap

13   Stomp **right** foot next to **left** foot
14   Stomp **left** foot in place

Crosses and Turns

15   Step **right** foot across **left** foot
16   Hold
17   Step **left** foot across **right** foot
18   Hold
19   Pivot on **both** feet ½ turn right
20   Hold

21   Step **right** foot across **left** foot
22   Hold
23   Step **left** foot across **right** foot
24   Hold
25   Pivot on **both** feet ½ turn right
26   Hold

Hitch and Shout, then a Vine

27   Hitch **right** leg and pull imaginary train whistle with left arm and call "Whoo!"
28   Pull imaginary train whistle with left arm and call "Whoo!"

29-32   Right vine with left stomp-up
         29   Step **right** foot to right side
         30   Step **left** foot behind **right** foot
         31   Step **right** foot to right side
         32   Stomp-up **left** foot next to **right** foot

33   Hitch **left** leg and pull imaginary train whistle with right arm and call "Whoo!"
34   Pull imaginary train whistle with right arm and call "Whoo!"

35-38   Left vine with ¼ turn left and right stomp-up
         35   Step **left** foot to left side
         36   Step **right** foot behind **left** foot
         37   Step **left** foot to left side and pivot ¼ turn left
         38   Stomp-up **right** foot next to **left** foot

Repeat Pattern

Rhythm Line:

```
secs      .....1.....2.....3.....4.....5.....6.....7.....8.....9....10
120bpm    1  2  3  4  1  2  3  4  1  2  3  4  1  2  3  4  1  2  3  4
foot      R  L  R  L  L  R  L  R  R  L  L  R  R  L  R  .  L  .  B  .
other           c        c        c

secs      ....11....12....13....14....15....16....17....18....19....20
120bpm    1  2  3  4  1  2  3  4  1  2  3  4  1  2  3  4  1  2  3  4
foot      R  .  L  .  B  .  R  .  R  L  R  L  L  .  L  R  L  R  repeat
other                       w  w              w  w
                         (whoo)
```

Cues:

right / left / right / kick
back / back / back / flick
right / kick / back / flick
stomp / stomp / cross / hold

cross / hold / turn / hold
cross / hold / cross / hold
turn / hold
whoo / whoo
right / behind / right / stomp
whoo / whoo
left / behind / turn / stomp

Norma Jean

About this dance: Donna Wasnick tells us that Norma Jean is the second dance she choreographed. She created it in 1992, inspired by the song "Norma Jean Riley". It now is a member of a repertoire of 25 dances she has choreographed, many of which have won praises at line dance competitions.

New Concepts, Steps and Combinations

New Steps

Lower foot   Instructs you to return one part of the designated foot to the floor. For example, "lower **left** heel" would most often follow a move that put your left heel in the air and tells you to return that heel to the floor. When lowering a toe or a heel, the move is like a touch, unless you are also told, in parentheses, to step that foot down. Some dance writers use "heel drop" to denote "lower heel".

New Combinations

Toe Strut   Instructs you to execute two movements of one foot in two beats of music. The strutting foot, and the direction of the strut (i.e., forward or backward) will be specified in the dance description. On beat one, the toe is touched in the direction of travel. On beat two, the heel is lowered and weight is transferred to that foot.

For example, "left toe strut forward" instructs you on "1" to touch your left toe forward. On "2", lower your left heel to the floor and step down on your left foot.

It is important to note that although "touch" is used to describe the movement on the first beat, in a toe strut this touch may bear some weight. This is especially true if the toe strut is involved in a turn.

The Dance

Difficulty Level: II   **Choreographer:** Donna Wasnick

Dance Faces: four directions   **Pattern Length:** 32 Beats

Suggested Music:

For practicing – "Can't Help It" by Scooter Lee (Track 2 on Free CD), "Talk Some" originally recorded by Billy Ray Cyrus (Track 3 on CD included with Book 1.)

For dancing – "Norma Jean Riley" by Diamond Rio, "Davey Crockett" by Kentucky Headhunters.

Beats	Description
	Toe Struts and Claps
1- 2	Right toe strut forward
	1 Touch **right** toe forward
	2 Lower **right** heel (step **right** foot down)
3- 4	Left toe strut forward
	3 Touch **left** toe forward
	4 Lower **left** heel (step **left** foot down)
5	Touch **right** toe forward
6	Clap
7	Lower **right** heel (step **right** foot down)
8	Step **left** foot next to **right** foot
9-10	Right toe strut forward
	9 Touch **right** toe forward
	10 Lower **right** heel (step **right** foot down)
11-12	Left toe strut forward
	11 Touch **left** toe forward
	12 Lower **left** heel (step **left** foot down)
13	Touch **right** toe forward
14	Clap
15	Lower **right** heel (step **right** foot down)
16	Step **left** foot next to **right** foot
	Step Back and to Sides
17	Step **right** foot diagonally back
18	Touch **left** foot next to **right** foot
19	Step **left** foot to left side
20	Touch **right** foot next to **left** foot
21	Step **right** foot to right side and pivot ¼ turn right
22	Touch **left** foot next to **right** foot
23	Step **left** foot to left side
24	Touch **right** foot next to **left** foot

Hitches and Scoots

25	Hitch **right** leg and scoot **left** foot forward
26	Touch **right** toe next to **left** foot
27	Hitch **right** leg and scoot **left** foot forward
28	Step **right** foot next to **left** foot

Split and Stomps

29-30	Heel Split
	29 Move heels apart
	30 Return heels to center
31	Stomp-up **right** foot in place
32	Stomp-up **right** foot in place

Repeat Pattern

Rhythm Line:

```
secs     .....1.....2.....3.....4.....5.....6.....7.....8.....9....10
120bpm   1  2  3  4  1  2  3  4  1  2  3  4  1  2  3  4  1  2  3  4
foot     R  R  L  L  R  .  R  L  R  R  L  L  R  .  R  L  R  L  L  R
other                      c                          c
                        (clap)
```

```
secs     ....11....12....13....14....15....16....17....18....19....20
120bpm   1  2  3  4  1  2  3  4  1  2  3  4  1  2  3  4  1  2  3  4
foot     R  L  L  R  B  R  B  R  B  B  R  R  repeat pattern
Other
```

Cues:

toe / strut / toe / strut
toe / clap / heel / together
toe / strut / toe / strut
toe / clap / heel / together

back / touch / left / touch
turn / touch / left / together
scoot / touch / scoot / together
split / center / stomp / stomp

Catfish

About this dance: We have found several variations for the last 8 beats of this dance, including shuffles and heel struts (both offered as variations) and varieties of boogey walks (something like the walking bumps in the featured pattern).

New Concepts, Steps and Combinations

New Combinations

Heel Strut   Instructs you to execute two moves in two beats of music. The foot involved in the strut will be specified in the dance description. On beat one, the heel of the specified foot is touched forward with the toe pointing up. On beat two, the toe of the specified foot is lowered as weight is transferred to that foot. Unlike toe struts, heel struts are always done moving forward. Keep in mind that, similar to toe struts, the touch on beat one may bear some weight, particularly when a turn is involved.

For example, "left heel strut" instructs you, on "1", to touch your left heel forward and on "2", to lower your left toe to the floor and step down.

Kick-Ball-Change   Instructs you to make three steps, in a specified order, to two beats of music. The foot that begins or leads the kick-ball-change will be specified in the dance description. On the first beat of a kick-ball-change, the leading foot is kicked forward (about six inches off the floor). On the half beat, the ball of the leading foot steps next to the following foot. On the second beat, the following foot steps in place. The dancer should note that this third movement is subtle. The following foot has not moved: it has simply stepped in place. An alternative way to think of this third movement is as a transfer of body weight from the leading foot to the following foot.

For example, "right kick-ball-change" instructs you to kick your right foot forward, step the ball of your right foot next to your left, and step your left foot in place, to a rhythm of "one-and-two".

The Dance

Difficulty Level: II

Choreographer: Jim Long

Dance Faces: four directions

Pattern Length: 32 Beats

Suggested Music:

For practicing – "Can't Help It" by Scooter Lee (Track 2 on **Free CD**), "The City Put The Country Back In Me" originally recorded by Neil McCoy (Track 2 on CD included with Book 1)

For dancing – "Little Miss Honky Tonk" by Brooks and Dunn, "Dog House Blues" by Ricky Lynn Gregg, and "Bigger Fish to Fry" by Boy Howdy.

Beats	Description
	Toe Touches
1	Touch **right** toe to right side
2	Touch **right** toe next to **left** foot
3	Touch **right** toe to right side
4	Touch **right** toe next to **left** foot
5	Touch **left** toe to left side
6	Touch **left** toe next to **right** foot
7	Touch **left** toe to left side
8	Touch **left** toe next to **right** foot
	Vines with Scuffs and Turn
9 -12	Left vine with right scuff
	9 Step **left** foot to left side
	10 Step **right** foot behind **left** foot
	11 Step **left** foot to left side
	12 Scuff **right** foot
13-16	Right vine with ¼ turn right and left scuff
	13 Step **right** foot to right side
	14 Step **left** foot behind **right** foot
	15 Step **right** foot to right side and pivot ¼ turn right
	16 Scuff **left** foot
	Walk Back
17	Step **left** foot back
18	Step **right** foot back
19	Step **left** foot back
20	Touch **right** toe next to **left** foot
	Kick and Stomp
21-22	Right kick-ball-change
	21 Kick **right** foot forward
	& Step ball of **right** foot next to **left** foot
	22 Step **left** foot in place
23	Stomp-up **right** foot next to **left** foot
24	Stomp-up **right** foot next to **left** foot

Walk and Bump

25	Step **right** foot diagonally forward and bump **right** hip diagonally forward
26	Bump **right** hip diagonally forward
27	Step **left** foot diagonally forward and bump **left** hip diagonally forward
28	Bump **left** hip diagonally forward
29	Step **right** foot diagonally forward and bump **right** hip diagonally forward
30	Bump **right** hip diagonally forward
31	Step **left** foot diagonally forward and bump **left** hip diagonally forward
32	Bump **left** hip diagonally forward

Repeat Pattern

Variations:

Heel strut instead of walk and bump (beats 25-32)

25-26	Right heel strut
	25 Touch **right** heel forward
	26 Lower **right** toe (step **right** foot down)
27-28	Left heel strut
	27 Touch **left** heel forward
	28 Lower **left** toe (step **left** foot down)
29-30	Right heel strut
31-32	Left heel strut

Shuffle instead of walk and bump (beats 25-32)

25-26	Right shuffle forward
	25 Step **right** foot forward
	& Step **left** foot next to **right** foot
	26 Step **right** foot forward
27-28	Left shuffle forward
	27 Step **left** foot forward
	& Step **right** foot next to **left** foot
	28 Step **left** foot forward
29-30	Right shuffle forward
31-32	Left shuffle forward

Rhythm Line:

```
secs    .... 1.....2.....3.....4.....5.....6.....7.....8.....9....10
120bpm  1  2  3  4  1  2  3  4  1  2  3  4  1  2  3  4  1  2  3  4
foot    R  R  R  R  L  L  L  L  L  R  L  R  R  L  R  L  L  R  L  R
Other

secs    ....11....12....13....14....15....16....17....18....19....20
120bpm  1 & 2  3  4  1  2  3  4  1  2  3  4  1  2  3  4  1  2  3  4
foot    RRL  R  R  R  .  L  .  R  .  L  .  repeat pattern
other               b  b  b  b  b  b  b  b
                       (hip bumps)
```

Cues:

right toe / close / toe / close
left toe / close / toe / close
left / behind / left / scuff
right / behind / turn / scuff

back / back / back / touch
kick - ball - change / stomp / stomp
right bump / bump / left bump / bump
right bump / bump / left bump / bump

God Blessed Texas

About this dance: This dance offers something extra. An eight beat pattern is offered as an "Introduction". It is danced only once, and is not repeated with the pattern. When danced to "God Blessed Texas" the "Introduction" begins eight beats after Little Texas concludes its "The Eyes of Texas Are Upon You" prelude.

New Concepts, Steps and Combinations

New Steps

Lower body
Instructs you to squat down a distance comfortable for you. If you are directed to lower your body over several contiguous beats, lower only slightly on each beat so that you finish the sequence in a comfortable squat.

Raise body or Rise
Generally instructs you to return your body from a squat position to your normal standing position. If you are directed to raise your body over several contiguous beats, raise only slightly on each beat so that you finish the sequence in your normal standing position. When told to "rise on ball of a foot", raise your body slightly by stepping the foot with ball/toe on the floor and heel in the air.

Raise foot
Instructs you to move one part of a foot independent of another. For example, "raise **right** toe" instructs you to lift the toe of your right foot off the floor while leaving the heel in place. When instructed to raise a heel, remember that you will need to bend the knee of that leg slightly in order to execute the move.

Swivel knee
Instructs you to bend the indentfied knee and turn it in the direction specified (i.e., left, right or center). Movement is executed by supporting the weight primarily on the foot opposite the swiveling knee. The knee that moves turns about 45 degrees in the direction indicated and the leg pivots on the ball of the foot.

For example, "swivel **left** knee to left side" instructs you to support your weight on right foot, raise your left heel and turn your leg to the left. "Swivel **left** knee to center" instructs you to support your weight on right foot, raise your left heel and turn your leg so that your feet are in parallel position.

The Dance

Difficulty Level: II

Dance Faces: two directions

Choreographer: Shirley K. Batson

Pattern Length: 32 Beats

Suggested Music:

For practicing – "Don't Walk Away" by Scooter Lee (Track 3 on **Free CD**), "South's Gonna Do It" originally recorded by Charlie Daniels Band (Track 6 on CD included with Book 1)

For dancing – "God Blessed Texas" by Little Texas.

Beats   Description

Introduction

(Keep knees bent slightly throughout the Introduction's eight beats)

Beats	Description
&	Raise heels
1	Lower heels
&	Raise heels
2	Lower heels
&	Raise heels
3	Lower heels
&	Raise heels
4	Lower heels
&	Raise heels
5	Lower heels
&	Raise heels
6	Lower heels
&	Raise heels
7	Lower heels
&	Raise heels
8	Lower heels

Main Pattern

Diagonal Steps and Touches

1	Step **left** foot diagonally forward
2	Touch **right** foot next to **left** foot
3	Step **right** foot diagonally back
4	Touch **left** foot next to **right** foot
5	Step **left** foot diagonally back and pivot ⅛ turn left
6	Touch **right** foot next to **left** foot
7	Step **right** foot to right side
8	Pivot on **right** foot ⅛ turn right and touch **left** foot next to **right** foot

Slaps and Knee Swivels

9	Stomp **left** foot to left side
10	Stomp **right** foot to right side (step only slightly to right side)
11	Lower body slightly and slap left hand on front of **left** thigh (left hand stays on thigh)
12	Slap right hand on front of **right** thigh (both hands stay on thighs)
13	Swivel **left** knee to left side (hands stay on thighs)
14	Swivel **left** knee to center (hands stay on thighs)
15	Swivel **right** knee to right side (hands stay on thighs)
16	Swivel **right** knee to center (hands stay on thighs) and raise body (as swivel is completed)

Vines

17-20	Right vine with left touch
	17 Step **right** foot to right side
	18 Step **left** foot behind **right** foot
	19 Step **right** foot to right side
	20 Touch **left** foot next to **right** foot
21-24	Left vine with right touch
	21 Step **left** foot to left side
	22 Step **right** foot behind **left** foot
	23 Step **left** foot to left side
	24 Touch **right** foot next to **left** foot

Kicks and Scoots

25	Step **right** foot forward
26	Kick **left** foot forward
27	Flick **left** foot and pivot on **right** foot ½ turn right
28	Step **left** foot forward
29	Scoot **left** foot forward and hitch **right** leg
30	Scoot **left** foot forward and hitch **right** leg
31	Step **right** foot forward
32	Scoot **right** foot forward and hitch **left** leg

Repeat Main Pattern

Rhythm Line:

```
Introduction
secs      .....1.....2.....3.....4..           Go to main pattern
120bpm    & 1 & 2 & 3 & 4 & 1 & 2 & 3 & 4
foot      B B B B B B B B B B B B B B B B
other
```

```
Main Pattern
secs      .....1.....2.....3.....4.....5.....6.....7.....8.....9....10
120bpm    1   2   3   4   1   2   3   4   1   2   3   4   1   2   3   4   1   2   3   4
foot      L   R   R   L   L   R   R   B   L   R   .   .   L   L   R   R   R   L   R   L
other                                             s   s   .
                                               (slaps)
```

```
secs      ....11....12....13....14....15....16....17....18....19....20
120bpm    1   2   3   4   1   2   3   4   1   2   3   4   1   2   3   4   1   2   3   4
foot      L   R   L   R   R   L   B   L   B   B   R   B repeat pattern
other
```

Cues:

(Introduction)
up-down- and - down - and - down - and - down
- and - down - and - down - and - down - and - down

(Main Pattern)
left / touch / back/ touch
turn / touch / right / turn
stomp / stomp / slap / slap
knee out / in / knee out / in
right / behind / right / touch
left / behind / left / touch
right / kick / turn / left
scoot / scoot / right / scoot

Hillbilly Rock

About this dance: Carol tells us that she choreographed this dance because she so much liked the song "Hillbilly Rock" by Marty Stuart. We're pleased that it was first performed at the 1990 Chicagoland (our neighborhood) Country-Western Dance Festival. Carol and her husband, Norm, have been teaching, choreographing and competing in Country-Western dance for 18 years. Carol has held local, state and regional offices in the National Teachers Association for Country Western Dance and is a past-president of that organization. They are currently teaching various forms of social dancing and have videos available on line dance, two-step, polka, waltz and east coast swing. You can reach them by telephoning them at (in the US) 651-429-4785.

"Hillbilly Rock" has become a favorite in most places where line dancing is done. When you dance it, make sure you begin just as the music does.

New Concepts, Steps and Combinations

New Combinations

Jazz Box   Instructs you to make three steps, in a specified order, to three beats of music. A jazz box will be described as either right or left, based on the foot that makes the crossing move and leads the jazz box. On beat "1", the leading foot steps across the following foot. On beat "2", the following foot steps back. On beat "3", the leading foot steps to the side (parallel to and shoulder width away from the following foot). Note that you will touch three corners of an imaginary square (or box) as you make these three steps. Jazz boxes are also called "jazz squares".

As with vines, a fourth, "finishing move" for the foot that is free to move after the jazz box is often specified (and, actually, may complete the box). In some dances, rather than having a "finishing move", the jazz box is preceded by a step (to make up 4 steps). Some jazz box instructions may include turns (giving a funny look to the imaginary box). That is, you will see directions like "right jazz box with left step" or "right step with left jazz box" or "right jazz box with ¼ turn right".

For example, "right jazz box with left step" instructs you to: on "1", step your right foot across your left foot, on "2", step your left foot back, on "3", step your right foot to the right side, and on "4", step your left foot next to your right foot, to a rhythm of 1,2,3,4.

The Dance

Difficulty Level: II   **Choreographer:** Carol Fritchie

Dance Faces: four directions   **Pattern Length:** 40 Beats

Suggested Music:

For practicing – "Can't Help It" by Scooter Lee (Track 2 on **Free CD**), "Redneck Girl" originally recorded by The Bellamy Brothers (Track 11 on CD included with Book 1.)

For dancing – "Hillbilly Rock" by Marty Stuart.

Beats	Description
	Heels and Vine with Turn
1	Touch **right** heel diagonally forward
2	Step **right** foot next to **left** foot
3	Touch **left** heel diagonally forward
4	Touch **left** foot next to **right** foot
5 - 8	Left vine with turn and right brush
	5 Step **left** foot to left side
	6 Step **right** foot behind **left** foot
	7 Step **left** foot to left side and pivot ¼ turn left
	8 Brush **right** foot forward
	Jazz Boxes and Toe Struts
9 -12	Right jazz box with left step
	9 Step **right** foot across **left** foot
	10 Step **left** foot back
	11 Step **right** foot to right side
	12 Step **left** foot next to **right** foot
13-14	Right toe strut forward
	13 Touch **right** toe forward
	14 Lower **right** heel (step **right** foot down) and snap fingers
15-16	Left toe strut forward
	15 Touch **left** toe forward
	16 Lower **left** heel (step **left** foot down) and snap fingers
17-18	Right toe strut forward
	17 Touch **right** toe forward
	18 Lower **right** heel (step **right** foot down) and snap fingers
19-20	Left toe strut forward
	19 Touch **left** toe forward
	20 Lower **left** heel (step **left** foot down) and snap fingers
21-24	Right jazz box with left step
	21 Step **right** foot across **left** foot
	22 Step **left** foot back
	23 Step **right** foot to right side
	24 Step **left** foot next to **right** foot

Toe Touches and Stomps

25	Touch **right** toe forward
26	Hold
27	Touch **right** toe back
28	Hold
29	Step **right** foot forward
30	Step **left** foot forward
31	Stomp-up **right** foot next to **left** foot
32	Stomp-up **right** foot next to **left** foot

Kicks and Knee Bends

33	Kick **right** foot forward
34	Kick **right** foot forward
35	Kick **right** foot forward
36	Step **right** foot next to **left** foot
37	Lower body
38	Raise body
39	Lower body
40	Raise body

Repeat Pattern

Rhythm Line:

```
secs    .....1.....2.....3.....4.....5.....6.....7.....8.....9....10
120bpm  1  2  3  4  1  2  3  4  1  2  3  4  1  2  3  4  1  2  3  4
foot    R  R  L  L  L  R  L  R  R  L  R  L  R  R  L  L  L  R  R  L  L
other                                          sn       sn       sn       sn
                                                  (finger snaps)


secs    ....11....12....13....14....15....16....17....18....19....20
120bpm  1  2  3  4  1  2  3  4  1  2  3  4  1  2  3  4  1  2  3  4
foot    R  L  R  L  R  .  R  .  R  L  R  R  R  R  R  R  .  .  .  .   repeat
other
```

Cues:

heel / together / heel / touch
left / behind / turn / brush
cross / back / side / together
toe / strut / toe / strut

toe / strut / toe / strut
cross / back / side / together
toe / hold / back / hold
right / left / stomp / stomp

kick / kick / kick / together
down / up / down / up

Bayou City Twister

About this dance: We like to guess why dances are given the names they have. Bayou City Twister has dancers spinning in several half-turns, making the cowgirls and cowboys look as if they are caught up in a tornado (along with the typical tornado debris).

New Concepts, Steps and Combinations

New Combinations

Jump- Cross- Turn	Instructs you to make two jumps and one turn in three beats of music. The direction of the turn will be specified in the dance description. On beat "1", the dancer jumps, landing with feet about shoulder width apart. On beat "2", the dancer jumps again, landing with the legs crossed. The leg which is named by the direction of the turn must be crossed behind the other leg. On beat "3", the dancer pivots ½ turn in the direction specified, "uncrossing" the legs. As with vines and many other three step combinations, a fourth, finishing move is often specified when a jump-cross-turn is used in 4/4 time music.

For example, "jump-cross-turn to the left" instructs you to: on "1", jump and land with feet apart; on "2", jump and land with left leg crossed behind right leg; and on "3", pivot ½ turn to the left on the balls of both feet.

Some dancers find jump-cross-turns too jarring, especially when several are done in rapid succession. Because of this, an alternative to the jump-cross-turn has been developed. It proceeds as follows: on "1", touch, to the side, the toe of the foot opposite the direction of the turn; on "2", step the foot opposite the direction of the turn across the other foot (leaving weight on both feet); and on "3", pivot ½ turn in the direction specified (as in the jump-cross-turn).

For example, (replacing a jump-cross-turn to the left): on "1", touch your right toe to the right side; on "21", step your right foot across your left foot; and on "3", pivot ½ turn to the left on the balls of both feet.

The Dance

Difficulty Level: II   **Choreographer:** Alfred Watkins
Dance Faces: four directions   **Pattern Length:** 32 Beats
Suggested Music:

For practicing – "Can't Help It" by Scooter Lee (Track 2 on **Free CD**), "Wher'm I Gonna Live When I Get Home" originally recorded by Billy Ray Cyrus (Track 9 on CD included with Book 1)

For dancing – "What You Gonna Do With A Cowboy" by Chris LeDoux.

Beats	Description
	Touches and Turn
1	Touch **right** heel forward
2	Step **right** foot next to **left** foot
3	Touch **left** heel forward
4	Step **left** foot next to **right** foot

5	Touch **right** heel forward
6	Touch **right** toe back
7	Pivot on **left** foot ½ turn right
8	Hook **right** legacross **left** leg

Shuffle and Rock

9-10	Right shuffle forward
	9 Step **right** foot forward
	& Step **left** foot next to **right** foot
	10 Step **right** foot forward
11	Rock-step **left** foot forward
12	Rock back on **right** foot

Shuffle and Turn

13-14	Left shuffle back
	13 Step **left** foot back
	& Step **right** foot next to **left** foot
	14 Step **left** foot back
15	Right ½ swing clockwise (begin forward) and pivot on **left** toe ½ turn right and step **right** toe next to **left** toe (as turn is completed)
16	Lower **both** heels

Vine and Turn

17-20	Right vine with left stomp
	17 Step **right** foot to right side
	18 Step **left** foot behind **right** foot
	19 Step **right** foot to right side
	20 Pivot on **right** foot ¼ turn right and step **left** foot next to **right** foot (as turn is completed)

21-24	Jump-cross-turn to the left with left touch
	21 Jump, landing with feet apart
	22 Jump, landing with **right** foot across **left** foot
	23 Pivot on **both** feet ½ turn left
	24 Touch **left** toe back

Shuffle and Turn

25-26	Left shuffle forward
	25 Step **left** foot forward
	& Step **right** foot next to **left** foot
	26 Step **left** foot forward
27-28	Military turn to the left
	27 Step **right** foot forward
	28 Pivot on **both** feet ½ turn left

Jazz Box and Turn

29-32	Right jazz box with ½ turn right
	29 Step **right** foot across **left** foot
	30 Step **left** foot back
	31 Step **right** foot to right side
	32 Pivot on **right** foot ½ turn right and step **left** foot next to **right** foot (as turn is completed) and clap

Repeat Pattern

Variations

Several kinds of variations are commonly seen with this dance. Perhaps to avoid the leg swing, some dancers do the following for beats Perhaps to avoid the leg swing, some dancers do the following for beats 15 and 16:

15   Pivot on **left** foot ½ turn right and step **right** foot forward (as turn is completed).

16   Stomp **left** foot next to **right** foot and clap

Maybe to add more twist to the Twister, some dancers replace the vine on beats 17-19 with a three-step-turn to the right and some do one and a half turns on beat 32! For those of you who wear hats while dancing, try lifting up your hat with both hands on beat 21 and returning it to your head on beat 22.

Another version of this dance, which we presented in UK Line Dance Favourites, has slightly different turns on beats 20 and 31-32. In that version there is no turn on beat 20 and instead of a ½ turn right on beat 32, there is a ¼ turn right on beat 31. Both versions get you to the same place—but through a slightly different sequence of turns.

Rhythm Line:

```
secs      .....1.....2.....3.....4.....5.....6.....7.....8.....9....10
120bpm    1  2  3  4  1  2  3  4  1 & 2  3  4  1 & 2  3  4  1  2  3  4
foot      R  R  L  L  R  R  L  R  R L R  L  R  L R L  B  L  R  L  R  L
other                                                  clap

secs      ....11....12....13....14....15....16....17....18....19....20
120bpm    1  2  3  4  1 & 2  3  4  1  2  3  4  1  2  3  4  1  2  3  4
foot      B  B  B  L  L R L  R  B  R  L  R  L  repeat pattern
```

Cues:

heel / together / heel / together
heel / toe / turn / hook

right-and-right / rock forward / back
back-and-back / turn / heels

right / behind / right / turn
jump / cross / turn / back

left-and-left / right / turn
cross / back / side / turn

Ridin'

About this dance: As country-western line dancing gains popularity around the world, more and more people are choreographing dances, and they're not all from the U.S. Dave Ingram, who choreographed Ridin', lives in Ottawa, Canada.

New Concepts, Steps and Combinations

New Combinations

Lindy   Instructs you to make a sideways shuffle and two rocks in four beats of music. The direction of movement will be specified in the dance description.

For example, "right Lindy" instructs you to: on "1&2", do a right shuffle to the right side; on "3", rock-step your left foot behind your right foot, as you face diagonally left; and on "4", rock forward on your right foot, still facing diagonally left.

This combination produces a look of pulling away from a starting point and being "sprung" back to it. The shuffle and the first rock smoothly move in one direction. On the last rock, you will look as though you are being tugged back towards your starting point.

Swing   Instructs you to lift the identified foot off the floor and move it in a smooth, fluid motion in an arc. The amount of movement ($\frac{1}{4}$ or $\frac{1}{2}$ circle), the direction of movement (clockwise or counterclockwise), the beginning position, and the beats in which the movement must be completed, will be specified in the dance description. Unless otherwise directed, lift your foot about six inches off the floor.

For example, "Right $\frac{1}{4}$ swing clockwise (begin forward)" instructs you to put your right foot forward, about six inches off the floor, and, leaving your leg in the air and extended, move your leg clockwise in a quarter circle, to the right side position.

A swing is like a *rondé*, except in a *rondé* the foot is on the floor. A swing is also known as a *rond de jambe en l'air*.

The Dance

Difficulty Level: II   **Choreographer:** Dave Ingram

Dance Faces: four directions   **Pattern Length:** 32 Beats

Suggested Music:

For practicing – "Honey Hush" by Scooter Lee (Track 5 on **Free CD**), "Shut Up And Kiss Me" originally recorded by Mary Chapin Carpenter (Track 8 on CD included with Book 1)

For dancing – "Ridin' Alone" by Rednex; "All You Ever Do Is Bring Me Down" by the Mavericks, "That's What I Like About You" by Trisha Yearwood.

Beats	Description
	Lindies
1 - 4	Right Lindy
	1 Step **right** foot to right side
	& Step **left** foot next to **right** foot
	2 Step **right** foot to right side
	3 Rock-step **left** foot behind **right** foot, face diagonally left
	4 Rock forward on **right** foot, face diagonally left
5 - 8	Left Lindy
	5 Step **left** foot to left side, face forward
	& Step **right** foot next to **left** foot
	6 Step **left** foot to left side
	7 Rock-step **right** foot behind **left** foot, face diagonally right
	8 Rock forward on **left** foot, face diagonally right
	Shuffles Forward and Turns
9-10	Right shuffle forward
	9 Step **right** foot forward, face forward
	& Step **left** foot next to **right** foot
	10 Step **right** foot forward
11-12	Military turn to the right
	11 Step **left** foot forward
	12 Pivot on **both** feet ½ turn right
13-14	Left shuffle forward
	13 Step **left** foot forward
	& Step **right** foot next to **left** foot
	14 Step **left** foot forward
15	Step **right** foot forward
16	Pivot on **right** foot ¼ turn left and step **left** foot next to **right** foot (as turn is completed)
17-18	Right shuffle forward
	17 Step **right** foot forward
	& Step **left** foot next to **right** foot
	18 Step **right** foot forward

19-20	Military turn to the right
	19 Step **left** foot forward
	20 Pivot on **both** feet ½ turn right

21-22	Left shuffle forward
	21 Step **left** foot forward
	& Step **right** foot next to **left** foot
	22 Step **left** foot forward
23	Step **right** foot forward
24	Pivot on **right** foot ¼ turn left and stomp **left** foot next to **right** foot (as turn is completed)

Kicks, Stomps and Swinging Turn

25	Kick **right** foot forward and pivot on **left** foot ¼ turn left
26	Flick **right** foot back
27	Stomp **right** foot next to **left** foot
28	Stomp **left** foot in place

29	Step **right** foot back
30	Hold
31	Left ½ swing counterclockwise (begin forward) and pivot on **right** foot ½ turn left and step **left** foot next to **right** foot (as turn is completed)
32	Hold

Repeat Pattern

Variation:

Some dancers find it easier to turn on beat 26 instead of beat 25:

25	Kick **right** foot forward
26	Flick **right** foot back and pivot on **left** foot ¼ turn left

Rhythm Line:

```
secs     .....1.....2.....3.....4.....5.....6.....7.....8.....9....10
120bpm   1 & 2   3   4   1 & 2   3   4   1 & 2   3   4   1 & 2   3   4   1 & 2   3   4
foot     R L R   L   R   L R L   R   L   R L R   L   B   L R L   R   B   R L R   L   B
Other
```

```
secs     ....11....12....13....14....15....16....17....18....19....20
120bpm   1 & 2   3   4   1   2   3   4   1   2   3   4   1   2   3   4   1   2   3   4
foot     L R L   R   B   B   R   R   L   R   .   B   .   repeat pattern
other
```

Cues:

right - and - right / rock back / forward
left - and - left / rock back / forward
right - and - right / left / turn
left - and - left / right / turn

right - and - right / left / turn
left - and - left / right / turn
turn / flick / stomp / stomp
right / hold / turn / hold

The Scooch

About this dance: This is another Jo Thompson dance and is named for its quick slides forward on the last eight beats. We think you'll enjoy gliding across the floor.

New Concepts, Steps and Combinations

New Combinations

Three-Step Turn

Instructs you to make one full turn in three steps to three beats of music. The turn will be labelled right or left, indicating the direction of the turn and the foot that leads the combination. Most often, a three-step turn will proceed as follows: On "1", step your lead foot to the side and pivot $\frac{1}{2}$ turn in the indicated direction. On "2", step your following foot to the side and pivot another $\frac{1}{2}$ turn in the indicated direction. On "3", step your lead foot to the side. On occasion, step one of a three-step turn will be the step to the side with the foot turned out, with the half turns being done on steps "2" and "3".

For example, a "three-step turn to left" means: on beat one, step your left foot to your left side and pivot $\frac{1}{2}$ turn left; on beat two, step your right foot to your right side and pivot $\frac{1}{2}$ turn to the left; and on beat three, step your left foot to your left.

If the movement of a three-step turn is not directly to the side, the direction of movement will be specified (for example, three-step turn to left moving forward)

Although we do not use this label, three-step turns are sometimes called "rolling vines". Three-step turns are often done as variations in place of vines or step-slide-step patterns. When three-step turns are used in 4/4 time music, a fourth finishing move is often specified with the turn.

The Dance

Difficulty Level: II
Dance Faces: two directions
Suggested Music:

Choreographer: Jo Thompson
Pattern Length: 32 Beats

For practicing — "Honey Hush" by Scooter Lee (Track 5 on **Free CD**), "Talk Some" originally recorded by Billy Ray Cyrus (Track 3 on CD included with Book 1)

For dancing — "Walkin' On Me" by Big House.

Beats	Description
	Stomps and Claps
1	Stomp-up **right** foot forward
2	Clap
&	Step **right** foot next to **left** foot
3	Stomp-up **left** foot forward
&	Step **left** foot next to **right** foot
4	Stomp-up **right** foot forward
&	Step **right** foot next to **left** foot
5	Stomp-up **left** foot forward
6	Clap
&	Step **left** foot next to **right** foot
7	Stomp-up **right** foot forward
&	Step **right** foot next to **left** foot
8	Stomp-up **left** foot forward
&	Step **left** foot next to **right** foot
	Rock and Shuffle Back
9	Rock-step **right** foot forward
10	Rock back on **left** foot
11-12	Right shuffle back
	11 Step **right** foot back, face diagonally right
	& Step **left** foot next to **right** foot, face diagonally right
	12 Step **right** foot back, face diagonally right
13-14	Left shuffle back
	13 Step **left** foot back, face diagonally left
	& Step **right** foot next to **left** foot, face diagonally left
	14 Step **left** foot back, face diagonally left
15	Rock-step **right** foot back, face forward
16	Rock forward on **left** foot
	Turns
17	Pivot on **left** foot ¼ turn left and step **right** foot to right side while shimmying
18	Snap fingers
&	Step **left** foot next to **right** foot
19	Step **right** foot to right side
20	Touch **left** foot next to **right** foot and clap

21	Step **left** foot to left side and pivot ½ turn left
22	Step **right** foot to right side and pivot ½ turn left
23	Step **left** foot to left side and pivot on **left** foot ¼ turn left
24	Clap

Slides
(During the Slides, your feet should remain shoulder width apart)

&	Slide **right** foot forward (slide only slightly forward)
25	Slide **left** foot next to **right** foot
26	Clap
&	Slide **right** foot back (slide only slightly back)
27	Slide **left** foot next to **right** foot
28	Clap
&	Slide **right** foot forward (slide only slightly forward)
29	Slide **left** foot next to **right** foot
&	Slide **right** foot forward (slide only slightly forward)
30	Slide **left** foot next to **right** foot
&	Slide **right** foot forward (slide only slightly forward)
31	Slide **left** foot next to **right** foot
&	Slide **right** foot forward (slide only slightly forward)
32	Slide **left** foot next to **right** foot

Repeat Pattern

Rhythm Line:

```
secs      .....1.....2.....3.....4.....5.....6.....7.....8.....9....10
120bpm    1   2 & 3 & 4 & 1   2 & 3 & 4 & 1   2   3 & 4   1 & 2   3   4   1   2 & 3   4
foot      R   . R L L R R L   . L R R L L R   L   R L R   L R L   R   L   B   . L R   L
other         c               c                                         sn          c
          (clap)                                          (finger snap)

secs      ....11....12....13....14....15....16....17....18....19....20
120bpm    1   2   3   4 & 1   2 & 3   4 & 1 & 2 & 3 & 4   1   2   3   4   1   2   3   4
foot      L   R   L   B R L   . R L   . R L R L R L R L   repeat pattern
other             c           c       c
```

Cues:

stomp / clap - and - stomp - and - stomp - and
stomp / clap - and - stomp - and - stomp - and
rock forward / back / right - and - right
left - and - left / rock back / forward

turn / snap - and - right / clap
turn / turn / together / turn
and - slide / clap - and - slide / clap
and - slide - and - slide - and - slide - and - slide

Progressive Cowboy

About this dance: Curtiss "Hoss" Marting, the choreographer of this dance, tells us that he created it in 1993. It was originally performed on Buena Vista Television's "Countdown at the Neon Armadillo". Since then, it has been performed on another TV program, Dick Clark's Rockin' New Year's Eve 1993, and by country-western enthusiasts in dance halls around the world. In addition to choreographing and teaching line dances, Hoss also coaches competition line dance teams.

Perhaps because of its creative hip work on beats 17 through 26, it has been nicknamed "Kool Dance". Hoss tells us that because the hip movements on beats 17 through 26 are so unusual, he varies that pattern when he teaches the dance, tailoring it to the preferences and capabilities of the particular group he is teaching. If you are not comfortable with the original hip sequence, try your own pattern. Just remember that the hip sequence must last for 10 beats.

New Concepts, Steps and Combinations

New Steps

Slide-up   Instructs you to move the designated foot while keeping it lightly in contact with the floor. This move produces a look of the foot being pulled from one position to the next. When a slide-up is completed, the sliding foot is touching the floor but bears no weight. Note that a slide is different from a slide-up. In a slide, the sliding foot bears weight; in a slide-up, it does not. For example, "slide-up **right** foot next to **left** foot" instructs you to move your right foot from its last position to a position next to your left foot, while keeping your right foot lightly in contact with the floor.

New Concepts

Lean   Instructs you to change, temporarily, the verticality of your body for the beats specified. Lean is used with foot directions to add body styling. When leaning accompanies hip bumps, the leaning is done from the waist up.

New Combinations

Toe Split   Instructs you to move your toes apart and then bring them back together in two beats of music. A toe split will begin from a position in which your feet are together and your weight is supported by both feet. On beat "1", move your toes apart. To execute this move, have your weight on the heels of your feet and move your right toe to the right and your left toe to the left. On beat "2", move your toes back together.

The Dance

Difficulty Level: II

Choreographer: Curtiss "Hoss" Marting

Dance Faces: four directions

Pattern Length: 40 Beats

Suggested Music:

For practicing – "Honey Hush" by Scooter Lee (Track 5 on **Free CD**), "Fast As You" originally recorded by Dwight Yoakam (Track 5 on CD included with Book 1)

For dancing – "Working For The Weekend" by Ken Mellons, "The Tribal Dance" by Two Unlimited.

Beats	Description
	Touches and Step-Slides
1	Touch **right** heel diagonally forward
2	Touch **right** toe next to **left** foot
3	Step **right** foot to right side (step as far to side as you can)
4	Slide-up **left** toe next to **right** foot
5	Touch **left** heel diagonally forward
6	Touch **left** toe next to **right** foot
7	Step **left** foot to left side (step as far to side as you can)
8	Slide-up **right** toe next to **left** foot
9	Touch **right** heel diagonally forward
10	Touch **right** toe next to **left** foot
11	Step **right** foot to right side (step as far to side as you can)
12	Slide-up **left** toe next to **right** foot
13	Touch **left** heel diagonally forward
14	Touch **left** toe next to **right** foot
15	Step **left** foot to left side (step as far to side as you can)
16	Slide **right** foot next to **left** foot
	Hip Bumps
17	Step **left** foot to left side and bump **left** hip to left side
18	Bump **left** hip to left side
19-20	Half hip roll, counterclockwise (begin left hip to left side)
21-22	Half hip roll, counterclockwise (begin left hip to left side)
23	Bump **left** hip to left side, lean forward
&	Bump **right** hip to right side, lean forward
24	Bump **left** hip to left side, lean forward
25	Bump **both** hips forward
26	Bump **both** hips forward
	Walk Forward
27	Step **right** foot forward
28	Step **left** foot forward
29	Step **right** foot forward
30	Step **left** foot forward

Touches, Turn and Jazz Box

31	Touch **right** heel forward
32	Touch **right** toe back
33	Step **right** foot forward and pivot ¼ turn right
34	Touch **left** toe to left side
35	Step **left** foot across **right** foot
36	Touch **right** toe to right side

37-40		Right jazz box with jump
	37	Step **right** foot across **left** foot
	38	Step **left** foot back
	39	Step **right** foot to right side
	40	Jump forward, landing with feet together

Repeat Pattern

Variation:

Some dancers, perhaps those less fond of hip bumps, make the following replacement:

25-26		Toe split
	25	Move toes apart
	26	Return toes to center

Some dancers add an extra jump at the end of the pattern:

&	Jump forward, landing with feet together
40	Jump forward, landing with feet together

Rhythm Line:

```
secs     .....1.....2.....3.....4.....5.....6.....7.....8.....9....10
120bpm   1   2   3   4   1   2   3   4   1   2   3   4   1   2   3   4   1   2   3   4
foot     R   R   R   L   L   L   L   R   R   R   R   L   L   L   L   R   L   .   .   .
other                                                            b   b   - h -
                                                            (hip bumps) (hip roll)

secs     ....11....12....13....14....15....16....17....18....19....20
120bpm   1 & 2   3 & 4   1 & 2   3   4   1   2   3   4   1   2   3   4   1   2   3   4
foot     .  .   .  .  .   .  .  .   R   L   R   L   R   R   R   L   L   R   R   L   R   B   repeat
Other    - h -   b b b   b b b
```

Cues:

right heel / toe / side / slide
left heel / toe / side / slide
right heel / toe / side / slide
left heel / toe / side / slide

left bump / bump
hip / roll / hip / roll
lean bump - and - bump / forward bump / bump

walk right / left / right / left
heel / toe / turn / side
cross / side
cross / back / side / jump

Little Squirt

About this dance: Bill Bader says that he likes to choreograph dances that are easy and fun. We think you will find both of those true of this dance. He also likes to find novel ways to get to new walls. He tells us that he created the last four beats of Little Squirt first, and built the rest of the dance around them. For extra fun, Bill suggests that you pantomime strumming a guitar during beats 9 through 20.

Bill has choreographed many dances that have become favorites and he has a collection of his dances for sale, "The Line Dance Choreography of Bill Bader – For All Levels of Line Dancers". You can reach him by writing to Bill Bader, Suite 1103, 1127 Barclay Street, Vancouver, British Columbia, Canada V6E 406.

New Concepts, Steps and Combinations

New Steps

Tap   Instructs you to move a particular part of your foot to the identified location without a weight transfer. In contrast to a touch, however, your foot will make only momentary contact with the floor. In a touch, your foot will stay in contact with the floor until the next step description. In a tap, raise your foot from the floor immediately after it makes contact with the floor. Directions to tap specify the part of the foot that should be used to execute the move. Frequently, when an instruction to tap is given, the toe or heel is moving in isolation. Please note that some dance writers use touch and tap synonymously. We do not. In our books, they are given different, specific definitions.

For example, "tap **left** heel in place (toe remains on floor from beat 5)" instructs you to bring your left heel to the floor, without moving your toe, and immediately lift your heel up from the floor.

New Combinations

Hip Scoop   Instructs you to move your hips in a half circle in a specified number of beats. The starting position of the hips (e.g., left side) will be specified in the dance description. The hip scoop is a continuous movement over the specified beats of music. The hips begin a hip scoop by moving down from their starting position, across the line of the body and up to finish at a position one half circle away from their starting position. In order to execute a hip scoop the knees must alternately straighten and bend. The leg under the beginning position will be straight while the other knee will be bent when the hip scoop begins. The straight leg bends its knee as the hips move across the line of the body, and the knee of the other leg straightens as the hip scoop is completed.

For example, "beats 1-4 Hip scoop (begin left hip to left side)" instructs you to move your hips to the left side position (if they are not already there) by straightening your left knee and bending your right knee, bend the knee of your left leg, push your hips in a straight line across your body, and straighten the knee of your right leg.

A hip scoop is very much like a half hip roll. However, in hip rolls the hips move around the body on a horizontal plane (or plane parallel to the floor) but in a hip scoop, the hips move across the line of the body on a vertical plane (or a plane perpendicular to the floor).

Sliding Toe Strut Instructs you to execute a toe strut, using a slide-up, instead of a touch, for the first movement. For example, "Right sliding toe strut forward" instructs you to, on beat "1" slide-up your right toe forward and on beat "2", lower your right heel, thereby stepping your right foot down. Keep in mind that, similar to toe struts, the slide-up on beat "1" may bear some weight, particularly when a turn is involved.

The Dance

Difficulty Level: II **Choreographer:** Bill Bader

Dance Faces: four directions **Pattern Length:** 32 Beats

Suggested Music:

For practicing – "Honey Hush" by Scooter Lee (Track 5 on **Free CD**), "Talk Some" originally recorded by Billy Ray Cyrus (Track 3 on CD included with Book 1).

For dancing – "Little Miss Honky Tonk" by Brooks and Dunn; "Honky Tonk World" by Chris LeDoux, "Girls With Guitars" by Wynonna

Beats	Description
	Sliding Toe Struts
1- 2	Sliding right toe strut forward
	1 Slide-up **right** toe forward (move only slightly forward)
	2 Lower **right** heel (step **right** foot down)
3 - 4	Sliding left toe strut forward
	3 Slide-up **left** toe forward (move only slightly forward)
	4 Lower **left** heel (step **left** foot down)
5- 6	Sliding right toe strut forward
	5 Slide-up **right** toe forward (move only slightly forward)
	6 Lower **right** heel (step **right** foot down)
7 - 8	Sliding left toe strut forward
	7 Slide-up **left** toe forward (move only slightly forward)
	8 Lower **left** heel (step **left** foot down)

Heel Taps and Turn

&	Slide-up **right** toe forward (move only slightly forward)
9	Tap **right** heel
10	Tap **right** heel
11	Tap **right** heel
12	Tap **right** heel
&	Pivot on **both** feet 1/4 turn left
13	Tap **left** heel
14	Tap **left** heel
15	Tap **left** heel
16	Tap **left** heel

Slow Twist and Steps, Slide And Hook

17-18	Slow twist ¼ turn right and hip scoop (begin right hip to right side)
19-20	Slow twist ¼ turn left and hip scoop (begin left hip to left side)
21	Step **left** foot forward
22	Slide **right** foot next to **left** foot
23	Step **left** foot forward
24	Hook **right** leg behind **left** leg (touching back of **left** knee with **right** leg)

Touches, Steps and Turn

25	Step **right** foot back
26	Tap **left** toe forward (only slightly forward)
27	Step **left** foot forward
28	Tap **right** toe back (only slightly back)
&	Step **right** foot back
29	Touch **left** heel forward
30	Step **left** foot forward
31	Touch **right** toe forward
32	Pivot on **left** foot ½ turn left

Repeat Pattern

Rhythm Line:

```
secs      .....1.....2.....3.....4.....5.....6.....7.....8.....9....10
120 bpm   1  2  3  4  1  2  3  4 &1  2  3  4 &1  2  3  4  1  2  3  4
foot      R  R  L  L  R  R  L  L RR  R  R  R BL  L  L  L (-B- )(-B- )
other                                                      slow  slow
secs      ....11....12....13....14....15....16....17....18....19....20
120 bpm   1  2  3  4  1  2  3  4 &1  2  3  4  1  2  3  4  1  2  3  4
foot      L  R  L  R  R  L  L  R RL  L  R  L repeat pattern
other
```

Cues:

slide / strut / slide / strut
slide / strut / slide / strut
slide - tap / tap / tap / tap
turn - tap / tap / tap / tap
slow / twist / slow / twist
left / slide / left / hook
back / tap / left / tap
back - heel / left / toe / turn

Ooo! Aah!

About this dance: We were really struck to learn that Sal Gonzalez's relationship with dancing is similar to Tony's. Sal, too, at one time, was not a dancer, but country-western dancing got him hooked! Now Sal dances (for fun and with competition teams), choreographs, and teaches line and partner dancing. Ooo! Aah! is choreographed to fit "Love Potion #9" by Hansel Martinez, beautifully. Sal would like you to know that the music is available from him. He can be reached by telephone at (in the US) 209-637-0597.

You need to stay alert when dancing Ooo! Aah!. In order for the dance to fit the music, the first five repetitions of the dance use all of the steps. After that, start each repetition with the step for beat 17.

New Concepts, Steps and Combinations

New Steps

Body Ripple

Describes a movement in which the body undulates like a wave. In a body ripple, the knees, hips, torso, shoulders and head move in sequence forward and back, or side to side. This move is difficult for many dancers and requires practice. A beginner's version of a body ripple might just include moving the hips and shoulders forward and back in opposition to one another.

New Combinations

Polka

Instructs you to make a shuffle and one other movement in two and a half beats of music. The direction of the polka (forward, backward, or to the side) and the foot that begins, or leads, the polka, will be specified in the dance description. The three shuffle steps take place on beats "1 & 2". The fourth step, which takes place on the next half-beat after beat "2", may be a kick, turn, or hop and will be specified in the dance description. The steps are done to a rhythm of "one-and-two-and".

For example, "right polka forward with $\frac{1}{2}$ turn left" instructs you to: on "1", step forward on your right foot; on "&", step the ball of your left foot next to heel of your right foot; on "2", step forward on your right foot; and on "&", pivot $\frac{1}{2}$ turn left on the ball of your right foot.

The Dance

Difficulty Level: II

Dance Faces: two directions

Choreographer: Sal Gonzalez

Pattern Length: 48 Beats

Suggested Music:

For practicing – "Honey Hush" by Scooter Lee (Track 5 on **Free CD**), "Fast As You" originally recorded by Dwight Yoakam (Track 5 on CD included with Book 1)

For dancing – "Love Potion # 9" by Hansel Martinez and "Cat Walk" by Lee Roy Parnell.

Beats	Description

Shuffles Forward

1 - 2	Right shuffle forward
	1 Step **right** foot forward
	& Step **left** foot next to **right** foot
	2 Step **right** foot forward
3 - 4	Left shuffle forward
	3 Step **left** foot forward
	& Step **right** foot next to **left** foot
	4 Step **left** foot forward
5 - 6	Right shuffle forward
	5 Step **right** foot forward
	& Step **left** foot next to **right** foot
	6 Step **right** foot forward
7 - 8	Left shuffle forward
	7 Step **left** foot forward
	& Step **right** foot next tc **left** foot
	8 Step **left** foot forward

Jazz Boxes with Turns

9 -12	Right jazz box with ¼ turn right and left brush
	9 Step **right** foot across **left** foot
	10 Step **left** foot back
	11 Step **right** foot to right side and pivot ¼ turn right
	12 Brush **left** foot across **right** foot
13-16	Left jazz box with ¼ turn left and right touch
	13 Step **left** foot across **right** foot
	14 Step **right** foot back
	15 Step **left** foot to left side and pivot ¼ turn left
	16 Touch **right** toe next to **left** foot

After the first five repetitions, the pattern omits the above steps and uses the remaining steps

Turning Shuffles to Sides

17-18   Right shuffle to side
      17   Step **right** foot to right side
      &   Step **left** foot next to **right** foot
      18   Step **right** foot to right side

19-20   Left shuffle to side with ½ turn right
      19   Pivot on **right** foot ½ turn right and step **left** foot to left side
            (as turn is completed)
      &   Step **right** foot next to **left** foot
      20   Step **left** foot to left side

21-22   Right shuffle to side with ½ turn left
      21   Pivot on **left** foot ½ turn left and step **right** foot to right side
            (as turn is completed)
      &   Step **left** foot next to **right** foot
      22   Step **right** foot to right side

23-24   Left kick-ball-change
      23   Kick **left** foot forward
      &   Step ball of **left** foot next to **right** foot
      24   Step **right** foot in place

25-26   Left shuffle to side
      25   Step **left** foot to left side
      &   Step **right** foot next to **left** foot
      26   Step **left** foot to left side

27-28   Right shuffle to side with ½ turn left
      27   Pivot on **left** foot ½ turn left and step **right** foot to right side
            (as turn is completed)
      &   Step **left** foot next to **right** foot
      28   Step **right** foot to right side

29-30   Left shuffle to side with ½ turn right
      29   Pivot on **right** foot ½ turn right and step **left** foot to left side
            (as turn is completed)
      &   Step **right** foot next to **left** foot
      30   Step **left** foot to left side

31-32   Right kick-ball-change
      31   Kick **right** foot forward
      &   Step ball of **right** foot next to **left** foot
      32   Step **left** foot in place

Rocks and Latin-Paddle Turn

33   Rock-step **right** foot forward
34   Rock back on **left** foot
35   Rock-step **right** foot back
36   Rock forward on **left** foot

37-40   ½ Latin-paddle turn to the left
      37   Latin-step **right** foot forward and pivot ¼ turn left
      38   Latin-step **left** foot in place
      39   Latin-step **right** foot forward and pivot ¼ turn left
      40   Latin-step **left** foot in place

Walk Forward and Body Ripple

41	Step **right** foot forward
42	Step **left** foot forward
43	Step **right** foot forward
44	Step **left** foot forward
45	Stomp **right** foot diagonally forward
46-48	Body ripple

Repeat Pattern

**Not thinking about the change in pattern,
Bessie invents the "OOPS, AHHH"!**

Variation:

Some people find it easier to turn on "shuffles" when they pivot on the half-beat after the shuffle. That is, they do a polka step. Thus, the multiple shuffles with alternating right and left half turns (beats 17-22 and 25-30), become easier if done as polkas with turns:

17-18	Right polka to side with ½ turn right	
	17	Step **right** foot to right side
	&	Step **left** foot next to **right** foot
	18	Step **right** foot to right side
	&	Pivot on **right** foot ½ turn right
19-20	Left polka to side with ½ turn left	
	19	Step **left** foot to left side
	&	Step **right** foot next to **left** foot
	20	Step **left** foot to left side
	&	Pivot on **left** foot ½ turn left
21-22	Right shuffle to side	
	21	Step **right** foot to right side
	&	Step **left** foot next to **right** foot
	22	Step **right** foot to right side
25-26	Left polka to side with ½ turn left	
	25	Step **left** foot to left side
	&	Step **right** foot next to **left** foot
	26	Step **left** foot to left side
	&	Pivot on **left** foot ½ turn left
27-28	Right polka to side with ½ turn right	
	27	Step **right** foot to right side
	&	Step **left** foot next to **right** foot
	28	Step **right** foot to right side
	&	Pivot on **right** foot ½ turn right
29-30	Left shuffle to side	
	29	Step **left** foot to left side
	&	Step **right** foot next to **left** foot
	30	Step **left** foot to left side

Rhythm Line:

This part is used in the first five repetitions of the full pattern.

```
secs    .....1.....2.....3.....4.....5.....6.....7.....8.....9....10
120bpm   1 & 2  3 & 4  1 & 2  3 & 4  1   2   3   4   1   2   3   4 continue below
foot     R L R  L R L  R L R  L R L  R   L   R   L   L   R   L   R
other
```

This part is used with above for first five repetitions and then by itself for the remainder of the dance.

```
secs    .....9....10....11....12....13....14....15....16....17....18
120bpm   1 & 2  3 & 4  1 & 2  3 & 4  1 & 2  3 & 4  1 & 2  3 & 4  1   2   3   4
foot     R L R  B R L  B L R  L L R  L R L  B L R  B R L  R R L  R   L   R   L
other
```

```
secs    ....19....20....21....22....23....24....25....26....27....28
120bpm   1   2   3   4   1   2   3   4   1   2   3   4   1   2   3   4   1   2   3   4
foot     R   L   R   L   R   L   R   L   R ————————          repeat pattern
other                                        body roll
```

Polka variation for beats 17-30

```
secs      .....9....10....11....12....13....14....15....16....17....18
120bpm    1 & 2 & 3 & 4 & 1 & 2  3 & 4  1 & 2 & 3 & 4 & 1 & 2  3 & 4  1  2  3  4
foot      R L R R L R L L R L R  L L R  L R L L R L R R L R L  R R L    as above
other
```

Cues:

right - and - right / left - and - left
right - and - right / left - and - left
cross / back / turn / brush
cross / back / turn / touch

right - and - right / turn - and - left
turn - and - right / kick - ball - change
left - and - left / turn - and - right
turn - and - left / kick - ball - change

rock forward / back / back / forward
turn / sway / turn / sway
right / left / right / left
stomp / r - o- ll

Polka variation for beats 17-32
right - and - right - turn - left - and - left - turn
right - and - right / kick - ball - change
left - and - left - turn - right - and - right - turn
left - and - left / kick - ball - change

Cruisin'

About this dance: This dance has been around for a while. Choreographed in 1989, it is still a favorite everywhere line dancing is done. Neil Hale is now an established line dance choreographer, but Cruisin' was one of his first attempts. He tells us that the dance was inspired by the song, "Still Cruisin' " by the Beach Boys. We think he's accomplished what he set out to do: capturing the song's message of "when you go cruisin' everything is all right." Like very few others, this dance is great at getting everyone out on the dance floor. Although choreographed as a line dance for individual dancers, we've often seen couples take a space on the dance floor and execute the turns while holding hands.

The Dance

Difficulty Level: II
Dance Faces: one direction

Choreographer: Neil Hale
Pattern Length: 32 Beats

Suggested Music:

For practicing – "Can't Help It" by Scooter Lee (Track 2 on **Free CD**), "Gulf of Mexico" originally recorded by Clint Black (Track 12 on CD included with Book 1)

For dancing – "Still Cruisin'" by the Beach Boys; "Tequila Sunrise" by Alan Jackson; "Heartache Tonight" by John Andersen; "What A Crying Shame" by The Mavericks, "Shadows in the Night" by Scooter Lee, "I Wanna Make You Mine" by Scooter Lee

---

Beats	Description
	Rocks Across and Cha-Chas
1	Rock-step **left** foot across **right** foot
2	Rock back on **right** foot
3 - 4	Left cha-cha in place
	3 Step **left** foot next to **right** foot
	& Step **right** foot in place
	4 Step **left** foot in place
5	Rock-step **right** foot across **left** foot
6	Rock back on **left** foot
7 - 8	Right cha-cha in place
	7 Step **right** foot next to **left** foot
	& Step **left** foot in place
	8 Step **right** foot in place
	Rocks Forward and Back and Cha-Chas
9	Rock-step **left** foot forward
10	Rock back on **right** foot
11-12	Left cha-cha back
	11 Step **left** foot back
	& Step **right** foot back
	12 Step **left** foot next to **right** foot
13	Rock-step **right** foot back
14	Rock forward on **left** foot
15-16	Right cha-cha forward
	15 Step **right** foot forward
	& Step **left** foot forward
	16 Step **right** foot next to **left** foot
	Military Turns
17-18	Military turn to the right
	17 Step **left** foot forward
	18 Pivot on **both** feet ½ turn right
19-20	Military turn to the right
	19 Step **left** foot forward
	20 Pivot on **both** feet ½ turn right

Vines and Turns

21-23   Left vine with ¼ turn left
         21   Step **left** foot to left side
         22   Step **right** foot behind **left** foot
         23   Step **left** foot to left side and pivot ¼ turn left

24-25   Military turn to the left
         24   Step **right** foot forward
         25   Pivot on **both** feet ½ turn left

26-28   Right vine with left and right turns
         26   Pivot on **left** foot ¼ turn left and step **right** foot to right side (as turn is completed)
         27   Step **left** foot behind **right** foot
         28   Step **right** foot to right side and pivot ¼ turn right

29-30   Military turn to the right
         29   Step **left** foot forward
         30   Pivot on **both** feet ½ turn right

Last Turn

31   Pivot on **right** foot ¼ turn right and step **left** foot to left side (as turn is completed)
32   Step **right** foot in place

Repeat Pattern

Rhythm Line:

```
secs    .....1.....2.....3.....4.....5.....6.....7.....8.....9....10
90bpm    1    2    3 & 4    1    2    3 & 4    1    2    3 & 4    1    2    3
foot     L    R    L R L    R    L    R L R    L    R    L R L    R    L    R

secs    ....11....12....13....14....15....16....17....18....19....20
90bpm   & 4    1    2    3    4    1    2    3    4    1    2    3    4    1    2
foot    L R    L    B    L    B    L    R    L    R    B    B    L    R    L    B

secs    ....21....22....23....24....25....26....27....28....29....30
90bpm    3    4    1    2    3    4    1    2    3    4    1    2    3    4    1
foot     B    R    repeat pattern
```

Cues:

cross / rock / cha - cha - cha
cross / rock / cha - cha - cha
rock forward / back / cha - cha - cha
rock back/ forward / cha - cha - cha

left / turn / left / turn

left / behind / turn
right / turn
turn / behind / turn
left / turn

turn / right

Level III

Kelly's Kannibals

About this dance: Liz and Bev Clarke tell us they were inspired to choreograph this dance on hearing "Cannibals" by Mark Knopfler. Why "Kelly's"? They dedicated it to Billy Kelly who at the time was organizing the Big, Big Country Festival in Glasgow, Scotland. Liz has been teaching and judging country-western dance for fourteen years. In September 1998, Liz and Bev are organizing the First Scottish Gathering of Country-Western Dance Championships. They can be reached by phone (in Scotland) at 01 436 675 798.

New Concepts, Steps and Combinations

New Steps

Flare Instructs you to make a low kick, keeping the foot parallel to the floor. While a kick generally brings the foot about six inches off the floor, in a flare the foot is lifted only high enough to avoid touching the floor. The direction of the flare will be specified in the dance description.

Right Flare Forward

Right Kick Forward

RIGHT LEG POSITIONS FOR FLARE AND KICK

New Combinations

Monterey Turn Instructs you to make four movements in four beats of music. The direction of the turn will be specified in the dance description. On "1", touch the lead foot

Right Chug

Right Hitch

(the foot in the direction of the turn) to the side. On "2", on the ball of the following foot, pivot ½ turn in the direction specified. Step the lead foot next to the following foot as the turn is completed. On "3", touch the toe of the following foot to the side. On "4", the following foot will be directed to touch or step next to the lead foot.

For example, "Monterey turn to the right" instructs you to: on "1", touch your right toe to the side; on "2", pivot ½ turn to the right on your left foot, stepping your right foot next to your left as you complete this turn; on "3", touch your left toe to the left side; on "4", step your left foot next to your right.

The Dance

Difficulty Level: III   **Choreographers:** Liz and Bev Clarke

Dance Faces: two directions   **Pattern Length:** 40 beats

Suggested Music:

For practicing – "Can't Help It" by Scooter Lee (Track 2 on **Free CD**), "Walkin' Away A Winner" originally recorded by Kathy Mattea (Track 1 on CD included with Book 1)

For dancing – "Cannibals" by Mark Knopfler.

Beats	Description
	Toe Struts
1 - 2	Right toe strut forward
	1 Touch **right** toe forward
	2 Lower **right** heel (step **right** foot down)
3 - 4	Left toe strut forward
	3 Touch **left** toe forward
	4 Lower **left** heel (step **left** foot down)
5 - 6	Right toe strut forward
	5 Touch **right** toe forward
	6 Lower **right** heel (step **right** foot down)
7 - 8	Left toe strut forward
	7 Touch **left** toe forward
	8 Lower **left** heel (step **left** foot down)
	Bumps
9	Step **right** foot to right side (step only slightly to the side) and bump **right** hip to right side
10	Hold
11	Bump **left** hip to left side
12	Hold
13	Bump **right** hip to right side
14	Bump **left** hip to left side
15	Bump **right** hip to right side
16	Bump **left** hip to left side
	Turning Jazz Boxes
17-20	Right jazz box with ¼ turn right and left step
	17 Step **right** foot across **left** foot
	18 Step **left** foot back
	19 Step **right** foot to right side and pivot ¼ turn right
	20 Step **left** foot next to **right** foot
21-24	Right jazz box with ¼ turn right and left step
	21 Step **right** foot across **left** foot
	22 Step **left** foot back
	23 Step **right** foot to right side and pivot ¼ turn right
	24 Step **left** foot next to **right** foot

Flares and Shuffles

25	Flare **right** foot forward
26	Flare **right** foot forward
27-28	Right shuffle in place
	27 Step **right** foot next to **left** foot
	& Step **left** foot in place
	28 Step **right** foot in place
29	Flare **left** foot forward
30	Flare **left** foot forward
31-32	Left shuffle in place
	31 Step **left** foot next to **right** foot
	& Step **right** foot in place
	32 Step **left** foot in place

Monterey Turns

33-36   Right Monterey turn
        33   Touch **right** toe to right side
        34   Pivot on **left** foot ½ turn right and step **right** foot next to **left** foot (as turn is completed)
        35   Touch **left** toe to left side
        36   Step **left** foot next to **right** foot
37-40   Right Monterey turn
        37   Touch **right** toe to right side
        38   Pivot on **left** foot ½ turn right and step **right** foot next to **left** foot (as turn is completed)
        39   Touch **left** toe to left side
        40   Step **left** foot next to **right** foot

Repeat Pattern

Variation:

On beats 10 and 12 replace holds with hip bumps
        10   Bump **right** hip to right side
        12   Bump **left** hip to left side

Rhythm Line:

```
secs      .....1.....2.....3.....4.....5.....6.....7.....8.....9....10
120bpm    1   2   3   4   1   2   3   4   1   2   3   4   1   2   3   4   1   2   3   4
foot      R   R   L   L   R   R   L   L   .   .   .   .   .   .   .   R   L   R   L
other                                     b       b       b   b   b   b
                                              (hip bumps)

secs      ....11....12....13....14....15....16....17....18....19....20
120bpm    1   2   3   4   1   2   3&4   1   2   3&4   1   2   3   4   1   2   3   4
foot      R   L   R   L   R   R   RLR   L   L   LRL   R   B   L   L   R   B   L   L   repeat
other
```

Cues:

toe / strut / toe / strut
toe / strut / toe / strut
bump right / hold / bump / hold
bump right / left / right / left

cross / back / turn / together
cross / back / turn / together
flare/ flare / right - and - right
flare/ flare / left - and - left

side / turn / side / together
side / turn / side / together

Sassy Stuff

About this dance: Sassy Stuff was the first dance that Dan and Sharon Ross jointly choreographed. They wanted to create a dance that would encourage younger dancers onto the dance floor and thought that the opportunity for individual expression offered in the final hip roll section might do that. This dance has been a favorite of dancers (of all ages) for awhile, so we think they've succeeded. Dan and Sharon have choreographed several other dances and teach line dancing at "Country World" in Virginia Beach, Virginia, USA. They encourage dancers to try their dances to different songs and would like to hear from people about the music to which they are dancing. They can be reached by telephone at 757-471-9147 or by e-mail at Dancrdan@aol.com. They also invite you to visit their internet site at http://members.aol.com/Dancrdan/index.html.

Sassy Stuff can be done in parallel lines or staggered contra lines. When this dance is done contra-style, the lines cross each other during the first eight beats. This dance will take some practice. The hip rolls in the last eight beats are fast. Remember that on beats 29 through 32&, the half hip-rolls with turns really form two full hip rolls. Try to keep these as continuous as possible.

New Combinations

Kick-Ball-Touch	Instructs you to make three steps, in a specified order, to two beats of music. The foot that begins or leads the kick-ball-touch will be specified in the dance description. On the first beat of a kick-ball-touch, the leading foot is kicked forward (about six inches off the floor). On the half-beat, the ball of the leading foot steps next to the following foot. On the second beat, the following foot touches as specified.
	For example, "right kick-ball-touch" instructs you to kick your right foot forward, step the ball of your right foot next to your left, and touch your left foot in place, to a rhythm of "one-and-two."

The Dance

Difficulty Level: III   **Choreographers:** Sharon and Dan Ross
Dance Faces: two directions   **Pattern Length:** 32 Beats
Suggested Music:

For practicing – "Honey Hush" by Scooter Lee (Track 5 on **Free CD**), "Shut Up And Kiss Me" originally recorded by Mary Chapin Carpenter (Track 8 on CD included with Book 1)

For dancing – "You Win My Love" and "Love Gets Me Every Time" by Shania Twain, "I'll Show You Mine if You Show Me Yours" by Tonja Rose, and "Give Me Some Love" by Gina G.

Beats   **Description**

Walking Hip Bumps

1   Step **right** foot diagonally forward and bump **right** hip diagonally
           forward
&   Bump **left** hip diagonally back
2   Bump **right** hip diagonally forward
3   Step **left** foot diagonally forward and bump **left** hip diagonally forward
&   Bump **right** hip diagonally back
4   Bump **left** hip diagonally forward
5   Step **right** foot diagonally forward and bump **right** hip diagonally
           forward
&   Bump **left** hip diagonally back
6   Bump **right** hip diagonally forward
7   Step **left** foot diagonally forward and bump **left** hip diagonally forward
&   Bump **right** hip diagonally back
8   Bump **left** hip diagonally forward

Kick-Ball-Touches, Turns and Shuffles

9-10   Right kick-ball-touch
           9   Kick **right** foot forward
           &   Step ball of **right** foot next to **left** foot
           10   Touch **left** toe to left side
11-12   Left kick-ball-touch
           11   Kick **left** foot forward
           &   Step ball of **left** foot next to **right** foot
           12   Touch **right** toe to right side

13   Step **right** foot behind **left** foot
14   Pivot on **both** feet ½ turn right
15-16   Left shuffle to left side
           15   Step **left** foot to left side
           &   Step **right** foot next to **left** foot
           16   Step **left** foot to left side

17-18   Right kick-ball-touch
           17   Kick **right** foot forward
           &   Step ball of **right** foot next to **left** foot
           18   Touch **left** toe to left side
19-20   Left kick-ball-touch
           19   Kick **left** foot forward
           &   Step ball of **left** foot next to **right** foot
           20   Touch **right** toe to **right** side

21   Step **right** foot behind **left** foot
22   Pivot on **both** feet ½ turn right
23-24   Left shuffle to left side
           23   Step **left** foot to left side
           &   Step **right** foot next to **left** foot
           24   Step **left** foot to left side

Half Hip Rolls and Bumps

25-&   Half hip roll, counter-clockwise (begin left hip to left side) and step
           right foot in place (as roll is completed)

26	Bump **left** hip diagonally forward
27-&	Half hip roll, clockwise (begin right hip to right side) and step **left** foot in place (as roll is completed)
28	Bump **right** hip diagonally forward

Full Hip Rolls with Turns

29-&	Half hip roll, counter-clockwise (begin left hip to left side) with turn
	29 Step **right** foot forward and begin half hip roll
	& Pivot on **both** feet ¼ turn left and complete half hip roll
30-&	Half hip roll, counter-clockwise (begin right hip to right side)
31-&	Half hip roll, counter-clockwise (begin left hip to left side) with turn
	31 Step **right** foot forward and begin half hip roll
	& Pivot on **both** feet ¼ turn left and complete half hip roll
32-&	Half hip roll, counter-clockwise (begin right hip to right side)

Repeat Pattern

Rhythm Line:

```
secs      .....1.....2.....3.....4.....5.....6.....7.....8.....9....10
120bpm    1 & 2   3 & 4   1 & 2   3 & 4   1 & 2   3 & 4   1   2   3 & 4   1 & 2   3 & 4
foot      R . .   L . .   R . .   L . .   R R L   L L R   R   B   L R L   R R L   L L R
other     b b b   b b b   b b b   b b b
          (hip bumps)
```

```
secs      ....11....12....13....14....15....16....17....18....19....20
120bpm    1   2   3 & 4   1 & 2   3 & 4   1 & 2 & 3 & 4 & 1   2   3   4   1   2   3   4
foot      R   B   L R L   . R .   . L .   R B . . R B . .       repeat pattern
other             -h-b   -h-b   -h-h-h-h-h-
                  (hip roll)
```

Cues:

bump right - and - right / bump left - and - left
bump right - and - right / bump left - and - left

right kick - ball - touch / left kick - ball - touch
behind / turn / left - and - left
right kick - ball - touch / left kick - ball - touch
behind / turn / left - and - left

hip- roll / bump left / hip - roll / bump right
roll - turn - hip - roll - roll - turn - hip - roll

You Know

About this dance: People all over the world are choreographing line dances. *You Know* was created by Gordon Elliot of Erskineville, NSW, Australia. It will be used as one of the competition dances at the UCWDC World Championships VII in January,1999. A former aerobics instructor, Gordon has been involved in line dancing for 8 years. Gordon teaches at the Wool Away Woolshed Line Dance Club in Picton and the John Edmonson Memorial Line Dance Club in Liverpool and conducts workshops throughout Australia and New Zealand. He frequently is a judge at line dance competitions including two recent UCWDC World Championships.

Gordon has prepared a series of line dance albums called "Australia's Favourite Line Dances". Each album contains up to fourteen musical tracks and dance steps descriptions. Gordon can be reached at (in Australia) 61-2-9550-6789.

New Concepts, Steps and Combinations

New Combinations

Sugar Foot   Instructs you to make a heel and toe touch of the designated foot to two beats of music and, for these two beats, the weight is supported by the other foot. In a sugar foot, sometimes the heel touches first and sometimes the toe touches first: the order will be specified in the dance description. The heel and toe touches are both done next to the weighted foot. On the heel touches, the foot is turned out. On the toe touches, the foot is turned in.

For example, "Right toe-heel sugar foot" instructs you to, on "1", touch your right toe next to your left foot (right foot turned in), and on "2", touch your right heel next to your left foot (right foot turned out).

The Dance

Difficulty Level: III   **Choreographer:** Gordon Elliott
Dance Faces: two directions   **Pattern Length:** 64 beats
Suggested Music:

For practicing – "Honey Hush" by Scooter Lee (Track 5 on Free CD), "The City Put The Country Back in Me" originally recorded by Neil McCoy (Track 2 on CD included with Book 1).

For dancing – "You Know Where I Am" by Scooter Lee

Beats	Description
	Side Steps and Crosses
&	Step **right** foot to right side
1	Stomp **left** foot in place
2	Hold
3	Step **right** foot across **left** foot
4	Hold
5	Step **left** foot to left side
6	Hold
7	Step **right** foot across **left** foot
8	Hold
&	Step **left** foot to left side
9	Stomp **right** foot in place
10	Hold
11	Step **left** foot across **right** foot
12	Hold
13	Step **right** foot to right side
14	Hold
15	Step **left** foot across **right** foot
16	Hold
	Steps and Struts
&	Step **right** foot back
17	Stomp **left** foot forward
18	Hold
19-20	Right heel strut
	19 Touch **right** heel forward
	20 Lower **right** toe (step **right** foot down)
21-22	Left heel strut
	21 Touch **left** heel forward
	22 Lower **left** toe (step **left** foot down)
23	Step **right** foot forward
24	Touch **left** foot next to **right** foot

Polkas and Turns

25-26   Left polka back with ½ turn right
25   Step **left** foot back
&   Step **right** foot next to **left** foot
26   Step **left** foot back
&   Pivot on **left** foot ½ turn right
27-28   Right polka forward with ½ turn right
27   Step **right** foot forward
&   Step **left** foot next to **right** foot
28   Step **right** foot forward
&   Pivot on **right** foot ½ turn right

29-30   Left shuffle back
29   Step **left** foot back
&   Step **right** foot next to **left** foot
30   Step **left** foot back
31   Step **right** foot back
32   Rock forward on **left** foot

Sugar Feet and Crosses

33-34   Right toe-heel sugar foot
33   Touch **right** toe *(turned in)* next to **left** foot
34   Touch **right** heel *(turned out)* next to **left** foot
35   Step **right** foot across **left** foot
&   Step **left** foot to left side
36   Step **right** foot across **left** foot

37-38   Left toe-heel sugar foot
37   Touch **left** toe *(turned in)* next to **right** foot
38   Touch **left** heel *(turned out)* next to **right** foot
39   Step **left** foot across **right** foot
&   Step **right** foot to right side
40   Step **left** foot across **right** foot

Rocks and Claps

41   Step **right** foot to right side
42   Rock to left side on **left** foot
43   Step **right** foot across **left** foot
44   Clap

45   Step **left** foot to left side
46   Rock to right side on **right** foot
47   Step **left** foot across **right** foot
48   Clap

Toe Struts Back

49-50   Right toe strut back
49   Touch **right** toe back
50   Lower **right** heel (step **right** foot down)
51-52   Left toe strut back
51   Touch **left** toe back
52   Lower **left** heel (step **left** foot down)

53-54   Right toe strut back
53   Touch **right** toe back
54   Lower **right** heel (step **right** foot down)

55-56	Left toe strut back
	55 Touch **left** toe back
	56 Lower **left** heel (step **left** foot down)

Shuffles with Turns

57-58	Right shuffle forward
	57 Step **right** foot forward
	& Step **left** foot next to **right** foot
	58 Step **right** foot forward
59-60	Military turn to the right
	59 Step **left** foot forward
	60 Pivot on **both** feet ½ turn right

61-62	Left shuffle forward
	61 Step **left** foot forward
	& Step **right** foot next to **left** foot
	62 Step **left** foot forward
63	Step **right** foot forward
64	Pivot on **both** feel ¼ turn left

Repeat Pattern

Rhythm Line:

```
secs      ....1....2....3....4....5....6....7....8....9...10...11...12
150bpm    &1 2 3 4 1 2 3 4&1 2 3 4 1 2 3 4&1 2 3 4 1 2 3 4 1&2&3&4&1&2
foot      RL . R . L . R .LR . L . R . L .RL . R R L L R L LRLLRLRRLRL
other

secs      ...13...14...15...16...17...18...19...20...21...22...23...24
150bpm    3 4 1 2 3&4 1 2 3&4 1 2 3 4 1 2 3 4 1 2 3 4 1 2 3 4 1&2 3 4
foot      R L R R RLR L L LRL R L R . L R L . R R L L R R L L RLR L B
other                                     c           c
                                       (clap)

secs      ...25...26...27...28...29...30...31...32...33...34...35...36
150bpm    1&2 3 4    repeat pattern
foot      LRL R B
other
```

Cues:

right - stomp / hold / cross / hold
left / hold / cross / hold
left - stomp / hold / cross / hold
right / hold / cross / hold

back - stomp / hold / heel / strut
heel / strut / right / together
back - and - back - turn - right - and - right - turn
back - and - back / back / forward

toe / heel / cross - and - cross
toe / heel / cross - and - cross
right / rock / cross / clap
left / rock / cross / clap

back / strut / back / strut
back / strut / back / strut
right - and - right / left / turn
left - and - left / right / turn

Louisiana Hot Sauce

About this dance: This dance is also called "My Little Jalepeño". It's hot! Four choreographers collaborated on this number. It is always done when the DJ plays Scooter Lee's "He's My Little Jalepeño".

New Concepts, Steps and Combinations

New Steps

Lunge-stomp Instructs you to move your foot to the indicated location, bending the knee of the moving leg and bringing it to the floor in a stomp. Move as far in the indicated direction as you are comfortably able to move.

The Dance

Difficulty Level: III   **Choreographers:** Joanne Brady, Gordon Elliott, Max Perry, and Jo Thompson

Dance Faces: 2 directions   **Pattern Length:** 32 Beats

Suggested Music:

For practicing – "Can't Help It " by Scooter Lee (Track 2 on **Free CD**), "Walkin' Away A Winner" originally recorded by Kathy Mattea (Track 1 on CD included with Book 1)

For dancing – "He's My Little Jalepeño" by Scooter Lee.

Beats	Description
	Foot Isolations
1	Touch **left** heel forward
&	Touch **left** toe forward
2	Tap **left** heel (toe remains in place from beat 1&)
&	Lower **left** heel (step **left** foot down)
3	Touch **right** heel forward
&	Touch **right** toe forward
4	Tap **right** heel (toe remains in place from beat 3&)
&	Lower **right** heel (step **right** foot down)
	Across, Unwind and Swivels
5	Step **left** foot across **right** foot
6	Pivot on **both** feet ½ turn right and swivel heels to left (as turn is completed)
7	Swivel heels to right
&	Swivel heels to left
8	Swivel heels to right
&	Clap

Jog Forward with a Hitch, Scoot and Clap

9	Step ball of **left** foot forward
&	Step ball of **right** foot forward
10	Step ball of **left** foot forward
&	Hitch **right** leg and scoot **left** foot forward and clap
11	Step ball of **right** foot forward
&	Step ball of **left** foot forward
12	Step ball of **right** foot forward
&	Hitch **left** leg and scoot **right** foot forward and clap

Back and Stomp

13	Step **left** foot directly in back of **right** foot
&	Hitch **right** leg and scoot **left** foot back
14	Step **right** foot directly in back of **left** foot
&	Step **left** foot directly in back of **right** foot
15	Lunge-stomp **right** foot diagonally forward
16	Hold

Cross Rocks with Knee Bends and Left Paddle Turn

17	Rock-step **left** foot across **right** foot, lowering body
&	Rock back on **right** foot, raising body
18	Step **left** foot to left side (step only slightly to left)
19	Rock-step **right** foot across **left** foot, lowering body
&	Rock back on **left** foot, raising body
20	Step **right** foot to right side (step only slightly to right)
21	Rock-step **left** foot across **right** foot, lowering body
&	Rock back on **right** foot, raising body
22-24	Full Paddle turn to the left
	22 Step **left** foot to left side (step only slightly to left) and pivot ⅓ turn left
	& Step **right** foot next to **left** foot
	23 Step **left** foot in place and pivot ⅓ turn left
	& Step **right** foot next to **left** foot
	24 Step **left** foot in place and pivot ⅓ turn left

Cross Rocks with Knee Bends and Right Paddle Turn

25	Rock-step **right** foot across **left** foot, lowering body
&	Rock back on **left** foot, raising body
26	Step **right** foot to right (step only slightly to right)
27	Rock-step **left** foot across **right** foot, lowering body
&	Rock back on **right** foot, raising body
28	Step **left** foot to left (step only slightly to left)
29	Rock-step **right** foot across **left** foot, lowering body
&	Rock back on **left** foot, raising body
30-32	Full Paddle turn to the right
	30 Step **right** foot to right side (step only slightly to right side) and pivot ⅓ turn right
	& Step **left** foot next to **right** foot
	31 Step **right** foot in place and pivot ⅓ turn right
	& Step **left** foot next to **right** foot
	32 Step **right** foot in place and pivot ⅓ turn right

Repeat Pattern

Rhythm Line:

```
secs      .....1.....2.....3.....4.....5.....6.....7.....8.....9....10
120bpm    1 & 2 & 3 & 4 & 1   2   3 & 4 & 1 & 2 & 3 & 4 & 1 & 2 & 3   4   1 & 2   3 & 4
foot      L L L L R R R L   B   B B B B L R L B R L R B L B R L R   .   L R L   R L R
other                                     c         c
                                        (clap)
```

```
secs      ....11....12....13....14....15....16....17....18....19....20
120bpm    1 & 2 & 3 & 4   1 & 2   3 & 4   1 & 2 & 3 & 4   1   2   3   4   1   2   3   4
foot      L R L R L R L   R L R   L R L   R L R L R L R   repeat pattern
other
```

Cues:

heel - toe - tap - down - heel - toe - down
cross / turn / right - left - right - clap
left - right - left - hitch - right - left - right - hitch
back - hitch - back - rock - stomp / hold

cross - rock - side / cross - rock - side
cross - rock - turn - together - turn - together - turn
cross - rock - side / cross - rock - side
cross - rock - turn - together - turn - together - turn

Lamtarra Rhumba

About this dance: As the name suggests, the standard rhumba pattern and rhumba syncopations are the basis for the choreography. The standard rhumba pattern consists of three steps to four beats of music: two quick steps (one beat each) and one slow step (taking two beats). This dance has a nice Latin feel and we think you will enjoy it. We have seen a variation in which the three steps of "quick, quick, slow" are interpreted as 3 quick (or regular steps) followed by a hold for one beat. If the steps are taken in this manner, the dance will have a more stacatto look.

New Concepts, Steps and Combinations

New Combinations

Weave   Instructs you to make a series of movements in which steps across and behind alternate with steps to the side. The number of beats involved in the weave will be specified in the dance description and each step will be done to one beat of music. The direction of the weave (e.g., "to left", "diagonally right") will be specified. A weave will be identified by its initial step(s): across, behind, side then across, or side then behind.

For example, "beats 1- 4 Weave to right (begin across)" tells you to: on "1", step your left foot across your right, on "2", step your right foot to the right side, on "3", step your left foot behind your right, and on "4", again step your right foot to the right side.

Doing a weave may feel very much like doing a vine. In fact, a weave is a special type of vine. It is different from the vines you have danced so far in that the crossing steps are alternately in front of and behind the weighted foot and weaves may be longer than three steps.

The Dance

Difficulty Level: III   **Choreographer:** Tony Chapman

Dance Faces: four directions   **Pattern Length:** 56 Beats

Suggested Music:

For practicing — "Can't Help It" by Scooter Lee (Track 2 on **Free CD**), "I Wanna Go Too Far" originally recorded by Trisha Yearwood (Track 4 on CD included with Book 1)

For dancing — "Cowboy Mambo" by Tom Russell, "Island Time" by Larry Joe Taylor, "New Train" by John Prine.

Beats	Description

Box Steps

Beats	Description
1	Step **left** foot to left side
2	Slide **right** foot next to **left** foot
3-4	Slow step **left** foot forward
5	Step **right** foot to right side
6	Slide **left** foot next to **right** foot
7-8	Slow step **right** foot back

Latin Steps in Place

Beats	Description
9	Latin-step **left** foot next to **right** foot
10	Latin-step **right** foot in place
11-12	Slow Latin-step **left** foot in place
13	Latin-step **right** foot in place
14	Latin-step **left** foot in place
15-16	Slow Latin-step **right** foot in place

Slow Steps and Rocks

Beats	Description
17-18	Slow step **left** foot forward
19-20	Slow step **right** foot forward
21	Rock-step **left** foot across **right** foot
22	Rock back on **right** foot
23-24	Slow step **left** foot back
25-26	Slow step **right** foot forward
27-28	Slow step **left** foot forward
29	Rock-step **right** foot across **left** foot
30	Rock back on **left** foot
31-32	Slow step **right** foot back

Side Step and Break

Beats	Description
33	Step **left** foot to left side
34	Step **right** foot next to **left** foot
35-36	Slow step **left** foot to left side
37	Step **right** foot behind **left** foot
38	Rock forward on **left** foot
39-40	Slow step **right** foot to right side

Weave and Turn

Beats	Description
41-48	Weave to the right (begin behind) with ¼ turn left
41	Step **left** foot behind **right** foot
42	Step **right** foot to right side
43	Step **left** foot across **right** foot
44	Step **right** foot to right side
45	Step **left** foot behind **right** foot
46	Step **right** foot to right side
47	Step **left** foot across **right** foot
48	Step **right** foot to right side and pivot on **both** feet ¼ turn left

Slow Steps and Turns

49-50	Slow step **right** foot forward
51-52	Slow step **left** foot forward
53	Step **right** foot forward and pivot ¼ turn left
54	Step **left** foot next to **right** foot
55-56	Slow pivot on **left** foot ¼ turn right and step **right** foot forward (as turn is completed)

Repeat Pattern

Rhythm Line:

```
secs      .....1.....2.....3.....4.....5.....6.....7.....8.....9....10
120bpm    1   2   3   4   1   2   3   4   1   2   3   4   1   2   3   4   1   2   3   4
foot      L   R  (-L-)  R   L  (-R-)  L   R  (-L-)  R   L  (-R-) (-L-) (-R-)
other         (slow)

secs      ....11....12....13....14....15....16....17....18....19....20
120bpm    1   2   3   4   1   2   3   4   1   2   3   4   1   2   3   4   1   2   3   4
foot      L   R  (-L-) (-R-) (-L-)  R   L  (-R-)  L   R  (-L-)  R   L  (-R-)
other

secs      ....21....22....23....24....25....26....27....28....29....30
120bpm    1   2   3   4   1   2   3   4   1   2   3   4   1   2   3   4   1   2   3   4
foot      L   R   L   R   L   R   L   B  (-R-) (-L-)  R   L  (-B-) repeat pattern
other
```

Cues:

left / slide / slow / left
right / slide / slow / right
left / right / slow / left
right / left / slow / right

slow / left / slow / right
rock cross / back / slow / back
slow / right / slow / left
rock cross / back / slow / back

left / together / slow / side
behind / rock / slow / side
behind / side / cross / side
behind / side / cross / turn

slow / right / slow / left
turn / together / slow / turn

West Coast Shuffle

About this dance: Donna Nussman and Greg Underwood are dance instructors and country-western dance competitors. They are fond of the partners' freestyle dance, West Coast Swing, but were dismayed that it wasn't popular in their area, Charlotte, North Carolina. That led to their choreographing West Coast Shuffle. Based on the 1,2,3,4,5&6 pattern of West Coast Swing, they thought it might help generate some interest in that dance style. It worked! West Coast Shuffle has been performed in many popular dance spots and is a favorite in many places where line dancing is done. This dance might take some practice to master. Because your feet are in "turned in" position on beats 13-16, you will appear to be swiveling as you walk forward. Also, note that on beats 29-31 your left foot bears no weight. The move will probably be easier to learn if you just don't think about your left foot!

New Concepts, Steps and Combinations

New Combinations

Coaster Step
Instructs you to make three back and forward steps in two beats of music. The foot that leads the sequence will be identified in the dance description. On beat "1", the lead foot steps back. On "&", the following foot steps next to the lead foot. On "2", the lead foot steps forward. Because of the quick change of direction involved, the first two steps should be taken on the balls of the feet. This movement produces a look of the feet backing away from the body.

For example, "right coaster step" instructs you to: on "1", step back on the ball of your right foot, on "&", step the ball of your left foot next to your right, and on "2", step forward on your right foot.

Swivel heels
Instructs you to turn one or both heels in the direction specified (i.e., left, right or center). Movement is executed by supporting the weight on the balls of the swiveling feet and turning the heels approximately 45 degrees in the direction indicated. While your feet move in this step, your body continues to face forward. Note that a "swivel" is different from a "twist" in which your body would be allowed to move with your feet. Note also, "swivel heels"(in which your heels are turned) is different from "swivel toes" (in which your toes are turned.)

For example, "swivel heels left" instructs you to put your body weight over the balls of both feet and turn your heels to the left. Note that when you complete this move, your toes will be pointed to the right. "Swivel heels center" instructs you to return your heels to their starting position under your body.

The Dance

Difficulty Level: III

Choreographers: Greg Underwood &
Donna Nussman

Dance Faces: four directions

Pattern Length: 32 Beats

Suggested Music:

For practicing — "Honey Hush" by Scooter Lee (Track 5 on **Free CD**), "Walkin' Away A Winner" originally recorded by Kathy Mattea (Track 1 on CD included with Book 1)

For dancing — "Wink" by Neal McCoy; "Heart's Desire" by Lee Roy Parnell, "Take It Back" by Reba McIntyre, "Be Bop A Lula" by Scooter Lee, "Heart Break Hotel" by Scooter Lee

Beats	Description
1	Step **right** foot forward
2	Step **left** foot forward
3	Kick **right** foot forward
4	Step **right** foot back
5 - 6	Left coaster step
5	Step **left** foot back
&	Step **right** foot next to **left** foot
6	Step **left** foot forward
7	Step **right** foot forward
8	Step **left** foot forward
9	Kick **right** foot forward
10	Step **right** foot back
11-12	Left coaster step
11	Step **left** foot back
&	Step **right** foot next to **left** foot
12	Step **left** foot forward

Swivel Walk Forward

Beats	Description
13	Step **right** foot *(turned in)* across **left** foot
14	Step **left** foot *(turned in)* across **right** foot
15	Step **right** foot *(turned in)* across **left** foot
16	Step **left** foot *(turned in)* across **right** foot

Jumping Side Steps

Beats	Description
17	Touch **right** toe to right side
18	Hold
&	Step **right** foot next to **left** foot
19	Touch **left** toe to left side
20	Hold
&	Step **left** foot next to **right** foot
21	Touch **right** toe to right side
&	Step **right** foot next to **left** foot
22	Touch **left** toe to left side
&	Step **left** foot next to **right** foot
23	Kick **right** foot forward
24	Kick **right** foot forward

Turns

25   Step **right** foot back
26   Pivot on **both** feet ½ turn right
27   Step **right** foot back
28   Pivot on **both** feet ¼ turn right

Swivel and Drag

(On beats 29-31&, your **right** foot bears your weight while the **left** foot is dragged
            along.)
29   Step **right** foot to right side (step only slightly to side)
29-31&   Draw-up **left** toe next to **right** foot while swivelling **right** toe and heel
            29   Swivel **right** toe to right and begin to draw-up **left** toe
            &   Swivel **right** heel to right and continue to draw-up **left** toe
            30   Swivel **right** toe to right and continue to draw-up **left** toe
            &   Swivel **right** heel to right and continue to draw up **left** toe
            31   Swivel **right** toe to right and continue to draw-up **left** toe
            &   Swivel **right** toe to center and end draw-up of **left** toe
32   Stomp **left** foot next to **right** foot

Repeat Pattern

Rhythm Line:

```
secs      .....1.....2.....3.....4.....5.....6.....7.....8.....9....10
120bpm    1   2   3   4   1 & 2   3   4   1   2   3 & 4   1   2   3   4   1   2 & 3   4
foot      R   L   R   R   LRL   R   L   R   R   LRL   R   L   R   L   R   .RL   .
other

secs      ....11....12....13....14....15....16....17....18....19....20
120bpm    & 1 & 2 & 3   4   1   2   3   4 & 1 & 2 & 3 & 4   1   2   3   4   1   2   3   4
foot      LRRLLR   R   R   B   R   BRBBBBBBL   repeat pattern
```

Cues:

right / left / kick / back
back - together - forward

right / left / kick / back
back - together - forward

swivel / swivel / swivel / swivel
touch / hold / - and - touch / hold
and- touch - and - touch - and - kick / kick

back / turn / back / turn - right
toe - heel - toe - heel - toe - heel - stomp

Funky Cowboy (II)

About this dance: We presented an older Funky Cowboy in book one. This one is newer and, perhaps, funkier. Style is everything in this dance so details are important. Note that on beats 13 to 16, your goal is to walk back in a straight, narrow line.

The choreographers of this dance, Kevin Johnson and Vickie Vance-Johnson, are well established in the country-western dance world. They are United Country Western Dance Council (UCWDC) Master competitors and are seven-time Division 1 National Grand Champions. They have choreographed other popular line dances and own and operate the Headquarters Dance Studio in Franklin, Tennessee.

New Concepts, Steps and Combinations

New Steps

Knock knees   Instructs you to, on the designated musical beat, bring your knees together (much as you bring your hands together in a clap.)

New Combinations

Side Jack   Instructs you to make four movements in two beats of music. The foot which leads the move will be identified in the dance description. On the half-beat before "1", the leading foot steps to the side. On "1", the following foot steps to the side. On "&", the leading foot steps home. On "2", the following foot steps home or as specified.

For example, "Side Jack (begin right)" instructs you to: on "&", step your right foot to the right side, on "1", step your left foot to the left side, on "&", step your right foot home, and on "2", step your left foot home.

Knee Roll   Instructs you to bend your knee and move it in a circular motion in a specified number of beats. The direction (clockwise or counter-clockwise), extent of rotation (half-circle or full circle) and the starting position of the knee (e.g., left diagonal forward) will be specified. The knee roll is a continuous movement over the specified beats of music. As with a knee swivel, knee rolls are generally easier to execute if the weight of the body is supported primarily on the foot opposite the rolling knee. The knee that rolls pivots on the ball of the foot.

For example, "beats 1-2 Full left knee roll, counter-clockwise (begin forward)" instructs you to push your knee forward (if it is not already there), move it in a circular motion left, then back, and continuing this circular motion, return it to its starting position

The Dance

Difficulty Level: III

Choreographers: Kevin Johnson and Vickie Vance-Johnson

Dance Faces: four directions

Pattern Length: 48 Beats

Suggested Music:

For practicing – "Honey Hush" by Scooter Lee (Track 5 on **Free CD**), "Talk Some" originally recorded by Billy Ray Cyrus (Track 3 on CD included with Book 1)

For dancing – "Funky Cowboy" by Ronnie McDowell.

Beats	Description
	Cross Hitches
1	Hitch **right** leg across **left** leg
2	Touch **right** toe to right side
3	Hitch **right** leg across **left** leg
4	Touch **right** toe to right side
	Swivels and Swings
5	Swivel **left** heel to right and touch **right** heel across **left** foot, face diagonally left
6	Swivel **left** toe to right and touch **right** heel diagonally forward, face diagonally right
7	Swivel **left** heel to right and touch **right** heel across **left** foot, face diagonally left
8	Swivel **left** toe to center and step **right** foot next to **left** foot, face forward
9	Stomp **left** foot in place
&	Pivot on **left** foot ¼ turn right
10	Touch **right** toe forward
11	Step **right** foot next to **left** foot
12	Left ½ swing counterclockwise (begin forward)
	Walk Back and Rock
13	Step **left** foot directly in back of **right** foot
14	Right ¼ swing clockwise (begin right side) and step **right** foot directly in back of **left** foot (as swing is completed)
15	Left ¼ swing counterclockwise (begin left side) and step **left** foot directly in back of **right** foot (as swing is completed)
&	Rock back on **left** heel
16	Rock forward on ball of **right** foot

Hip Rolls with Turns, Stomp and Touches

17-18   Full hip roll, counterclockwise (begin right hip to right side) with turn
         17   Begin full hip roll
         18   Pivot on **left** foot ⅛ turn left and complete full hip roll
19-20   Full hip roll, counterclockwise (begin right hip to right side) with turn
         19   Begin full hip roll
         20   Pivot on **left** foot ⅛ turn left and complete full hip roll

21   Stomp **right** foot next to **left** foot
22   Touch **left** heel forward
&   Step **left** foot next to **right** foot
23   Touch **right** toe next to **left** foot
24   Hold

Knee Rolls

25-26   Full right knee roll, clockwise (begin forward)
27-28   Full left knee roll, clockwise (begin forward)

29-&   Full right knee roll, clockwise (begin forward)
30-&   Full right knee roll, clockwise (begin forward)
31   Knock knees
32   Knock knees

Steps, Slides, and Touches

33   Step **right** foot to right side
34   Slide **left** foot next to **right** foot
35   Step **right** foot to right side and pivot ¼ turn right
36   Slide-up **left** foot next to **right** foot

37   Pivot on **right** foot ⅛ turn right and step **left** foot forward (as turn is completed)
38   Touch **right** toe next to **left** instep
39   Pivot on **left** foot ¼ turn right and step **right** foot forward (as turn is completed)
40   Pivot on **right** foot ⅛ turn left and touch **left** toe next to **right** instep

Side-Jack and Turn

&- 42   Side jack (begin left)
         &   Step **left** foot to left side
         41   Step **right** foot to right side
         &   Step **left** foot home
         42   Step **right** foot across **left** foot
43   Pivot on **both** feet ½ turn left
44   Hold

Hip Thrusts and Ripples

&   Bump **both** hips back and extend both arms forward
45   Bump **both** hips forward and pull arms back to body
&   Bump **both** hips back and extend both arms forward
46   Bump **both** hips forward and pull arms back to body
47-48   Body ripple

Repeat Pattern

Funky Cowboy (II)

Rhythm Line:

```
secs     .... 1.....2.....3.....4.....5.....6.....7.....8.....9....10
120bpm   1   2   3   4   1   2   3   4   1&2  3   4   1   2  3&4  1   2   3   4
foot     R   R   R   R   B   B   B   B   LLB  R-L-L    R  LRL  .   L   .   L
other                                                  sw      sw  sw      hip rolls
                                                     (swing)

secs     ....11....12....13....14....15....16....17....18....19....20
120bpm   1   2&3  4   1   2   3   4   1&2&3    4   1   2   3   4   1   2   3   4
foot     R   LLR  .   R-R  L-L  RRLLB    B   R   L   R   L   L   R   R   L
other             kr   kr   kr kr (knee
                 (knee rolls)    knocks)

secs     ....21....22....23....24....25....26....27....28....29....30
120bpm   &1&2  3   4&1&2    3   4   1   2   3   4   1   2   3   4   1   2   3   4
foot     LRLR  B   .....     .  .   repeat pattern
other          b b b b   ripple
              (bumps)
```

Cues:

hitch / side / hitch / side
swivel / swivel / swivel / together
stomp - and - touch / together / swing
step / back / back - rock - rock

roll / turn / roll / turn
stomp / heel - ball - toe / hold
knee / roll / knee / roll
knee roll / knee roll / knock / knock

right / slide / right / slide
turn / touch / turn / turn
out - out - in - cross / turn / hold
arms - bump - arms - bump / body / ripple

Cowboy Stomp

About this dance: Rick and Deborah have choreographed many line dances and several partnered round dances. Rick Bates tells us that the inspiration for this dance came when he was reading an interview with Curtis Day, who recorded "The Cowboy Stomp". In the interview, Day suggested that his new song would be perfect for a high energy dance. Intrigued, Rick purchased the CD, listened to the track, and in an hour, the dance was formed. We're sure you'll like it. Illusions are important here. The side rocks on beats and half-beats happen so quickly that you will appear to be pushing away from one step to get to the next.

Note that the pattern begins on the half-beat before the lyrics start. We have seen descriptions of this dance that place the first step on the first beat of the lyrics, but our description reflects the choreographer's design.

New Concepts, Steps and Combinations

New Steps

Leap   Instructs you to move the identified foot by lifting off from the other foot and landing on the ball of the identified foot in the specified location. As in a jump, in a leap both feet will be off the floor, if only for a moment.

For example, "leap **right** foot forward" instructs you to lift off from your left foot and land forward on the ball of your right foot. This move will be more comfortable to execute if you bend, slightly, the knee of your right leg.

The Dance

Difficulty Level: III   **Choreographers:** Rick and Deborah Bates

Dance Faces: four directions   **Pattern Length:** 48 Beats

Suggested Music:

For practicing – "Can't Help It" by Scooter Lee (Track 2 on **Free CD**), "Fast As You" originally recorded by Dwight Yoakam (Track 5 on CD included with Book 1).

For dancing – "The Cowboy Stomp" by Curtis Day.

Beats	Description
	Jumps Forward and Back with Claps
&	Leap **right** foot forward
1	Leap **left** foot next to **right** foot
2	Clap
&	Leap **right** foot back
3	Leap **left** foot next to **right** foot
4	Clap
	Hip Bumps
5	Bump **right** hip to right side
6	Bump **right** hip to right side
7	Bump **left** hip to left side
8	Bump **left** hip to left side
	Side Rocks and Turn
9	Rock-step ball of **right** foot to right side
&	Rock to left side on **left** foot
10	Step **right** foot next to **left** foot
11	Rock-step ball of **left** foot to left side
&	Rock to right side on **right** foot
12	Step **left** foot next to **right** foot

13-16	Jump-cross-turn to the left with clap
	13 Jump, landing with feet apart
	14 Jump, landing with **right** foot across **left** foot
	15 Pivot on **both** feet ½ turn left
	16 Clap

Jumps Forward and Back with Claps

&	Leap **right** foot forward
17	Leap **left** foot next to **right** foot
18	Clap
&	Leap **right** foot back
19	Leap **left** foot next to **right** foot
20	Clap

Jazz Box with Turn

21-24	Right jazz box with ¼ turn right and left step
	21 Step **right** foot across **left** foot
	22 Step **left** foot back
	23 Step **right** foot to right side and pivot ¼ turn right
	24 Step **left** foot next to **right** foot

Shuffles Forward and Back with Turns and Rocks

25-26	Right shuffle forward
	25 Step **right** foot forward
	& Step **left** foot next to **right** foot
	26 Step **right** foot forward
27-28	Left shuffle forward
	27 Step **left** foot forward
	& Step **right** foot next to **left** foot
	28 Step **left** foot forward
29-30	Right shuffle forward with ½ turn left
	29 Step **right** foot forward and pivot ½ turn left
	& Step **left** foot next to **right** foot
	30 Step **right** foot back
31	Rock-step **left** foot back
32	Rock forward on **right** foot
33-34	Left shuffle forward
	33 Step **left** foot forward
	& Step **right** foot next to **left** foot
	34 Step **left** foot forward
35-36	Right shuffle forward
	35 Step **right** foot forward
	& Step **left** foot next to **right** foot
	36 Step **right** foot forward
37-38	Left shuffle forward with ½ turn right
	37 Step **left** foot forward and pivot ½ turn right
	& Step **right** foot next to **left** foot
	38 Step **left** foot back
39	Rock-step **right** foot back
40	Rock forward on **left** foot

Jumps and Shimmies

41	Jump forward, landing with feet together
&	Lower body while shimmying
42	Lower body while shimmying
43	Raise body while shimmying
&	Raise body while shimmying
44	Clap
45	Jump forward, landing with feet together
&	Lower body while shimmying
46	Lower body while shimmying
47	Raise body while shimmying
&	Raise body while shimmying
48	Clap

Repeat Pattern

Rhythm Line:

```
secs        ....1.....2.....3.....4.....5.....6.....7.....8.....9....10
180 bpm     1&2 3&4 1 2 3 4 1&2 3&4 1 2 3 4 1&2 3&4 1 2 3 4 1&2 3&4 1&2
foot        RL. RL. . . . . RLR LRL B B B . RL. RL. R L R L RLR LRL RLR
other         c   c b b b b             c   c   c
            (clap) (hip bump)

secs        ....11....12....13....14....15....16....17....18....19....20
180 bpm     3 4 1&2 3&4 1&2 3 4 1&2 3&4 1&2 3&4 1 2 3 4 1 2 3 4 1 2 3 4
foot        L R LRL RLR LRL R L B.. ... B.. ... repeat pattern
                                ss ssc  ss ssc
Other                           (shimmy)
```

Cues:

run - run - clap / run - run - clap
bump right / right / left / left
right - rock - together / left - rock - together
jump / cross / turn / clap

run - run - clap / run - run - clap
cross / back / turn / together
right - and - right / left - and - left
turn - and - back / rock back / forward

left - and - left / right - and - right
turn - and - back / rock back / forward
jump - shimmy - down / shimmy - up - clap
jump - shimmy - down / shimmy - up - clap

Black Coffee

About this dance: Helen O'Malley tells us that she choreographed Black Coffee as a tribute to her brother, Johnny, on the occasion of his wedding anniversary. Helen is very involved in line dance. Along with Johnny, and brother Dermott and his wife, Diedre, she runs a dance club, "The Nash Villains" that meets weekly. She choreographs line dances and visits spots around the world as a special guest instructor. She is also the force behind the International Line Dance Charity Marathons.

New Concepts, Steps and Combinations

New Concepts

Half-time Instructs you to take twice as long to perform the designated combination as you would ordinarily take. For example, "half-time right vine" instructs you to execute a right vine on beats "1" to "6" instead of on beats "1", "2" and "3" as the vine would be more customarily done. The step description will tell you either to make the steps of the vine "slow" steps, or to take the steps of the vine on beats "1", "3" and "5" with "holds" or other movements specified for the intervening beats.

The Dance

Difficulty Level: III   **Choreographer:** Helen O'Malley

Dance Faces: 4 directions   **Pattern Length:** 48 Beats

Suggested Music:

For practicing – "Can't Help It" by Scooter Lee (Track 2 on **Free CD**), "I'm So Miserable Without You" originally recorded by Billy Ray Cyrus (Track 7 on CD included with Book 1).

For dancing – "Black Coffee" by Lacy J. Dalton.

Beats	Description
	Kick and Shuffle
1	Kick **right** foot forward
2	Kick **right** foot forward
3-4	Right shuffle in place
	3 Step **right** foot home
	& Step **left** foot in place
	4 Step **right** foot in place

5	Kick **left** foot forward
6	Kick **left** foot forward
7-8	Left shuffle in place
	7 Step **left** foot home
	& Step **right** foot in place
	8 Step **left** foot in place

Toe Touches and Turns

9	Touch **right** toe forward
10	Pivot on **both** feet ⅛ turn left
11	Touch **right** toe forward
12	Pivot on **both** feet ⅛ turn left

Rocks and Shuffles with Turns

13	Rock-step **right** foot forward
14	Rock back on **left** foot
15-16	Right shuffle in place with ½ turn right
	15 Step **right** foot next to **left** foot and pivot ¼ turn right
	& Step **left** foot next to **right** foot and pivot ¼ turn right
	16 Step **right** foot next to **left** foot

17	Rock-step **left** foot forward
18	Rock back on **right** foot
19-20	Left shuffle in place with ½ turn left
	19 Step **left** foot next to **right** foot and pivot ¼ turn left
	& Step **right** foot next to **left** foot and pivot ¼ turn left
	20 Step **left** foot next to **right** foot

Heel Touches and Clap

21	Touch **right** heel diagonally forward
&	Step **right** foot home
22	Touch **left** heel diagonally forward
&	Step **left** foot home
23	Touch **right** heel diagonally forward
24	Clap (**right** foot remains diagonally forward from beat #23)

Side Steps and Shimmies

25-26	Slow step **right** foot to right side while shimmying
27	Step **left** foot next to **right** foot
28	Hold
29-30	Slow step **right** foot to right side while shimmying
31	Step **left** foot next to **right** foot
32	Hold

Vine and Scuff

33-36	Left vine with right scuff
	33 Step **left** foot to left side
	34 Step **right** foot behind **left** foot
	35 Step **left** foot to left side
	36 Scuff **right** foot

Half-Time Weave

37-44 Half-time weave to right (begin side then behind) with finger snaps
- 37 Step **right** foot to right side
- 38 Snap fingers in front, shoulder high
- 39 Step **left** foot behind **right** foot
- 40 Snap fingers behind hips
- 41 Step **right** foot to right side
- 42 Snap fingers in front, shoulder high
- 43 Step **left** foot across **right** foot
- 44 Snap fingers behind hips

Military Turns

45-46 Military turn to the left
- 45 Step **right** foot forward
- 46 Pivot on **both** feet ½ turn left

47-48 Military turn to the left
- 47 Step **right** foot forward
- 48 Pivot on **both** feet ½ turn left

Repeat Pattern

Rhythm Line:

```
secs     .....1.....2.....3.....4.....5.....6.....7.....8.....9....10
120bpm   1   2   3 & 4   1   2   3 & 4   1   2   3   4   1   2   3 & 4   1   2   3 & 4
foot     R   R   RLR     L   L   LRL     R   B   R   B   R   L   RLR     L   R   LRL
other

secs     ....11....12....13....14....15....16....17....18....19....20
120bpm   1 & 2 & 3   4   1   2   3   4   1   2   3   4   1   2   3   4   1   2   3   4
foot     R & B & B   .  —R—  L   .  —R—  L   .   L   R   L   R   R   .   L   .
other                    c shimmy      shimmy                          sn      sn
             (Clap)                                                        (snap)

secs     ....21....22....23....24....25....26....27....28....29....30
120bpm   1   2   3   4   1   2   3   4   1   2   3   4   1   2   3   4   1   2   3   4
foot     R   .   L   .   R   B   R   B   repeat pattern
other        sn      sn
```

Cues:

kick / kick / right - and - right
kick / kick / left - and - left
toe / turn / toe / turn

rock forward / back / turn - turn - together
rock forward / back / turn - turn - together
heel - and - heel - and - heel / clap

slow / step / together / hold
slow / step / together / hold
left / behind / left / scuff

right / snap / behind / snap
right / snap / cross / snap
right / turn / right / turn

Forever Waltz

About this dance: This is another dance choreographed by Helen O'Malley. It is very new, but we are sure it will become a favorite. Helen says it was choreographed in honor of the 48th wedding anniversary of her parents, John and Mona Fitzsimons.

New Concepts, Steps and Combinations

New Combinations

Chassé	Instructs you to make a series of movements in which a step is taken on the lead foot and then the following foot quickly replaces the lead foot as the lead foot steps again. The foot that leads the combination and the direction of the chassé will be specified in the dance description. The number of beats involved in the chassé also will be specified and steps will be taken on each beat and half-beat in the series.
	For example, "beats 1-3, left chassé to left side" instructs you to step your left foot to the left side, step your right foot next to your left foot, step your left foot to the left side, step your right foot next to your left foot, and step your left foot to the left side, to a rhythm of "one-and-two-and-three".
	Chassés often create the look of the following foot "chasing" the leading foot. To effect this illusion, chassés are best done on the balls of the feet and on "&", the following foot should step very close to the leading foot. Shuffles are very much like three-step chassés and sometimes those names are used interchangeably.
Twinkle	Instructs you to make a three step movement to three beats of music. A twinkle will involve taking all three steps at the same point on the floor and making a specified degree of turn. The foot that leads the twinkle, the location at which you step, and the degree of turn involved in the twinkle will be specified in the dance description. On beat one, step to the identified location with your lead foot, on beat two, step your following foot very close to your lead foot, and on beat three, step your lead foot in place. You will be instructed to make some degree of turn in the twinkle and most often this turn will take place on the first beat.
	For example, "beats 1-3, Left twinkle across, $\frac{1}{8}$ turn left" instructs you to: on beat 1, step your left foot across your right foot and pivot $\frac{1}{8}$ turn left, on beat 2, step your right foot very close to your left foot, and on beat three step your left foot in place.
	Twinkles are different from spirals in that in a twinkle, all three steps are taken at the same point on the floor but in a spiral the three steps are in different locations. Both a twinkle and spiral involve a change in the orientation of your body, but in spirals the change is always small and temporary while in twinkles the change is more variable.

The Dance

Difficulty Level: III   **Choreographer:** Helen O'Malley

Dance Faces: four directions   **Pattern Length:** 42 beats

Suggested Music:

For practicing– "Old Friend" by Scooter Lee (Track 1 on **Free CD**), "You Got Me Over A Heartache Tonight" originally recorded by Dolly Parton (Track 10 on CD included with Book 1)

For dancing– "Their Hearts Are Dancing" by the Forrester Sisters

Beats	Description
	Crosses, Chassés and Turns
1	Step **left** foot across **right** foot
2-3	Right chassé to right side
	2 Step **right** foot to right side
	& Step **left** foot next to **right** foot
	3 Step **right** foot to right side
4	Pivot on **right** foot ¼ turn right and step **left** foot forward (as turn is completed)
5	Step **right** foot in place and pivot ¾ turn right
6	Step **left** foot to left side
7	Step **right** foot across **left** foot
8-9	Left chassé to left side
	8 Step **left** foot to left side
	& Step **right** foot next to **left** foot
	9 Step **left** foot to left side
10	Pivot on **left** foot ¼ turn left and step **right** foot forward (as turn is completed)
11	Step **left** foot in place and pivot ¾ turn left
12	Step **right** foot to right side
	Forward with Military Turns
13	Step **left** foot forward
14-15	Military turn to the left
	14 Step **right** foot forward
	15 Pivot on **both** feet ½ turn left
16	Step **right** foot forward
17-18	Military turn to the right
	17 Step **left** foot forward
	18 Pivot on **both** feet ½ turn right

Weave and Rock

19-21	Weave to the right (begin across)
	19 Step **left** foot across **right** foot
	20 Step **right** foot to right side
	21 Step **left** foot behind **right** foot
22	Rock-step **right** foot to right side
23	Rock to left side on **left** foot
24	Rock to right side on **right** foot

Turns and Rocks

25-27	Three-step turn to the left
	25 Step **left** foot to left side
	26 Pivot on **left** foot ½ turn left and step **right** foot to right side (as turn is completed)
	27 Pivot on **right** foot ½ turn left and step **left** foot to left side (as turn is completed)
28	Rock-step **right** foot across **left** foot
29	Rock back on **left** foot
30	Step **right** foot to right side
31	Step **left** foot across **right** foot
32	Pivot on **left** foot ¼ turn left and step **right** foot back (as turn is completed)
33	Pivot on **right** foot ¼ turn left and step **left** foot to left side (as turn is completed)
34	Rock-step **right** foot across **left** foot
35	Rock back on **left** foot
36	Step **right** foot to right side

Twinkle and Turn

37-39	Left twinkle forward, ¼ turn left
	37 Step **left** foot forward and pivot ¼ turn left
	38 Step **right** foot next to **left** foot
	39 Step **left** foot in place
40	Step **right** foot back
41	Pivot on **right** foot ½ turn left and step **left** foot forward (as turn is completed)
42	Step **right** foot to right side

Repeat Pattern

Rhythm Line:

```
secs    .....1.....2.....3.....4.....5.....6.....7.....8.....9....10
90bpm    1    2 & 3   1    2    3    1    2 & 3   1    2    3    1    2    3
foot     L    R L R   B    R    L    R    L R L   B    L    R    L    R    B

secs    ....11....12....13....14....15....16....17....18....19....20
90bpm    1    2    3    1    2    3    1    2    3    1    2    3    1    2    3
foot     R    L    B    L    R    L    R    L    R    L    B    B    R    L    R

secs    ....21....22....23....24....25....26....27....28....29....30
90bpm    1    2    3    1    2    3    1    2    3    1    2    3 repeat pattern
foot     L    B    B    R    L    R    L    R    L    R    B    R
```

Cues:

cross / side - and - side
turn / turn / side
cross / side - and - side
turn / turn / side

left / right / turn
right / left / turn

cross / side / behind
rock / rock / rock

turn / turn / side
cross / back / side
cross / turn / turn
cross / back / side

turn / together / place
back / turn / side

José Cuervo

About this dance: Danced to José Cuervo by Kimber Clayton, this dance is sure to become a "friend of yours". A note to phrasing perfectionists: because of a difference of two beats, this dance fits the "dance mix" version of "José Cuervo" better than it fits the music orginally released.

The choreographer, Max Perry, would like you to be able to reach him. He is in Danbury Connecticut, USA at 203-798-9312. He also has an internet site at http://www.maxperry.com.

New Concepts, Steps and Combinations

New Combinations

Sailor step Instructs you to make three foot movements in two beats of music. The foot to lead (begin) the pattern, and whether it steps across or behind, will be specified. On beat one, the lead foot steps across or behind the following foot. On the half-beat, the following foot steps to the side. On beat two, the lead foot steps to the side (or as specified). When a sailor step is completed, the feet are about shoulder width apart. In a sailor step, the body leans slightly in the direction of the foot to move first.

For example, "right sailor step (begin behind)" instructs you to step your right foot behind your left, step your left foot to the left side and step your right foot to the right side. These movements are done to a count of "one and two". Throughout a right sailor step, you would lean slightly to the right.

Sailor steps are sometimes called sailor shuffles. Sailor steps that begin across are sometimes called across-ball-changes.

Direction of travel

Direction of lean

A SAILOR STEP

The Dance

Difficulty Level: III   **Choreographer:** Max Perry
Dance Faces: four directions   **Pattern Length:** 32 Beats
Suggested Music:

For practicing – "Can't Help It" by Scooter Lee (Track 2 on **Free CD**), "The City Put the Country Back in Me" originally recorded by Neil McCoy (Track 2 on CD included with Book 1).

For dancing – "José Cuervo" by Kimber Clayton.

Beats	Description
	Crosses and Sailor Steps
1	Step **left** foot across **right** foot
2	Step **right** foot to right side
3 - 4	Left sailor step (begin behind)
	3 Step **left** foot behind **right** foot (leaning body slightly left)
	& Step **right** foot to right side
	4 Step **left** foot to left side
5	Step **right** foot across **left** foot
6	Step **left** foot to left side
7 - 8	Right sailor step (begin behind)
	7 Step **right** foot behind **left** foot (leaning body slightly right)
	& Step **left** foot to left side
	8 Step **right** foot to right side
	Weave and Turns
9 -11	Weave to the right (begin across)
	9 Step **left** foot across **right** foot
	10 Step **right** foot to right side
	11 Step **left** foot behind **right** foot
12	Pivot on **left** foot ¼ turn right and step **right** foot forward (as turn is completed)
13-14	Military turn to the right
	13 Step **left** foot forward
	14 Pivot on **both** feet ½ turn right
15-16	Left shuffle in place with turns
	15 Step **left** foot next to **right** foot and pivot ½ turn right
	& Step **right** foot next to **left** foot and pivot ½ turn right
	16 Step **left** foot next to **right** foot
	Forward Steps and Kick-Ball-Changes
17	Step **right** foot forward
18	Step **left** foot forward
19-20	Right kick-ball-change
	19 Kick **right** foot forward
	& Step ball of **right** foot next to **left** foot
	20 Step **left** foot in place

21-22	Right kick-ball-change
	21 Kick **right** foot forward
	& Step ball of **right** foot next to **left** foot
	22 Step **left** foot in place
23	Step **right** foot forward
24	Step **left** foot forward

Turn and Shuffle, Stomp and Kick

25-28	Right Monterey turn
	25 Touch **right** toe to right side
	26 Pivot on **left** foot ½ turn right and step **right** foot next to **left** foot (as turn is completed)
	27 Touch **left** toe to left side
	28 Step **left** foot next to **right** foot

29-30	Right shuffle to side
	29 Step **right** foot to right side
	& Step **left** foot next to **right** foot
	30 Step **right** foot to right side
31	Stomp-up **left** foot next to **right** foot
32	Kick **left** foot forward

Repeat Pattern

Variation:

The choreographer suggests that, if you do not like to turn a lot, the turning shuffle (beats 15-16) can be done as a shuffle in place.

15-16	Left shuffle in place
	15 Step **left** foot next to **right** foot
	& Step **right** foot in place
	16 Step **left** foot in place

Rhythm Line:

```
secs     ....1.....2.....3.....4.....5.....6.....7.....8.....9....10
120bpm   1  2  3 & 4  1  2  3 & 4  1  2  3  4  1  2  3 & 4  1  2  3 & 4
foot     L  R  LRL   R  L  RLR   L  R  L  B  L  B  LRL   R  L  RRL
other
```

```
secs     ....11....12....13....14....15....16....17....18....19....20
120bpm   1 & 2  3  4  1  2  3  4  1 & 2  3  4  1  2  3  4  1  2  3  4
foot     RRL   R  L  R  B  L  L  RLR   L  L  repeat pattern
other
```

Cues:

left cross / side / behind - side - side
right cross / side / behind - side - side
left cross / side / behind / turn
left / turn / turn - turn - together

right / left / kick - ball - change
kick - ball - change / right / left
right / turn / left / together
right - and - right / stomp / kick

Dizzy

About this dance: This dance is well named—it is loaded with turns! Also, it is very well phrased to fit its recommended music, "Dizzy" by Scooter Lee. However, two beats of the song will remain after you finish the last repetition of the pattern. For these two beats, Jo Thompson recommends a right and left stomp in place to finish things off.

The Dance

Difficulty Level: III

Choreographer: Jo Thompson

Dance Faces: four directions

Pattern Length: 32 beats

Suggested Music:

For practicing – "Can't Help It" by Scooter Lee (Track 2 on **Free CD**), "I'm So Miserable Without You" originally recorded by Billy Ray Cyrus (Track 7 on CD included with Book 1).

For dancing – "Dizzy" by Scooter Lee

Beats	Description
	Rocks and Coaster
1	Rock-step **right** foot forward
2	Rock back on **left** foot
3-4	Right coaster step
3	Step **right** foot back
&	Step **left** foot next to **right** foot
4	Step **right** foot forward
	Full Turn
5-6	Military turn to the right
5	Step **left** foot forward
6	Pivot on **both** feet ½ turn right
7-8	Military turn to the right
7	Step **left** foot forward
8	Pivot on **both** feet ½ turn right
	Crosses and Sailor Steps
9	Step **left** foot across **right** foot
10	Step **right** foot to right side
11-12	Left sailor step (begin behind), face diagonally left
11	Step **left** foot behind **right** foot, face diagonally left
&	Step **right** foot to right side, face diagonally left
12	Step **left** foot to left side, face diagonally left
13	Step **right** foot across **left** foot
14	Step **left** foot to left side
15-16	Right sailor step (begin behind), face diagonally right
15	Step **right** foot behind **left** foot, face diagonally right
&	Step **left** foot to left side, face diagonally right
16	Step **right** foot to right side, face face diagonally right
	More Turns
17	Step **left** foot across **right** foot
18	Step **right** foot to right side and pivot ¼ turn left
19-20	Left shuffle back
19	Step **left** foot back
&	Step **right** foot next to **left** foot
20	Step **left** foot back

21	Rock-step **right** foot (*turned out*) back, face diagonally right
22-24	Three-step turn to left moving forward
	22 Step **left** foot in place and pivot ½ turn left
	23 Step **right** foot back and pivot ½ turn left
	24 Step **left** foot forward

Shuffles and Turns

25-26	Right shuffle forward
	25 Step **right** foot forward
	& Step **left** foot next to **right** foot
	26 Step **right** foot forward
27-28	Military turn to the right
	27 Step **left** foot forward
	28 Pivot on **both** feet ½ turn right
29-30	Left shuffle forward
	29 Step **left** foot forward
	& Step **right** foot next to **left** foot
	30 Step **left** foot forward
31-32	Military turn to the left
	31 Step **right** foot forward
	32 Pivot on **both** feet ½ turn left

Repeat Pattern

Rhythm Line:

```
secs      ......1.......2.......3.......4.......5.......6.......7....
120bpm    1   2   3 & 4   1   2   3   4   1   2   3 & 4   1   2   3
foot      R   L   R L R   L   B   L   B   L   R   L R L   R   L   R

secs      ...8.......9......10......11......12......13......14......15
120bpm    & 4   1   2   3 & 4   1   2   3   4   1 & 2   3   4   1 & 2
foot      L R   L   R   L R L   R   L   R   L   R L R   L   B   L R L

secs      ......16......17......18......19......20......21......22....
120bpm    3   4    repeat pattern
foot      R   B
```

Cues:

rock forward / back / right - and - right
left / turn / left / turn
cross / side / behind - and - side
cross / side / behind - and - side

cross / turn / back - and - back
rock back / turn / turn / forward
right - and - right / left / turn
left - and - left / right / turn

Bad Thang

About this dance: Max Perry is a prolific choreographer and Bad Thang is yet another one of his "dood things". He is the winner of UK *Line dancer Magazine's* "International Choreographer of the Year" award for 1997.He invites you to check his web site (http://www.maxperry.com) periodically to hear of his appearances and new dances. If the Cuban steps on beats 21 through 24 are difficult for you, try the steps without Cuban motion first.

New Concepts, Steps and Combinations

New Concepts

Cuban 'Cuban-" is used as a prefix with a variety of steps and instructs you to prepare for a step by bending the knee, and lifting the heel of the leg that will move and straightening the knee and pushing out the hip of the weighted leg. The act of bending the knee of the moving leg and straightening the knee of the other leg results in the hip of the moving leg being lower than the hip of the other leg. A Cuban-step is completed by straightening the knee of the moving leg, pushing its hip out, and bending the knee of the other leg. When you take a Cuban-step, bend your knee, step your toe to the indicated location, then lower your heel as you allow your knee to straighten, pushing your hip out.

For example, "Cuban-step left foot forward" instructs you to straighten your right knee, pushing its hip out, bend your left knee, step forward with the ball of your left foot, then lower your left heel as you allow your left knee to straighten, pushing its hip out, and your right knee to bend.

A Cuban-step is different from a Latin-step. In a Latin-step, the hip of the *moving* foot sways out at the beginning of the step. In a Cuban-step, the hip of the *non-moving* foot sways out at the beginning of the step. Both Cuban and Latin motion add hip movement styling to the steps you take. Many dancers find Cuban motion difficult at first, and it is a style that requires practice.

New Combinations

Running Man Instructs you to make two movements on a beat and half beat. A running man will be identified as "right" or "left" depending upon which foot moves forward or "leads" the combination. The first movement will involve stepping the leading foot forward and the other foot back. This movement is quick and requires practice. It may help to think of it as jumping and landing with your feet apart. The second movement involves sliding the leading foot to its home position and hitching the other leg. As the name implies, a running man produces the look of running although you will not change your location on the dance floor.

For example, "right running man" instructs you to: on "1" step your right foot forward and your left foot back and, on "&" slide your right foot home and hitch your left leg.

Charleston Swivel   Instructs you to swivel your heels alternately in and out to a syncopated rhythm (e.g., &, 1, &, 2, etc.) Keep your weight over the balls of your feet when you do this movement. When you swivel your heels "in", your toes will point away from each other and both feet will be *turned out*. When you swivel your heels "out", your toes will point toward each other and both feet will be *turned in*. Charleston swivels often accompany other steps and are used for extra styling.

The Dance

Difficulty Level: III

Choreographer: Max Perry

Dance Faces: four directions

Pattern Length: 32 beats

Suggested Music:

For practicing – "Can't Help It" by Scooter Lee (Track 2 on **Free CD**), "Walkin' Away A Winner" originally recorded by Kathy Mattea (Track 1 on CD included with Book 1)

For dancing – "You Bad Thang" by Scooter Lee

Beats	Description
	Heel Taps
1	Touch **left** foot forward
2	Tap **left** heel (toe remains in place from beat 1)
3	Tap **left** heel (toe remains in place from beat 1)
4	Tap **left** heel (toe remains in place from beat 1)
&	Step **left** foot next to **right** foot
5	Touch **right** foot forward
6	Tap **right** heel (toe remains in place from beat 5)
7	Tap **right** heel (toe remains in place from beat 5)
8	Tap **right** heel (toe remains in place from beat 5)
	Sailor Steps
9 -10	Right sailor step (begin behind)
	9 Step **right** foot behind **left** foot
	& Step **left** foot to left side
	10 Step **right** foot to right side
11-12	Left sailor step (begin behind)
	11 Step **left** foot behind **right** foot
	& Step **right** foot to right side
	12 Step **left** foot to left side
	Ins and Outs
13	Step **right** foot forward
&-14	Charleston swivel
	& Swivel **both** heels in
	14 Swivel **both** heels out
&	Step **right** foot to right side (step only slightly to right side)
15	Step **left** foot to left side (step only slightly to left side)
16	Clap
	Running Men
17-&	Right running man
	17 Step **right** foot forward and step **left** foot back
	& Slide **right** foot home and hitch **left** leg

18-&	Left running man
	18 Step **left** foot forward and step **right** foot back
	& Slide **left** foot home and hitch **right** leg
19-&	Right running man
	19 Step **right** foot forward and step **left** foot back
	& Slide **right** foot home and hitch **left** leg
20-&	Left running man
	20 Step **left** foot forward and step **right** foot back
	& Slide **left** foot home and hitch **right** leg

Paddle Turn

21-24	¼ Cuban-Paddle turn to the left
	21 Cuban-step **right** foot forward and pivot ⅛ turn left
	22 Cuban-step **left** foot in place
	23 Cuban-step **right** foot forward and pivot ⅛ turn left
	24 Cuban-step **left** foot in place

Walk Back with Charleston Swivels

&	Swivel **both** heels out
25-&	Charleston swivel with right step back
	25 Step **right** foot back and swivel **both** heels in
	& Swivel **both** heels out
26-&	Charleston swivel with left step back
	26 Step **left** foot back and swivel **both** heels in
	& Swivel **both** heels out
27-&	Charleston swivel with right step back
	27 Step **right** foot back and swivel **both** heels in
	& Swivel **both** heels out
28-&	Charleston swivel
	28 Swivel **both** heels in
	& Swivel **both** heels out
29-&	Charleston swivel with left step back
	29 Step **left** foot back and swivel **both** heels in
	& Swivel **both** heels out
30-&	Charleston swivel with right step back
	30 Step **right** foot back and swivel **both** heels in
	& Swivel **both** heels out
31-32	Left coaster step
	31 Step **left** foot back
	& Step **right** foot next to **left** foot
	32 Step **left** foot forward
&	Step **right** foot next to **left** foot

Repeat Pattern

Variation:

If the Charleston swivels on beats &25-30& are difficult for you, try leaving them out. Your movement then would look like:

25	Step **right** foot back
26	Step **left** foot back
27	Step **right** foot back
28	Hold
29	Step **left** foot back
30	Step **right** foot back

Rhythm Line:

```
secs       .......1.......2.......3.......4.......5.......6.......7....
120bpm     1   2   3   4 & 1   2   3   4   1 & 2   3 & 4   1 & 2 & 3
foot       L   L   L   L L R   R   R   R   R L R   L R L   R B B R L
Other

secs       ...8.......9......10......11......12......13......14......15
120bpm     4   1 & 2 & 3 & 4 & 1   2   3   4 & 1 & 2 & 3 & 4 & 1 & 2
foot       .   B B B B B B B B R   L   R   L B B B B B B B B B B B B
other      c
           (clap)
secs       ......16......17......18......19......20......21......22....
120bpm     & 3 & 4 &       repeat pattern
foot       B L R L R
other
```

Variation Rhythm Line (beats 25-30):

```
secs       ...8.......9......10......11......12......13......14......15
120bpm                                     1   2   3   4   1   2
foot                                       R   L   R   .   L   R
                                           ——- Variation ——-
```

Cues:

toe / tap / tap / tap
home - toe / tap / tap / tap
behind - and - side / behind - and - side
right - heels - heels - out - out / clap

apart - hitch - apart - hitch - apart - hitch - apart - hitch
turn / step / turn / step
and - back - and - back - and - back - and - in
and - back - and - back - and - back - together - forward - and

Scotia Samba

About this dance: This is another Liz and Bev Clarke dance. How did it come about? As written by Liz: "I received a promo disc with the Maverick's 'Dance the Night Away', put it in my CD player, and honestly, within 15 minutes, Beverley and myself had put together the dance".

We think you will enjoy the feel of this dance. It brings the "1 and 2, 3 and 4" rhythm of the samba to life by using lots of sailor steps, shuffles, and other triple step patterns. Liz and Bev Clarke mention that Scotia Samba can be danced to any nice samba or cha-cha music.

The Dance

Difficulty Level: III

Dance Faces: four directions

Suggested Music:

Choreographer: Liz and Bev Clarke

Pattern Length: 64 beats

For practicing – "Can't Help It" by Scooter Lee (Track 2 on your **Free CD**), "Gulf of Mexico" originally recorded by Clint Black (Track 12 on CD included with Book 1)

For dancing – "Dance the Night Away" by The Mavericks

Beats	Description
	Triples and Kicks
1	Touch **right** heel diagonally forward, face diagonally right
&	Step ball of **right** foot back, face diagonally right
2	Step **left** foot across **right** foot, face diagonally right
3	Touch **right** heel diagonally forward, face diagonally right
&	Step ball of **right** foot back, face diagonally right
4	Step **left** foot across **right** foot, face diagonally right
5	Kick **right** foot forward
6	Kick **right** foot to right side
7-8	Right sailor step (begin behind)
7	Step **right** foot behind **left** foot
&	Step **left** foot to left side
8	Step **right** foot to right side

9	Touch **left** heel diagonally forward, face diagonally left
&	Step ball of **left** foot back, face diagonally left
10	Step **right** foot across **left** foot, face diagonally left
11	Touch **left** heel diagonally forward, face diagonally left
&	Step ball of **left** foot back, face diagonally left
12	Step **right** foot across **left** foot, face diagonally left

13	Kick **left** foot forward
14	Kick **left** foot to left side
15-16	Left sailor step (begin behind)
	15 Step **left** foot behind **right** foot
	& Step **right** foot to right side
	16 Step **left** foot to left side

Paddle Turn

17-24	½ Paddle turn to the left
	17 Step **right** foot forward and pivot ⅛ turn left
	18 Step **left** foot in place
	19 Step **right** foot forward and pivot ⅛ turn left
	20 Step **left** foot in place
	21 Step **right** foot forward and pivot ⅛ turn left
	22 Step **left** foot in place
	23 Step **right** foot forward and pivot ⅛ turn left
	24 Step **left** foot in place

Rocks and Turning Shuffles

25	Rock-step **right** foot across **left** foot
26	Rock back on **left** foot
27-28	Right shuffle forward with ½ turn right
	27 Pivot on **left** foot ½ turn right and step **right** foot forward (as turn is completed)
	& Step **left** foot next to **right** foot
	28 Step **right** foot forward

29	Rock-step **left** foot across **right** foot
30	Rock back on **right** foot
31-32	Left shuffle forward with ½ turn left
	31 Pivot on **right** foot ½ turn left and step **left** foot forward (as turn is completed)
	& Step **right** foot next to **left** foot
	32 Step **left** foot forward

Side Touches and Claps

33	Touch **right** toe to right side
&	Clap (Hands to left side at shoulder height)
34	Clap (Hands to left side at shoulder height)
&	Step **right** foot next to **left** foot
35	Touch **left** toe to left side
&	Clap (Hands to right side at shoulder height)
36	Clap (Hands to right side at shoulder height)

&	Step **left** foot next to **right** foot
37	Touch **right** toe to right side
&	Step **right** foot next to **left** foot
38	Touch **left** toe to left side

&	Step **left** foot next to **right** foot
39	Touch **right** toe to right side
&	Clap (Hands to left side at shoulder height)
40	Clap (Hands to left side at shoulder height)

Steps, Slides and Turn

41	Step **right** foot to right side
42	Slide **left** foot next to **right** foot
43	Step **right** foot back
44	Hold

45	Step **left** foot to left side
46	Slide **right** foot next to **left** foot
47	Step **left** foot forward
48	Hold

49	Step **right** foot to right side
50	Slide **left** foot next to **right** foot
51	Step **right** foot across **left** foot
52	Hold

53	Step **left** foot to left side
54	Slide **right** foot next to **left** foot
55	Step **left** foot across **right** foot
56	Hold

57	Step **right** foot to right side
58-60	Draw **left** foot next to **right** foot

61	Step **right** foot across **left** foot
62-63	Slow pivot on **both** feet ¾ turn left
&	Clap
64	Clap

Repeat Pattern

Rhythm Line:

```
secs      ......1.......2.......3.......4.......5.......6.......7....
120bpm    1 & 2   3 & 4   1   2   3 & 4   1 & 2   3 & 4   1   2   3
foot      R R L   R R L   R   R   R L R   L L R   L L R   L   L   L
other

secs      ...8.......9......10......11......12......13......14......15
120bpm    & 4   1   2   3   4   1   2   3   4   1   2   3 & 4   1   2
foot      R L   R   L   R   L   R   L   R   L   R   L   B L R   L   R
other

secs      ......16......17......18......19......20......21......22....
120bpm    3 & 4   1 & 2 & 3 & 4 & 1 & 2 & 3 &.4   1   2   3   4   1
foot      B R L   R . . R L . . L R R L L R . .   R   L   R   . L
other             c c     c c                 c c
                  (claps)
secs      ..23......24......25......26......27......28......29......30
120bpm    2   3   4   1   2   3   4   1   2   3   4   1   2   3   4
foot      R   L   .   R   L   R   .   L   R   L   .   R   — — L — —
other                                                         draw

secs      ......31......32......33......34......35......36......37....
120bpm    1   2   3 & 4   repeat pattern
foot      R   (-B-)  . .
other         slow  c c
```

Cues:

heel - and - cross / heel - and - cross
kick / kick / behind - and - side
heel - and - cross / heel - and - cross
kick / kick / behind - and - side
turn / place / turn / place
turn / place / turn / place
cross / back / turn - and - forward
cross / back / turn - and - forward
side - clap - clap - and - side - clap - clap - and
side - and - side - and - side - clap - clap
right / slide / right / hold
left / slide / left / hold
right / slide / right / hold
left / slide / left / hold
right / draw / draw / together
cross / turn / turn - clap - clap

Ribbon of Highway

About this dance: Neil Hale, the choreographer of this dance, also created the long-time favorite line dance, Cruisin'. More and more dances are being choreographed following the rhythmic patterns of classic dance forms. In Ribbon of Highway you will have fun with the eight-beat "slow, slow, quick, quick, slow" rhythm of tango.

The Dance

Difficulty Level: III   **Choreographer:** Neil Hale

Dance Faces: one direction   **Pattern Length:** 64 beats

Suggested Music:

For practicing – "Don't Walk Away" by Scooter Lee (Track 3 on **Free CD**), "I Wanna Go Too Far" originally recorded by Trisha Yearwood   (Track 4 on CD included with Book 1).

For dancing – "Ribbon of Highway" by Scooter Lee, "Don't Walk Away " by Scooter Lee

Beats	Description
	To the Sides
1 - 2	Slow step **right** foot to right side
3 - 4	Slow step **left** foot next to **right** foot
5	Step **right** foot to right side (step only slightly to right side)
6	Step **left** foot next to **right** foot
7 - 8	Slow step **right** foot to right side (step only slightly to right side)
9 -10	Slow step **left** foot to left side
11-12	Slow step **right** foot next to **left** foot
13	Step **left** foot to left side (step only slightly to left side)
14	Step **right** foot next to **left** foot
15-16	Slow step **left** foot to left side (step only slightly to left side)
	Forward and Back
17	Step **right** foot forward
18	Step **left** foot next to **right** foot
19-20	Slow step **right** foot back
21-22	Slow step **left** foot back
23-24	Slow step **right** foot back
25	Step **left** foot back
26	Step **right** foot next to **left** foot
27-28	Slow step **left** foot forward
29-30	Slow step **right** foot forward
31-32	Slow step **left** foot forward
	Turns
33-34	Slow step **right** foot forward
35-36	Slow rock back on **left** foot
37	Step **right** foot back and pivot $\frac{1}{4}$ turn right
38	Step **left** foot next to **right** foot
39-40	Slow step **right** foot in place and pivot $\frac{1}{4}$ turn right
41-42	Slow step **left** foot forward
43-44	Slow rock back on **right** foot
45	Step **left** foot back and pivot $\frac{1}{4}$ turn left
46	Step **right** foot next to **left** fool
47-48	Slow step **left** foot in place and pivot $\frac{1}{4}$ turn left

49-52	Half-time military turn to the left
	49-50 Slow step **right** foot forward
	51-52 Slow pivot on **both** feet ½ turn left
53	Step **right** foot forward and pivot ¼ turn left
54	Step **left** foot next to **right** foot
55-56	Slow step **right** foot in place and slow pivot ¼ turn left

Touches

57	Touch **left** heel forward
58	Step **left** foot next to **right** foot
59	Touch **right** heel forward
60	Step **right** foot next to **left** foot
61	Touch **left** heel forward
62	Step **left** foot next to **right** foot
63-64	Slow touch **right** toe next to **left** foot

Repeat Pattern

Rhythm Line:

```
secs       .....1.....2.....3.....4.....5.....6.....7.....8.....9....10
180bpm     1 2 3 4 1 2 3 4 1 2 3 4 1 2 3 4 1 2 3 4 1 2 3 4 1 2 3 4 1 2
foot       (R-)(L-)R L (R-)(L-)(R-)R L (L-)R L (R-)(L-)(R-)L R (L-)(R-)
           S   S       S   S   S       S       S   S   S       S   S
           (Slow)

secs       ....11....12....13....14....15....16....17....18....19....20
180bpm     3 4 1 2 3 4 1 2 3 4 1 2 3 4 1 2 3 4 1 2 3 4 1 2 3 4 1 2 3 4
foot       (L-)(R-)(L-)R L (R-)(L-)(R-)L R (L-)(R-)(B-)R L (R-)L L R R
           S   S   S       S   S   S       S   S   S       S

secs       ....21....22....23....24....25....26....27....28....29....30
180bpm     1 2 3 4 1 2 3 4 1 2 3 4 1 2 3 4 1 2 3 4 1 2 3 4 1 2 3 4 1 2
foot       L L (R-) repeat pattern
               S
```

Cues:

slow / side / slow / together
side / together / slow / side

slow / side / slow / together
side / together / slow / side

forward / together / slow / back
slow / back / slow / back

back / together / slow / forward
slow / forward / slow / forward

slow / forward / slow / back
turn / together / slow / turn

slow / forward / slow / back
turn / together / slow / turn

slow / forward / slow / turn
turn / together / slow / turn

heel / together / heel / together
heel / together / slow / touch

OeeOeeO (The English Language)

About this dance: Here's another fun dance from Max Perry.

New Concepts, Steps and Combinations

New Concept

Syncopated pattern   Indicates a set of steps that deviate from the standard step pattern for a particular type of dance or combination.

New Combination

Vaudeville Kick   Instructs you to make four movements to two beats of music. The foot that begins (leads) the combination is specified. On beat "1", the lead foot steps across the following foot. On "&", the following foot steps back (or as specified). On "2", the lead heel touches forward, and, on "&", the lead foot steps home. To complete the vaudevillian look, try leaning slightly back as you touch your heel forward.

For example, "Right Vaudeville kick" instructs you: On "1", step your right foot across your left foot; On "&", step your left foot back; On "2", touch your right heel forward; On "&", step your right foot home.

The Dance

Difficulty Level: III   **Choreographer:** Max Perry

Dance Faces: four directions   **Pattern Length:** 32 beats

Suggested Music:

For practicing – "Honey Hush" by Scooter Lee (Track 5 on **Free CD**), "I'm So Miserable Without You" originally recorded by Billy Ray Cyrus (Track 7 on CD included with Book 1).

For dancing – "OeeOeeO" by Scooter Lee

Beats	Description
	Touches and Steps
1	Touch **left** toe to left side
&	Step **left** foot next to **right** foot
2	Touch **right** toe to right side
&	Step **right** foot next to **left** foot
3	Touch **left** heel forward
&	Step **left** foot next to **right** foot
4	Touch **right** heel forward
&	Step **right** foot next to **left** foot

Steps and Claps

5	Step **left** foot forward
6	Clap
&	Step **right** foot *(turned out)* next to **left** instep
7	Step **left** foot forward
8 -	Clap

Sailor Steps Moving Back

9-10   Right sailor step (begin behind)
        9   Step **right** foot behind **left** foot
        &   Step **left** foot to left side
        10   Step **right** foot in place

11-12   Left sailor step (begin behind)
        11   Step **left** foot behind **right** foot
        &   Step **right** foot to right side
        12   Step **left** foot in place

Turns and Shuffle

13   Step **right** foot forward and pivot on **both** feet ½ turn left
14   Step **left** foot in place
15-16   Right shuffle in place with ½ turn left
        15   Step **right** foot forward next to **left** foot and pivot ¼ turn left
        &   Step **left** foot in place and pivot ¼ turn left
        16   Step **right** foot in place

Weave and Vaudeville Kicks

17-19   Syncopated weave to the left (begin side then behind)
        17   Step **left** foot to left side
        18   Step **right** foot behind **left** foot
        &   Step **left** foot to left side
        19   Step **right** foot across **left** foot
        &   Step **left** foot to left side
20   Touch **right** heel diagonally forward
&   Step **right** foot next to **left** foot

21-22& Left Vaudeville kick
        21   Step **left** foot across **right** foot
        &   Step **right** foot to **right** side
        22   Touch **left** heel diagonally forward
        &   Step **left** foot home

23-24& Right Vaudeville kick
        23   Step **right** foot across **left** foot
        &   Step **left** foot to **left** side
        24   Touch **right** heel diagonally forward
        &   Step **right** foot home

Crosses, ¾ Turn and Shuffle

25	Step **left** foot across **right** foot
26	Hold
&	Step **right** foot to right side
27	Step **left** foot across **right** foot
&	Step **right** foot to right side
28	Step **left** foot across **right** foot

29   Step **right** foot to right side and pivot ¼ turn right
30   Step **left** foot across **right** foot and pivot on **both** feet ½ turn right
31-32   Right shuffle forward
            31   Step **right** foot forward
            &   Step **left** foot next to **right** foot
            32   Step **right** foot forward

Repeat Pattern

Rhythm Line:

```
secs      .......1.......2.......3.......4.......5.......6.......7....
120bpm    1 & 2 & 3 & 4 & 1   2 & 3   4   1 & 2   3 & 4   1   2   3
foot      L L R R L L R R L   . R L   .   R L R   L R L   R   L   R
other                                c       c
                               (clap)

secs      ...8.......9......10......11......12......13......14......15
120bpm    & 4   1   2 & 3 & 4 & 1 & 2 & 3 & 4 & 1   2 & 3 & 4   1   2
foot      L R   L   R L R L R R L R L L R L R R L   . R L R L   R   B
other

secs      ......16......17......18......19......20......21......22....
120bpm    3 & 4    repeat pattern
foot      R L R
other
```

Cues:

left - and - right - and - heel - and - heel - and
left / clap - and - left / clap
behind - and - back / behind - and - back
turn / left / turn - turn - together

side / behind - and - cross - and - heel - and
cross - side - heel - home - cross - side - heel - home
cross / hold - and - cross - and - cross
turn / turn / right - and - right

Fly Like A Bird

About this dance: Hedy McAdams choreographed this dance in September of 1995. She tells us she tried to capture the feeling of flying in the movements. We think she's succeeded, as do many others. This dance is New Zealand's "Most Influential Overseas Choreographed Dance" for 1997. (It was also New Zealand's favorite for 39 straight weeks until it was dethroned by Love Letters, another Hedy McAdams dance.) Fly Like A Bird has also been a finalist in Canada's Outstanding Dance Achievement Competition, took second place in Las Vegas' Desert Sands competition in 1995 and was voted Dance of the Year in Vancouver. The steps in this dance are not difficult, but it has many turns and changes of direction. It will take some practice to master!

The Dance

Difficulty Level: III   **Choreographer:** Hedy McAdams
Dance Faces: two directions   **Pattern Length:** 32 Beats
Suggested Music:

For practicing – "Can't Help It " by Scooter Lee (Track 2 on **Free CD**), "Wher'm I Gonna Live When I Get Home" originally recorded by Billy Ray Cyrus (Track 9 on CD included with Book 1).

For dancing – "Fly Like A Bird" by Boz Scaggs, "Tulsa Shuffle" by The Tractors.

Beats	Description
	Rock and ¼ Turns
1	Step **left** foot to left side
2	Rock to right side on **right** foot
3	Pivot on **both** feet ¼ turn left
4	Hold
5	Pivot on **left** foot ¼ turn left and step **right** foot to right side (as turn is completed)
6	Rock to left side on **left** foot
7	Pivot on **both** feet ¼ turn right
8	Hold
9	Pivot on **right** foot ¼ turn right and step **left** foot to left side (as turn is completed)
10	Rock to right side on **right** foot
11	Pivot on **both** feet ¼ turn left
12	Hold

Kick-Ball-Changes

13-14	Right kick-ball-change with turn
	13 Kick **right** foot forward
	& Step ball of **right** foot next to **left** foot and pivot ¼ turn left
	14 Step **left** foot next to **right** foot
15-16	Right kick-ball-change
	15 Kick **right** foot forward
	& Step ball of **right** foot next to **left** foot
	16 Step **left** foot in place

Crosses and Turn

17	Step **right** foot across **left** foot
18	Pivot on **both** feet ½ turn left
19	Step **left** foot across **right** foot
&	Step **right** foot to right side (step only slightly to right side)
20	Step **left** foot across **right** foot

Shuffle and Turns

21-22	Right shuffle to right side with ¼ turn right
	21 Step **right** foot to right side and pivot ¼ turn right
	& Step **left** foot next to **right** foot
	22 Step **right** foot forward
23	Pivot on **right** foot ¼ turn right and step **left** foot to left side (as turn is completed)
24	Pivot on **left** foot ½ turn left and step **right** foot to right side (as turn is completed)

Crosses and Turns

25	Step **left** foot across **right** foot, lower body
26	Touch **right** toe to right side, raise body
27	Step **right** foot across **left** foot
28	Pivot on **both** feet ½ turn left
29	Step **left** foot across **right** foot
&	Step **right** foot to right side (step only slightly to right side)
30	Step **left** foot across **right** foot
31	Step **right** foot to right side (step as far to the right as you can)
32	Slide-up **left** toe next to **right** foot

Repeat Pattern

Rhythm Line:

```
secs     .... 1.....2.....3.....4.....5.....6.....7.....8.....9....10
120bpm   1  2  3  4  1  2  3  4  1  2  3  4  1&2  3&4  1  2  3&4
foot     L  R  B  .  B  L  B  .  B  R  B  .  RRL  RRL  R  B  LRL
other

secs     ....11....12....13....14....15....16....17....18....19....20
120bpm   1&2  3  4  1  2  3  4  1&2  3  4  1  2  3  4  1  2  3  4
foot     RLR  B  B  L  R  R  B  LRL  R  L  repeat pattern
other
```

Cues:

left / rock / turn / hold
turn / rock / turn / hold
turn / rock / turn / hold
kick - turn - change / kick - ball - change
cross / turn / cross - right - cross
turn - and - right / turn / turn
cross / side / cross / turn
cross - side - cross / right / slide

Level IV

Honky Tonk Twist

About this dance: This parallel line dance has a sequel, "Honky Tonk Twist II", by the same choreographer, Max Perry. We think that this version, the original dance, is slightly more difficult than the sequel. Max Perry received a CDMA (Country Dance Music Award) nomination for this dance (and he has received other awards as well). In July of 1997, Max was named "Honorary President of Line Dancing" by the British "Country Music in the Arts" organization. Max Perry is available by phone (in the U.S. at 203-798-9312) and through his internet site (http://www.maxperry.com).

New Concepts, Steps and Combinations

New Combinations

Boot hook combination
Instructs you to make a sequence of four movements, one of which will be a hook, in four beats of music. The four movements are executed by the identified leg, while the other leg supports the weight of the body. On beat "1", the heel will touch diagonally forward, with foot turned out. On beat "2", the foot is hooked in front of the weighted leg. On beat "3", the heel is touched diagonally forward, with foot turned out. On beat "4", the foot steps or touches next to the weighted foot.

For example, "left boot hook combination" instructs you to: On "1", touch your left heel, with foot turned out, diagonally forward; On "2", hook your left leg in front of your right leg; On "3", touch your left heel, with foot turned out, diagonally forward; On "4", step your left foot next to your right.

Swivet
Instructs you to swivel both feet, on the heel of one and ball of the other. Both feet turn approximately 45 degrees in the direction specified and then back to center in two beats of music. The direction of the swivet identifies the direction your toes will point on the first movement. The foot named in the direction of the swivet swivels its toe and the other foot swivels its heel. While swiveling, your weight will be on the heel of one foot and the ball of the other. At the completion of a swivet, both feet will be centered under your body and flat on the floor.

SWIVEL HEELS TO LEFT

SWIVEL TOES TO RIGHT

For example, "swivet to right" instructs you to: on "1", swivel your right toe to the right and your left heel to the left; and on "2", swivel your right toe to center and your left heel to center.

SWIVET TO RIGHT

Heel and Toe Swivels and a Swivet that result in similar foot positions

The Dance

Difficulty Level: IV
Dance Faces: four directions

Choreographer: Max Perry
Pattern Length: 64 Beats

Suggested Music:

For practicing — "Don't Walk Away" by Scooter Lee (Track 3 on **Free CD**), "South's Gonna Do It" originally recorded by Charlie Daniels Band (Track 6 on CD included with Book 1).

For dancing — "Honky Tonk Twist" by Scooter Lee, "Honky Tonk Superman" by Aaron Tippin, "Honky Tonk Attitude" by Joe Diffie, "Honky Tonk Crowd" by Rick Trevino.

Beats	Description
	Swivels and Boot Hooks
1	Swivel heels to right
2	Swivel heels to center
3	Swivel heels to right
4	Swivel heels to center
5 - 8	Right boot hook combination
	5 Touch **right** heel diagonally forward
	6 Hook **right** leg across **left** leg
	7 Touch **right** heel diagonally forward
	8 Step **right** foot next to **left** foot
9	Swivel heels to left
10	Swivel heels to center
11	Swivel heels to left
12	Swivel heels to center
13-16	Left boot hook combination
	13 Touch **left** heel diagonally forward
	14 Hook **left** leg across **right** leg
	15 Touch **left** heel diagonally forward
	16 Touch **left** foot next to **right** foot
	Charleston Kicks and Turn
17-20	Left Charleston kick
	17 Step **left** foot forward
	18 Kick **right** foot forward
	19 Step **right** foot back
	20 Touch **left** toe back
21-24	Left Charleston kick with ¼ turn right
	21 Step **left** foot forward
	22 Kick **right** foot forward
	23 Step **right** foot back and pivot ¼ turn right
	24 Touch **left** foot next to **right** foot

Vines with Stomps and Claps

25-28   Left vine with right stomp-up
    25   Step **left** foot to left side
    26   Step **right** foot behind **left** foot
    27   Step **left** foot to left side
    28   Stomp-up **right** foot and clap

29-32   Right vine with left stomp
    29   Step **right** foot to right side
    30   Step **left** foot behind **right** foot
    31   Step **right** foot to right side
    32   Stomp **left** foot next to **right** foot and clap

Swivets

33-34   Swivet to left
    33   Swivel **left** toe to left and swivel **right** heel to right
    34   Swivel **left** toe to center and swivel **right** heel to center
35-36   Swivet to left
    35   Swivel **left** toe to left and swivel **right** heel to right
    36   Swivel **left** toe to center and swivel **right** heel to center

37-38   Swivet to right
    37   Swivel **right** toe to right and swivel **left** heel to left
    38   Swivel **right** toe to center and swivel **left** heel to center
39-40   Swivet to right
    39   Swivel **right** toe to right and swivel **left** heel to left
    40   Swivel **right** toe to center and swivel **left** heel to center

Walk Back and Clap

41   Step **right** foot back
42   Clap
43   Step **left** foot back
44   Clap

45   Step **right** foot back
46   Clap
47   Step **left** foot back
48   Clap

Step and Slide Forward

49   Step **right** foot forward
50   Slide **left** foot next to **right** foot
51   Step **right** foot forward
52   Scuff **left** foot

53   Step **left** foot forward
54   Slide **right** foot next to **left** foot
55   Step **left** foot forward
56   Scuff **right** foot

Crossing Walk Forward

57   Step **right** foot across **left** foot
58   Hold
59   Step **left** foot across **right** foot
60   Hold

61	Step **right** foot across **left** foot
62	Hold
63	Stomp **left** foot next to **right** foot
64	Hold

Repeat Pattern

Variation:

Max said that when he did this on the TV show "Club Dance", the last step was a stomp:

| 64 | Stomp **right** foot next to **left** foot |

Rhythm Line:

```
secs      .....1.....2.....3.....4.....5.....6.....7.....8.....9....10
180 bpm   1 2 3 4 1 2 3 4 1 2 3 4 1 2 3 4 1 2 3 4 1 2 3 4 1 2 3 4 1 2
foot      B B B B R R R R B B B B L L L L L R R L L R R L L R L R R L
other

secs      ....11....12....13....14....15....16....17....18....19....20
180 bpm   3 4 1 2 3 4 1 2 3 4 1 2 3 4 1 2 3 4 1 2 3 4 1 2 3 4 1 2 3 4
foot      R L B B B B B B B B B R . L . R . L . R L R L L R L R R . L .
other                             c   c   c   c
                                  (claps)

secs      ....21....22....23....24....25....26....27....28....29....30
180 bpm   1 2 3 4 1 2 3 4 1 2 3 4 1 2 3 4 1 2 3 4 1 2 3 4 1 2 3 4 1 2
foot      R . L . repeat pattern
other
```

Cues:

heels right / center / right / center
heel / hook / heel / together
heels left / center / left / center
heel / hook / heel / touch

left / kick / back / touch
left / kick / turn / touch
left / behind / left / stomp
right / behind / right / stomp

left / swivet / left / swivet
right / swivet / right / swivet
back / clap / back / clap
back / clap / back / clap

right / slide / right / scuff
left / slide / left / scuff
cross / hold / cross / hold
cross / hold / stomp / hold

Swing City Jive

About this dance: "Swing City" by Roger Brown seems to be very popular dance music just about anywhere line dancing is done. Swing City Jive is one dance often done to that music. Although Rick had choreographed several dances before, this dance marks the debut of Rick and Linda as a choreography team. Rick is involved, not only in dance, but in several areas of country-western music. In January of 1997 he was named the American Disc Jockey Association's Country-Western Deejay of the Year.

Rick produces and sells music that he finds particularly "danceable" performed by artists from around the world. You can reach him by writing to R 2 Box 150 A, Haubstadt, Indiana, 47639 USA. His telephone and fax numbers, in the US, are 812-867-3401 and 812-867-1082. You can also e-mail him at HillbillyR@aol.com or visit his internet site at http://www.hillbillyrick.com.

The Dance

Difficulty Level: IV   **Choreographers:** Hillbilly Rick and The Lovely Linda

Dance Faces: four directions   **Pattern Length:** 64 Beats

Suggested Music:

For practicing – "Honey Hush" by Scooter Lee (Track 5 on **Free CD**), "Fast As You" originally recorded by Dwight Yoakam (Track 5 on CD included with Book 1).

For dancing – "Swing City" by Roger Brown and Swing City.

Beats	Description
	Rocks Forward and Back
1	Rock-step **right** foot forward
2	Rock back on **left** foot
3	Rock-step **right** foot back
4	Rock forward on **left** foot
5	Rock-step **right** foot forward
6	Rock back on **left** foot
7	Step **right** foot next to **left** foot
8	Hold
	Left Touches and Travelling to the Right
9	Touch **left** toe to left side
10	Hold
11	Touch **left** foot next to **right** foot
12	Hold

13	Touch **left** toe to left side
14	Touch **left** toe next to **right** foot
15	Touch **left** toe to left side
16	Hold

17	Step **left** foot behind **right** foot
18	Step **right** foot to right side
19	Step **left** foot next to **right** foot
20	Hold

Right Touches and Travelling to the Left

21	Touch **right** toe to right side
22	Hold
23	Touch **right** foot next to **left** foot
24	Hold

25	Touch **right** toe to right side
26	Touch **right** toe next to **left** foot
27	Touch **right** toe to right side
28	Hold

29	Step **right** foot behind **left** foot
30	Step **left** foot to left side
31	Step **right** foot next to **left** foot
32	Hold

Rocks Forward and Back

33	Rock-step **left** foot forward
34	Rock back on **right** foot
35	Rock-step **left** foot back
36	Rock forward on **right** foot

37	Rock-step **left** foot forward
38	Rock back on **right** foot
39	Step **left** foot next to **right** foot
40	Hold

Walk Forward

41	Step **right** foot forward
42	Hold
43	Step **left** foot forward
44	Hold

45	Step **right** foot across **left** foot
46	Step **left** foot across **right** foot
47	Step **right** foot across **left** foot
48	Hold

Forward and Turns

49	Step **left** foot forward
50	Hold
51	Pivot on **both** feet ½ turn right
52	Hold

53	Step **left** foot forward
54	Slide **right** foot foward to lock behind **left** foot
55	Step **left** foot forward
56	Scuff **right** foot and pivot on **left** foot ¼ turn left

Jazz Box and Splits

57-60	Right jazz box with left step
	57 Step **right** foot across **left** foot
	58 Step **left** foot back
	59 Step **right** foot to right side
	60 Step **left** foot next to **right** foot

61-62	Heel Split
	61 Move heels apart
	62 Return heels to center
63-64	Toe Split
	63 Move toes apart
	64 Return toes to center

Repeat Pattern

Rhythm Line:

```
secs       .....1.....2.....3.....4.....5.....6.....7.....8.....9....10
180 bpm    1 2 3 4 1 2 3 4 1 2 3 4 1 2 3 4 1 2 3 4 1 2 3 4 1 2 3 4 1 2
foot       R L R L R L R . L . L . L L L . L R L . R . R . R R R . R L
other

secs       ....11....12....13....14....15....16....17....18....19....20
180 bpm    3 4 1 2 3 4 1 2 3 4 1 2 3 4 1 2 3 4 1 2 3 4 1 2 3 4 1 2 3 4
foot       R . L R L R L R L . R . L . R L R . L . B . L R L B R L R L
other

secs       ....21....22....23....24....25....26....27....28....29....30
180 bpm    1 2 3 4 1 2 3 4 1 2 3 4 1 2 3 4 1 2 3 4 1 2 3 4 1 2 3 4 1 2
foot       B B B B repeat pattern
other
```

Cues:

rock forward / back / back / forward
rock forward / back / together / hold

left touch / hold / touch / hold
touch / touch / touch / hold
behind / right / together / hold

right touch / hold / touch / hold
touch / touch / touch / hold
behind / left / together / hold

rock forward / back / back / forward
rock forward / back / together / hold

right / hold / left / hold
cross / cross / cross / hold
left / hold / turn / hold
left / slide / left / turn

cross / back / side / together
split / close / split / close

Swing Time Boogie

About this dance: This is one of two dances in this book that is choreographed to "Swing City" by Roger Brown. Scott Blevins tells us that songs always provide the inspiration for his dances and we think he has certainly captured the spirit of "Swing City" in Swing Time Boogie. The dance won a first runner-up placement at the Outstanding Dance Achievement Awards for International Choreographer of the Year. In competition, the choreography includes some smooth arm movements on the stomp steps (beats 1, 5, 9, 10, 13-16), however, unless done smoothly, the arm movements might look awkward!

Swing Time Boogie fits the music of "Swing City" perfectly, but the dancer must be alert for two breaks in the pattern. On the first repetition, the last two steps are modified and the second repetition starts halfway through the full pattern. You dance beat 63 as "Step **right** foot next to **left** foot" and beat 64 as "Touch **left** foot next to **right** foot". Then you start the second repetition on beat 33 (omitting beats 1 to 32). The full 64 beat pattern is done for the third and all remaining repetitions.

Scott would like you to be able to reach him, for information on the dance or regarding instructional videos. He is in Highland, Indiana, USA at 219-922-6398. You can also e-mail him at Blevscot@aol.com.

The Dance

Difficulty Level: IV

Choreographer: Scott Blevins

Dance Faces: four directions

Pattern Length: 64 Beats

Suggested Music:

For practicing– "Honey Hush" by Scooter Lee (Track 5 on **Free CD**), "Fast As You" originally recorder by Dwight Yoakam (Track 5 on CD included with Book 1).

For dancing – "Swing City" by Roger Brown.

Beats	Description
	Stomps Forward
1	Stomp **right** foot forward (move as far forward as you can)
2	Hold
3	Hold
4	Hold

5	Stomp **left** foot forward (move as far forward as you can)
6	Hold
7	Hold
8	Hold

9	Stomp **right** foot forward
10	Hold
11	Stomp **left** foot forward
12	Hold

13	Stomp **right** foot forward (move only slightly forward)
14	Stomp **left** foot forward (move only slightly forward)
15	Stomp **right** foot forward (move only slightly forward)
16	Stomp **left** foot forward (move only slightly forward)

Turns

17-20	Right Monterey turn
17	Touch **right** toe to right side
18	Pivot on **left** foot ½ turn right and step **right** foot next to **left** foot (as turn is completed)
19	Touch **left** toe to left side
20	Step **left** foot next to **right** foot

21-22	Military turn to the left
21	Step **right** foot forward
22	Pivot on **both** feet ½ turn left
23	Step **right** foot forward
24	Kick **left** foot forward

Steps and Touches

25	Step **left** foot back
26	Step **right** foot across **left** foot

27	Touch **left** toe next to **right** foot
28	Touch **left** heel to left side (touch only slightly to left side)
29	Step **left** foot across **right** foot

30	Touch **right** toe next to **left** foot
31	Touch **right** heel to right side (touch only slightly to right side)
32	Step **right** foot across **left** foot

33	Step **left** foot to left side
34	Step **right** foot to right side
35	Step **left** foot across **right** foot
36	Clap

Hip Bumps, Stomps and Claps

37	Step **right** foot to right side and bump **right** hip to right side
38	Bump **right** hip to right side
39	Bump **left** hip to left side
40	Bump **left** hip to left side

41	Stomp **right** foot forward
42	Clap
43	Stomp **left** foot forward
44	Clap

Shuffles and Turns

45-46   Right polka back with ½ turn left
       45   Step **right** foot back
       &   Step **left** foot next to **right** foot
       46   Step **right** foot back
       &   Pivot on **right** foot ½ turn left

47-48   Left shuffle forward
       47   Step **left** foot forward
       &   Step **right** foot next to **left** foot
       48   Step **left** foot forward

49-50   Military turn to the left
       49   Step **right** foot forward
       50   Pivot on **both** feet ½ turn left
51   Step **right** foot forward
52   Step **left** foot to left side (shoulder width apart)

Heel Swivels

53   Swivel heels to left
54   Swivel heels to right
55   Swivel heels to left
56   Swivel heels to center

Shuffle, Turns and Rocks

57-58   Right shuffle forward
       57   Step **right** foot forward
       &   Step **left** foot next to **right** foot
       58   Step **right** foot forward
59-60   Military turn to the right
       59   Step **left** foot forward
       60   Pivot on **both** feet ½ turn right

61-62   Left shuffle in place with ¾ turn right
       61   Pivot on **right** foot ¼ turn right and step **left** foot next to **right** foot (as turn is completed)
       &   Pivot on **left** foot ½ turn right and step **right** foot next to **left** foot (as turn is completed)
       62   Step **left** foot in place
63   Rock-step **right** foot back
64   Rock forward on **left** foot

Repeat Pattern

NOTE: For the first repetition (the first time through the dance pattern), use the following:
63   Step **right** foot next to **left** foot
64   Touch **left** foot next to **right** foot
Go to beat 33

Rhythm Line:

```
secs     .....1.....2.....3.....4.....5.....6.....7.....8.....9....10
180 bpm  1 2 3 4 1 2 3 4 1 2 3 4 1 2 3 4 1 2 3 4 1 2 3 4 1 2 3 4 1 2
foot     R . . . L . . . R . L . R L R L R B L L R B R L L R L L L R
Other


secs     ....11....12....13....14....15....16....17....18....19....20
180 bpm  3 4 1 2 3 4 1 2 3 4 1 2 3 4 1&2&3&4 1 2 3 4 1 2 3 4 1&2 3 4
foot     R R L R L . R . . . R . L . RLRBLRL R B R L B B B B RLR L B
other                c              c  c
                  (clap)


secs     ....21....22....23....24....25....26....27....28....29....30
180 bpm  1&2 3 4 1 2 3 4 1 2 3 4 1 2 3 4 1 2 3 4 1 2 3 4 1 2 3 4 1 2
foot     BBL R L repeat pattern
other
```

Cues:

stomp right / hold / hold / hold
stomp left / hold / hold / hold
stomp right / hold / stomp left / hold
right / left / right / left

touch / turn / touch / together
right / turn / right / kick
back / cross
toe / heel / cross
toe / heel / cross

side / side / cross / clap
bump right / right / left / left
stomp right / clap / stomp left / clap
back - and - back - turn - left - and - left

right / turn / right / left
heels left / right / left / center
right - and - right / left / turn
turn - turn - left / rock back / forward

Swamp Thang

About this dance: There is a very interesting story behind the name of this dance. Max Perry originally choreographed it for "Wheel of Love" by Rick Tippe and it was called "Heart Like A Wheel". Dancers found they also liked dancing it to "Swamp Thang" by The Grid. It now has an official alias: Swamp Thang. Having seen the movie "Swamp Thing" too many times, Tony's image of the dance is probably different from most.

The choreographer, Max Perry, would like you to be able to reach him. He is in Danbury Connecticut, USA at 203-798-9312. He also has an internet site at http://www.maxperry.com.

The Dance

Difficulty Level: IV
Dance Faces: 4 directions
Suggested Music:

Choreographer: Max Perry
Pattern Length: 40 Beats

For practicing – "Honey Hush" by Scooter Lee (Track 5 on **Free CD**), "The City Put The Country Back In Me" originally recorded by Neil McCoy (Track 2 on CD included with Book 1).

For dancing – "Swamp Thang" by The Grid, "C-O-U-N-T-R-Y" by Joe Diffie, "Wheel of Love" by Rick Tippe, "Some Things Are Meant To Be" by Linda Davis, "Rodeo Man" by Ronna Reeves.

Beats	Description
	Rocks and Coaster Steps
1	Rock-step **left** foot forward
2	Rock back on **right** foot
3-4	Left coaster step
	3 Step **left** foot back
	& Step **right** foot next to **left** foot
	4 Step **left** foot forward (step only slightly forward)
5	Rock-step **right** foot forward
6	Rock back on **left** foot
7-8	Right coaster step
	7 Step **right** foot back
	& Step **left** foot next to **right** foot
	8 Step **right** foot forward (step only slightly forward)
	Side Rock and Cha-Cha
9	Rock-step **left** foot to left side
10	Rock in place on **right** foot

11-12	Left shuffle in place
	11 Step **left** foot next to **right** foot
	& Step **right** foot in place
	12 Step **left** foot in place

13	Rock-step **right** foot to right side
14	Rock in place on **left** foot
15-16	Right shuffle in place
	15 Step **right** foot in place
	& Step **left** foot next to **right** foot
	16 Step **right** foot in place

Vines, Chassés and Rocks

17-19	Left vine with ¼ turn left
	17 Step **left** foot to left side
	18 Step **right** foot behind **left** foot
	19 Step **left** foot to left side and pivot ¼ turn left
20	Step **right** foot forward and pivot on **right** foot ¾ turn left

21-22	Left chassé to left side
	21 Step **left** foot to left side
	& Step **right** foot next to **left** foot
	22 Step **left** foot to left side
23	Rock-step **right** foot back
24	Rock forward on **left** foot

25-27	Right vine with ¼ turn right
	25 Step **right** foot to right side
	26 Step **left** foot behind **right** foot
	27 Step **right** foot to right side and pivot ¼ turn right
28	Step **left** foot forward and pivot on **left** foot ¾ turn right

29-30	Right chassé to right side
	29 Step **right** foot to right side
	& Step **left** foot next to **right** foot
	30 Step **right** foot to right side
31	Rock-step **left** foot back
32	Rock forward on **right** foot

33-35	Syncopated left chassé to left side
	33 Step **left** foot to left side
	34 Clap
	& Step **right** foot next to **left** foot
	35 Step **left** foot to left side and clap
36	Step **right** foot next to **left** foot

Turns

37	Pivot on **right** foot ¼ turn left and step **left** foot forward (as turn is completed)
38	Step **right** foot forward and pivot on **both** feet ½ turn left
39	Step **left** foot in place
40	Stomp **right** foot next to **left** foot

Repeat Pattern

Rhythm Line:

```
secs      .....1.....2.....3.....4.....5.....6.....7.....8.....9....10
120bpm    1  2  3 & 4   1  2  3 & 4   1  2'  3 & 4   1  2  3 & 4   1  2  3  4
foot      L  R  L R L   R  L  R L R   L  R  L R L   R  L  R L R   L  R  L  R
other

secs      ....11....12....13....14....15....16....17....18....19....20
120bpm    1 & 2  3  4   1  2  3  4   1 & 2  3  4   1  2 & 3  4   1  2  3  4
foot      L R L  R  L   R  L  R  L   R L R  L  R   L  .R L  R  B  B  L  R   repeat
other                                             c
                                               (clap)
```

Cues:

rock forward / back / left - and - left
rock forward / back / right - and - right
side / rock / left - and - left
side / rock / right - and - right

left / behind / turn / turn
left - chase - left / rock back / forward
right / behind / turn / turn
right - chase - right / rock back / forward

left / clap / chase - left / together
turn / turn / step / stomp

Dancin' Feet

About this dance: This dance is very popular in our area and had an interesting conception. Susan and Harry Brooks tell us that they like to dance patterns that are unique and try to choreograph dances that involve novel pairings of steps. Dancin' Feet got its start when Harry suggested putting together sailor steps that begin across and behind. Susan tried dancing the two in sequence and found that it felt unusual, but nice. So, on that day she came up with steps for 36 more beats to accompany them! We do this dance to both slow and medium tempo music. Done to slower music, we think this dance has a very nice, "soft-shoe" feel to it.

The Dance

Difficulty Level: IV   **Choreographers:** Susan and Harry Brooks

Dance Faces: 2 directions   **Pattern Length:** 40 Beats

Suggested Music:

For practicing — "Can't Help It" by Scooter Lee (Track 2 on **Free CD**), "Wher'm I Gonna Live When I Get Home" originally recorded by Billy Ray Cyrus (Track 9 on CD included with Book 1).

For dancing— "Feelin Kind of Lonely Tonight" by Shelby Lynne, "Wipeout" by the Beach Boys, "Be Bop A Lula" by Scooter Lee.

Beats	Description
	Two Sailor Steps, Cross and a Sailor Step
1-2	Right sailor step (begin across)
	1 Step **right** foot across **left** foot (leaning body slightly right)
	& Step **left** foot to left side
	2 Step **right** foot to right side
3-4	Left sailor step (begin behind)
	3 Step **left** foot behind **right** foot (leaning body slightly left)
	& Step **right** foot to right side
	4 Step **left** foot to left side
5	Step **right** foot across **left** foot
6	Step **left** foot to left side
7-8	Right sailor step (begin behind)
	7 Step **right** foot behind **left** foot (leaning body slightly right)
	& Step **left** foot to left side
	8 Step **right** foot to right side

Two Sailor Steps, Cross and a Sailor Step

9-10   Left sailor step (begin across)
     9   Step **left** foot across **right** foot (leaning body slightly left)
     &   Step **right** foot to right side
     10   Step **left** foot to left side
11-12 Right sailor step (begin behind)
     11   Step **right** foot behind **left** foot (leaning body slightly right)
     &   Step **left** foot to left side
     12   Step **right** foot to right side

13   Step **left** foot across **right** foot
14   Step **right** foot to right side
15-16 Left sailor step (begin behind)
     15   Step **left** foot behind **right** foot (leaning body slightly left)
     &   Step **right** foot to right side
     16   Step **left** foot to left side

Weave, Turns and Shuffle

17-20 Weave to the left (begin across) with body rise and $\frac{1}{4}$ turn left
     &   Rise on ball of **left** foot
     17   Step **right** foot across **left** foot
     &   Rise on ball of **right** foot
     18   Step **left** foot to left side
     &   Rise on ball of **left** foot
     19   Step **right** foot behind **left** foot
     &   Rise on ball of **right** foot
     20   Step **left** foot to left side and pivot $\frac{1}{4}$ turn left

21-22 Military turn to the left
     21   Step **right** foot forward
     22   Pivot on **both** feet $\frac{1}{2}$ turn left
23-24 Right shuffle forward
     23   Step **right** foot forward
     &   Step **left** foot next to **right** foot
     24   Step **right** foot forward

Weave, Turns and Shuffle

25-28 Weave to the right (begin across) with body rise and $\frac{1}{4}$ turn right
     &   Rise on ball of **right** foot
     25   Step **left** foot across **right** foot
     &   Rise on ball of **left** foot
     26   Step **right** foot to right side
     &   Rise on ball of **right** foot
     27   Step **left** foot behind **right** foot
     &   Rise on ball of **left** foot
     28   Step **right** foot to right side and pivot $\frac{1}{4}$ turn right

29-30 Military turn to the right
     29   Step **left** foot forward
     30   Pivot on **both** feet $\frac{1}{2}$ turn right
31-32 Left shuffle forward
     31   Step **left** foot forward
     &   Step **right** foot next to **left** foot
     32   Step **left** foot forward

Turning Kick-Ball Changes

33-34	Right kick-ball-change with ¼ turn left
	33 Kick **right** foot forward
	& Step ball of **right** foot next to **left** foot and pivot ¼ turn left
	34 Step **left** foot in place
35-36	Right kick-ball-change with ¼ turn left
	35 Kick **right** foot forward
	& Step ball of **right** foot next to **left** foot and pivot ¼ turn left
	36 Step **left** foot in place

Kick, Side-Jack and Clap

37	Kick **right** foot forward
38-39	Side-jack (begin right)
	& Step **right** foot to right side
	38 Step **left** foot to left side
	& Step **right** foot home
	39 Step **left** foot next to **right** foot
40	Clap

Repeat Pattern

Variation:

On the weaves (beats 17-20 and beats 25-28), you can omit the body rises on the half-beats (&s).

Rhythm Line:

```
secs      .....1.....2.....3.....4.....5.....6.....7.....8.....9....10
120bpm    1 & 2   3 & 4   1   2   3 & 4   1 & 2   3 & 4   1   2   3 & 4 & 1 & 2 & 3 & 4
foot      R L R   L R L   R   L   R L R   L R L   R L R   L   R   L R L L R R L L R R L
other

secs      ....11....12....13....14....15....16....17....18....19....20
120bpm    1   2   3 & 4 & 1 & 2 & 3 & 4   1   2   3 & 4   1 & 2   3 & 4   1 & 2 & 3   4
foot      R   B   R L R R L L R R L L R   L   B   L R L   R R L   R R L   R R L R L   .    repeat
other                                                                                 c
                                                                                   (clap)
```

Cues:

across - side - side / behind - side - side
cross / side / behind - side - side
across - side - side / behind - side - side
cross / side / behind - side - side

and - cross - and - side - and - behind - and - turn
right / turn / right - and - right
and - cross - and - side - and - behind - and - turn
left / turn / left - and - left

kick - turn - change / kick - turn - change
kick - out - out - in - in / clap

Honky Tonk Habit

New Concepts, Steps and Combinations

New Combinations

Electric Kick

Instructs you to make four movements in two beats of music. The foot which "kicks" will be identified in the dance description while the other foot "supports" the weight during the kick. On the half-beat before "1", the support foot steps diagonally back. On "1", the heel of the kicking foot touches diagonally forward. On "&", the kicking foot steps home. On "2", the support foot touches or steps next to the kicking foot, depending on the action required next.

For example, "left electric kick" instructs you to: on "&", step diagonally back on your right foot, on "1", touch your left heel diagonally forward, on "&", step your left foot home, and on "2", touch your right foot next to your left foot.

Most dancers find the electric kick very difficult to do at first. As with all dance steps, it gets easier with practice. Practice it very slowly and mechanically at first. Start by practicing small movements, and then try separating your feet more and more as you gain familiarity with the moves. As you become proficient with this combination, your four movements will begin to look like two, and your kicking leg will appear to be "flying" to its heel touch. Electric Kicks are also known as "Romps".

Heel Jack

Instructs you to make four movements in four beats of music. Heel Jacks are half-time (or low voltage!) electric kicks. The foot which "kicks" will be identified in the dance description while the other foot supports the weight. On "1", the support foot steps diagonally back. On "2", the heel of the kicking foot touches diagonally forward. On "3", the kicking foot steps home. On "4", the support foot touches or steps next to the kicking foot, depending on the action required next.

For example, "left heel jack" instructs you to: on "1", step diagonally back on your right foot, on "2", touch your left heel diagonally forward, on "3", step your left foot home, and on "4", touch your right foot next to your left foot.

The Dance

Difficulty Level: IV

Choreographers: Chris Gibbons, Helen Morgan and Stephanie Corrick

Dance Faces: two directions

Pattern Length: 64 Beats

Suggested Music:

For practicing – "Can't Help It" by Scooter Lee (Track 2 on **Free CD**), "The City Put The Country Back In Me" originally recorded by Neil McCoy (Track 2 on CD included with Book 1).

For dancing – "Honky Tonk Habits" by Emilio, "Put Some Drive In Your Country" by Travis Tritt, "Here Comes That Train" by Joe Diffie.

Beats	Description

Kick-Ball-Changes and Military Turns

1 - 2	Right kick-ball-change
	1 Kick **right** foot forward
	& Step ball of **right** foot next to **left** foot
	2 Step **left** foot in place
3 - 4	Right kick-ball-change
	3 Kick **right** foot forward
	& Step ball of **right** foot next to **left** foot
	4 Step **left** foot in place
5 - 6	Military turn to the left
	5 Step **right** foot forward
	6 Pivot on **both** feet ½ turn left
7	Stomp **right** foot next to **left** foot
8	Stomp **left** foot in place
9 -10	Right kick-ball-change
	9 Kick **right** foot forward
	& Step ball of **right** foot next to **left** foot
	10 Step **left** foot in place
11-12	Right kick-ball-change
	11 Kick **right** foot forward
	& Step ball of **right** foot next to **left** foot
	12 Step **left** foot in place
13-14	Military turn to the left
	13 Step **right** foot forward
	14 Pivot on **both** feet ½ turn left
15	Stomp **right** foot next to **left** foot
16	Touch **left** foot in place

Vines and Monterey Turns

17-20　Left vine with right touch
　　17　Step **left** foot to left side
　　18　Step **right** foot behind **left** foot
　　19　Step **left** foot to left side
　　20　Touch **right** foot next to **left** foot

21-24　Right Monterey turn
　　21　Touch **right** toe to right side
　　22　Pivot on **left** foot ½ turn right and step **right** foot next to **left** foot (as turn is completed)
　　23　Touch **left** toe to left side
　　24　Touch **left** foot next to **right** foot

25- 28　Left vine with right touch
　　25　Step **left** foot to left side
　　26　Step **right** foot behind **left** foot
　　27　Step **left** foot to left side
　　28　Touch **right** foot next to **left** foot

29-32　Right Monterey turn
　　29　Touch **right** toe to right side
　　30　Pivot on **left** foot ½ turn right and step **right** foot next to **left** foot (as turn is completed)
　　31　Touch **left** toe to left side
　　32　Step **left** foot next to **right** foot

Heel Jacks

33-36　Left heel jack
　　33　Step **right** foot diagonally back
　　34　Touch **left** heel diagonally forward
　　35　Step **left** foot home
　　36　Step **right** foot home

37-40　Right heel jack
　　37　Step **left** foot diagonally back
　　38　Touch **right** heel diagonally forward
　　39　Step **right** foot home
　　40　Step **left** foot home

Electric Kicks

41-42　Left electric kick
　　&　Step **right** foot diagonally back
　　41　Touch **left** heel diagonally forward
　　&　Step **left** foot home
　　42　Step **right** foot home

43-44　Right electric kick
　　&　Step **left** foot diagonally back
　　43　Touch **right** heel diagonally forward
　　&　Step **right** foot home
　　44　Step **left** foot home

Turn and Bumps

45-48	Jump-cross-turn to the left with stomp and clap
	45 Jump, landing with feet apart
	46 Jump, landing with **right** foot across **left** foot
	47 Pivot on **both** feet ½ turn left
	48 Stomp **right** foot diagonally forward and clap

49	Bump **right** hip diagonally forward
50	Bump **right** hip diagonally forward
51	Bump **left** hip diagonally back
52	Bump **left** hip diagonally back

53	Bump **right** hip diagonally forward
54	Bump **left** hip diagonally back
55	Bump **right** hip diagonally forward
56	Bump **left** hip diagonally back

Pendulum Legs and Stomps

57	Touch **right** toe to right side
58	Hold
&	Step **right** foot next to **left** foot
59	Touch **left** toe to left side
60	Hold

&	Step **left** foot next to **right** foot
61	Touch **right** toe to right side
&	Step **right** foot next to **left** foot
62	Touch **left** toe to left side
&	Step **left** foot next to **right** foot
63	Stomp-up **right** foot next to **left** foot
64	Stomp-up **right** foot next to **left** foot

Repeat Pattern

Rhythm Line:

```
secs     .....1.....2.....3.....4.....5.....6.....7.....8.....9....10
120bpm   1 & 2   3 & 4   1   2   3   4   1 & 2   3 & 4   1   2   3   4   1   2   3   4
foot     R R L   R R L   R   B   R   L   R R L   R R L   R   B   R   L   L   R   L   R
other

secs     ....11....12....13....14....15....16....17....18....19....20
120bpm   1   2   3   4   1   2   3   4   1   2   3   4   1   2   3   4   1   2   3   4
foot     R   B   L   L   L   R   L   R   R   B   L   L   R   L   L   R   L   R   R   L
other

secs     ....21....22....23....24....25....26....27....28....29....30
120bpm   & 1 & 2 & 3 & 4   1   2   3   4   1   2   3   4   1   2   3   4   1   2 & 3   4
foot     R L L R L R R L   B   B   B   R   .   .   .   .   .   .   .   R   . R L   .
other                                     c   b   b   b   b   b   b   b   b
                                        (clap)      (hip bumps)

secs     ....31....32....33....34....35....36....37....38....39....40
120bpm   & 1 & 2 & 3   4   1   2   3   4   1   2   3   4   1   2   3   4   1   2   3   4
foot     L R R L L R   R   repeat pattern
other
```

Cues:

right kick - ball - change / right kick - ball - change
right / turn / stomp / stomp
right kick - ball - change / right kick - ball - change
right / turn / stomp / touch

left / behind / left / touch
side / turn / side / touch
left / behind / left / touch
side / turn / side / together

back / right heel / home / home
back / left heel / home / home
back - heel - home - home - back - heel - home - home
jump / cross / turn / stomp

bump right / right / left / left
bump right / left / right / left
right side / hold / switch - side / hold
switch - side - switch - side - switch - stomp / stomp

Fever

About this dance: Parry Spence won The Crystal Boot Award as Country Dance Choreographer of the Year for this dance. She also won a Teli award for the instructional video for Fever. She is the choreographer and leader of "Rampage", a Nashville based show dance troupe. She also does seminars and workshops on country dance. You can year Parry by writing to "Country With An Edge", P O.Box 158056, Nashville, TN, USA 37215 or by phoning her at (in the USA) 615 292 4794.

New Concepts, Steps and Combinations

New Steps

Lunge   Instructs you to take a long step in the indicated direction, bending the knee of the stepping leg. When the step is forward, the move is like a fencing lunge.

Skate   Instructs you to move the identified foot by bending the knee of that leg and sliding the foot from a position under the center of the body to the specified location, at which the leg is straightened. When a skate is completed, all or most of the weight is on the skating foot. A skate is usually easier to execute on the ball of the foot.

For example, "skate left0 foot to left side" instructs you to move your left foot home (if it is not already there), bend your left knee, and slide your left foot to the left side. You would "unbend" or straighten your leg (to a normal standing position) as your foot reaches the left side.

New Combinations

Stroll   Instructs you to make three steps diagonally forward to three beats of music. A stroll will be described as either a right stroll or left stroll, indicating the direction of movement and the foot that leads the move. On the first beat, the leading foot steps diagonally forward. On the second beat, the other foot slides to a position where it is locked behind the leading foot. On the third beat, the leading foot, moves diagonally forward.

For example, "right stroll" instructs you to: on beat one, step your right foot diagonally forward, on beat two, slide your left foot to lock behind your right foot, and on beat three, step your right foot diagonally forward.

As with vines, when strolls are used in 4/4 time music, a fourth, "finishing move" for the foot that is free to move after the stroll is often specified with the stroll.

The Dance

Difficulty Level: IV

Dance Faces: four directions

Choreographer: Parry Spence

Pattern Length: 48 Beats

Suggested Music:

For practicing — "Can't Help It" by Scooter Lee (Track 2 on **Free CD**), "Talk Some" originally recorded by Billy Ray Cyrus (Track 3 on CD included with Book 1).

For dancing — "Fever" by Jeff Moore.

Beats	Description
	Rocks and Roll
1	Rock-step **right** foot forward
2	Rock back on **left** foot
3	Rock-step **right** foot back
4	Rock forward on **left** foot
5	Rock-step **right** foot forward
6	Rock back on **left** foot
7	Lunge **right** foot forward
8	Quarter hip roll, counter-clockwise (begin right hip forward) and raise body to standing position
	Turns and Stomps
9	Step **right** foot back
10	Pivot on **both** feet ½ turn right
11-12	Military turn to the right
	11 Step **left** foot forward
	12 Pivot on **both** feet ½ turn right
13	Step **left** foot forward
14	Scuff **right** foot
15	Stomp **right** foot next to **left** foot
16	Stomp **left** foot in place and clap
	Slaps and Skates
17	Step **right** foot diagonally forward
18	Hitch **left** leg and slap **left** knee with right hand
19	Step **left** foot diagonally forward
20	Hitch **right** leg and slap **right** knee with left hand
21	Skate **right** foot to right side
22	Skate **left** foot to left side
23	Skate **right** foot to right side and pivot ¼ turn right
24	Stomp **left** foot next to **right** foot and clap

Strolls and Slides

25-28   Right stroll with left slide-up
- 25   Step **right** foot diagonally forward
- 26   Slide **left** foot to lock behind **right** foot
- 27   Step **right** foot diagonally forward
- 28   Slide-up **left** foot next to **right** foot

29-32   Left stroll with right slide
- 29   Step **left** foot diagonally forward
- 30   Slide **right** foot to lock behind **left** foot
- 31   Step **left** foot diagonally forward
- 32   Slide **right** foot next to **left** foot

Electric Kicks with Twists and Swivels

33-34   Right electric kick
- &   Step **left** foot diagonally back
- 33   Touch **right** heel diagonally forward
- &   Step **right** foot home
- 34   Step **left** foot home

35   Twist ½ turn left
&   Swivel heels to right
36   Swivel heels to center

37-38   Right electric kick
- &   Step **left** foot diagonally back
- 37   Touch **right** heel diagonally forward
- &   Step **right** foot home
- 38   Step **left** foot home

39   Twist ½ turn left
&   Swivel heels to right
40   Swivel heels to center

Lunges and Bumps

41   Lunge **right** foot to right side (raise right forearm to forehead)
42   Bump **right** hip to right side
43   Step **right** foot next to **left** foot (lower right arm)
44   Clap

45   Lunge **left** foot to left side (raise left forearm to forehead)
46   Bump **left** hip to left side
47   Step **left** foot next to **right** foot (lower right arm)
48   Clap

Repeat Pattern

Variation

Parry suggests an easy alternative to the electric kicks with half-turn twists and swivels on beats 33-40.

33	Step **right** toe across left foot
34	Pivot on **both** feet ½ turn left
35	Twist left
&	Twist right
36	Twist centre
37	Step **right** toe across **left** foot
38	Pivot on **both** feet ½ turn left
39	Twist left
&	Twist right
40	Twist centre

Rhythm Line:

```
secs    .... 1.....2.....3.....4.....5.....6.....7.....8.....9....10
120bpm  1   2   3   4   1   2   3   4   1   2   3   4   1   2   3   4   1   2   3   4
foot    R   L   R   L   R   L   R   .   R   B   L   B   L   R   R   L   R   L   L   R
other                           hip                         c       s       s
                                roll                      (clap) (knee slaps)

secs    ....11....12....13....14....15....16....17....18....19....20
120bpm  1   2   3   4   1   2   3   4   1   2   3   4&1&2  3&4&1&2  3&4
foot    R   L   R   L   R   L   R   L   L   R   L  RLRRL  BBBLRRL  BBB
other           c

secs    ....21....22....23....24....25....26....27....28....29....30
120bpm  1   2   3   4   1   2   3   4   1   2   3   4   1   2   3   4   1   2   3   4
foot    R   .   R   .   L   .   L   .  repeat pattern
other       b       c       b       c
            (bump)
```

Cues:

rock forward / back / back / forward
rock forward / back / lunge / roll
back / turn / left / turn
left / scuff / stomp / stomp

right / hitch / left / hitch
skate / skate / turn / stomp
right / stroll / right / slide
left / stroll / left / slide

back - heel - home - home / twist - heels - center
back - heel - home - home / twist - heels - center
lunge / bump / together / clap
lunge / bump / together / clap

New Jack Swing

About this dance: Deb Crew tells us that the song "If I Had No Loot" really inspired this dance. The song was a favorite of her co-choreographer, Steve Morrison, and in one 22-hour marathon, they created this dance! The dance is named for Jackie, Deb's daughter and Steve's partner. Deb is very active in Canada's country-western dance community. She developed and hosts the North Country/Rick Tippe outstanding Dance Achievement Awards. When we last spoke with Deb, she was busy planning the next ODAA event to be held in Toronto, Ontario, Canada in April of 1999. You can reach her by phone at (in Canada) 705-429-0265.

This dance begins with an introductory eight beat pattern that is repeated a number of times, depending on the particular song, at the beginning of the dance. The remainder of the dance consists of a pattern of 64 beats. The choreographer suggests that if the dance is done to "If I Had No Loot", the dance starts after the first 16 beats of music and the introductory pattern is done four times (for musical beats 17-48). If the dance is done to "No One Else On Earth", the dance also starts after the first 16 beats, but the introductory pattern is done twice (for musical beats 17-32). The use of the introductory and main patterns can also be varied to fit the phrasing of other songs.

The Dance

Difficulty Level: IV   **Choreographers:** Deb Crew and Steve Morrison
Dance Faces: four directions   **Pattern Length:** Two different patterns:
8 and 64 Beats

Suggested Music:

For practicing – "Honey Hush" by Scooter Lee (Track 5 on **Free CD**), "I'm So Miserable Without You" originally recorded by Billy Ray Cyrus (Track 7 of CD included with Book 1).

For dancing – "If I Had No Loot" by Tony, Toni, Tone, "No One Else on Earth" by Wynonna Judd.

Introductory Pattern

Beats	Description
1-2	Right shuffle in place
	1 Step **right** foot in place
	& Step **left** foot next to **right** foot
	2 Step **right** foot in place
&	Touch **left** toe *(turned in)* next to **right** instep
3	Touch **left** heel forward
&	Clap
4	Clap

5-6	Left shuffle in place
	5 Step **left** foot next to **right** foot
	& Step **right** foot next to **left** foot
	6 Step **left** foot in place
&	Touch **right** toe *(turned in)* next to **left** instep
7	Touch **right** heel forward
&	Clap
8	Clap

Repeat Pattern as indicated

Main Pattern

Beats	**Description**
	Toe Struts to Side and Rock
1-2	Right toe strut across left foot
	1 Touch **right** toe across **left** foot
	2 Lower **right** heel (step **right** foot down) and clap
3-4	Left toe strut to left side
	3 Touch **left** toe to left side
	4 Lower **left** heel (step **left** foot down) and clap
5-6	Right toe strut across left foot
	5 Touch **right** toe across **left** foot
	6 Lower **right** heel (step **right** foot down) and clap
7	Rock-step **left** foot to left side
8	Rock to right side on **right** foot
9-10	Left toe strut across right foot
	9 Touch **left** toe across **right** foot
	10 Lower **left** heel (step **left** foot down) and clap
11-12	Right toe strut to right side
	11 Touch **right** toe to right side
	12 Lower **right** heel (step **right** foot down) and clap
13-14	Left toe strut across right foot
	13 Touch **left** toe across **right** foot
	14 Lower **left** heel (step **left** foot down) and clap
15	Rock-step **right** foot to right side
16	Rock to left side on **left** foot
	Vaudeville Kicks
17-18&	Right Vaudeville kick
	17 Step **right** foot across **left** foot
	& Step **left** foot back
	18 Touch **right** heel forward
	& Step **right** foot home
19-20&	Left Vaudeville kick
	19 Step **left** foot across **right** foot
	& Step **right** foot back
	20 Touch **left** heel forward
	& Step **left** foot home

21-22&	Right Vaudeville kick
21	Step **right** foot across **left** foot
&	Step **left** foot back
22	Touch **right** heel forward
&	Step **right** foot home

23-24&	Left Vaudeville kick
23	Step **left** foot across **right** foot
&	Step **right** foot back
24	Touch **left** heel forward
&	Step **left** foot home

Kicks and Coaster Steps

25	Kick **right** foot forward
26	Kick **right** foot forward
27-28	Right coaster step
27	Step **right** foot back
&	Step **left** foot next to **right** foot
28	Step **right** foot forward

29	Kick **left** foot forward
30	Kick **left** foot forward
31-32	Left coaster step
31	Step **left** foot back
&	Step **right** foot next to **left** foot
32	Step **left** foot forward

Kick-Ball-Touch and Cross-Unwind

33-34	Right kick-ball-touch
33	Kick **right** foot forward
&	Step ball of **right** foot next to **left** foot
34	Touch **left** foot to left side
35	Step **left** foot across **right** foot
36	Pivot on **both** feet ½ turn right
37-38	Right kick-ball-touch
37	Kick **right** foot forward
&	Step ball of **right** foot next to **left** foot
38	Touch **left** foot to left side

39	Step **left** foot across **right** foot
40	Pivot on **both** feet ½ turn right

Bump, Toe Touch and Clap

41	Step **right** foot to right side and bump **both** hips forward
42	Bump **both** hips forward
43	Touch **left** toe next to **right** foot
44	Clap

45	Step **left** foot to left side and bump **both** hips forward
46	Bump **both** hips forward
47	Touch **right** toe next to **left** foot
48	Clap

Pendulum Legs and Jazz Box

49	Step **right** foot to right side

50	Step **left** foot behind **right** foot
51	Touch **right** toe to right side
&	Step **right** foot next to **left** foot
52	Touch **left** toe to left side
&	Step **left** foot next to **right** foot

53	Touch **right** toe to right side
54-56	Right jazz box
	54 Step **right** foot across **left** foot
	55 Step **left** foot back
	56 Step **right** foot to right side

Pendulum Legs and Jazz Box with Turn

57	Step **left** foot in place
58	Step **right** foot behind **left** foot
59	Touch **left** toe to left side
&	Step **left** foot next to **right** foot
60	Touch **right** toe to right side
&	Step **right** foot next to **left** foot
61	Touch **left** toe to left side
62-64	Left jazz box with $\frac{1}{4}$ turn left
	62 Step **left** foot across **right** foot
	63 Step **right** foot back and pivot $\frac{1}{4}$ turn left
	64 Step **left** foot to left side (step only slightly to left side)

Repeat Pattern

Rhythm Line:

Introductory Pattern

```
secs      .....1.....2.....3.....4.....5.....6.....7.....8.....9....10
120bpm    1 & 2 & 3 & 4   1 & 2 & 3 & 4   1 & 2 & 3 & 4   1 & 2 & 3 & 4   1 & 2 & 3 & 4
foot      R L R L L . .   L R L R R . .   repeat pattern as indicated
other           c c             c c
          (claps)
```

Main Pattern

```
secs      .....1.....2.....3.....4.....5.....6.....7.....8.....9....10
120bpm    1   2   3   4   1   2   3   4   1   2   3   4   1   2   3   4   1 & 2 & 3 & 4
foot      R   R   L   L   R   R   L   R   L   L   R   R   L   L   R   L   R L R R L R L
other     c       c       c               c       c       c
          (clap)

secs      ....11....12....13....14....15....16....17....18....19....20
120bpm    & 1 & 2 & 3 & 4 & 1   2   3 & 4   1   2   3 & 4   1 & 2   3   4   1 & 2   3   4
foot      L R L R R L R L L R   R   R L R   L   L   L R L   R R L   L   B   R R L   L   B
other

secs      ....21....22....23....24....25....26....27....28....29....30
120bpm    1   2   3   4   1   2   3   4   1   2   3 & 4 & 1   2   3   4   1   2   3 & 4
foot      R   .   L   .   L   .   R   .   R   L   R R L L R   R   L   R   L   R   L L R
other     b   b       c   b   b       c
          (hip bumps)

secs      ....31....32....33....34....35....36....37....38....39....40
120bpm    & 1   2   3   4   1   2   3   4   1   2   3   4   1   2   3   4   1   2   3   4
foot      R L   L   R   L   repeat pattern
other
```

Cues:

Introductory Pattern

right - and - right - toe - heel - clap - clap
left - and - left - toe - heel - clap - clap

Main Pattern

toe / strut / toe / strut
toe / strut / rock / rock
toe / strut / toe / strut
toe / strut / rock / rock

cross - back - heel - home - cross - back - heel - home
cross - back - heel - home - cross - back - heel - home
kick / kick / back - and - forward
kick / kick / back - and - forward

kick - ball - touch / cross / turn
kick - ball - touch / cross / turn
right bump / bump / touch / clap
left bump / bump / touch / clap

right / behind / side - switch - side - switch
side / cross / back / side
left / behind / side - switch - side - switch
side / cross / turn / side

Girls' Night Out

About this dance: Country-Western line dancing has become very popular in Australia. This dance, choreographed by Terry Hogan of Clayfield, Queensland, Australia, has been named Australian Lane Dance of the Year at the Tamworth Country Music Festival in 1995. You can phone Terry at (in Australia) 61-7-3357 9947 or be e-mail: thogan@powerup.com.au. by the way, Tony thinks women dancers love to do turns and hip bumps. If that is true, this dance is truly a "girl's night out".

New Concepts, Steps and Combinations

New Combinations

Reverse three-step turn
Instructs you to make one full turn in three steps to three beats of music. The turn will be labelled "to the right" or "to the left", indicating the direction of travel and the foot that leads the combination. Unlike a three-step turn, however, in a reverse three-step turn the direction of turn is opposite (reverse) the direction of travel and opposite the foot that leads the combination. In other words, in a "Reverse three-step turn to the right" the first foot to move will be your right foot and you will be moving to the right, but you will make two half turns left. Most often, a reverse three-step turn will proceed as follows: on "1", step your lead foot turned in to the side. On "2", pivot on your lead foot $\frac{1}{2}$ turn in the reverse direction and step your following foot to the side as the turn is completed. On "3", pivot on your following foot $\frac{1}{2}$ turn in the reverse direction and step your lead foot to the side as the turn is completed. On occasion, steps "1" and "2" of a reverse three-step turn will be the turning steps with a step to the side being done on step "3".

For example, a "reverse three-step turn to left" means: on beat one, step your left foot to your left side; on beat two, pivot on your left foot $\frac{1}{2}$ turn right and step your right foot to your right side as the turn is completed; on beat three, pivot on your right foot $\frac{1}{2}$ turn right and step your left foot to your left side as the turn is completed.

If the movement of a reverse three-step turn is not directly to the side, the direction of movement will be specified (for example, reverse three-step turn to left moving forward).

When reverse three-step turns are used in 4/4 time music, a fourth finishing move is often specified with the turn.

The Dance

Difficulty Level: IV

Choreographer: Terry Hogan

Dance Faces: two directions

Pattern Length: 64 Beats

Suggested Music:

For practicing – "Honey Hush" by Scooter Lee (Track 5 on **Free CD**)"I Wanna Go Too Far" originally recorded by Trisha Yearwood (Track 4 on CD included with Book 1).

For dancing – "Girls' Night Out" by Gina Jeffreys, "Wrong Place, Wrong Time" by Mark Chestnutt.

Beats	Description
	Kick and Three Turns
1	Kick **right** foot forward
2	Rock-step ball of **right** foot back
3	Step **left** foot in place and pivot ¼ turn left
4	Latin-step **right** foot to right side
5	Latin-step **left** foot in place and pivot ¼ turn right
6	Step **right** foot back
7	Step **left** foot in place and pivot ¼ turn right
8	Step **right** foot next to **left** foot
	Reverse Three-Step Turn
9 -12	Reverse three-step turn to left with a touch
	9 Step **left** foot (turned in) to left side
	10 Pivot on **left** foot ½ turn right and step **right** foot to right side (as turn is completed)
	11 Pivot on **right** foot ½ turn right and step **left** foot to left side (as turn is completed)
	12 Touch **right** foot next to **left** foot
	Steps and Three More Turns
13	Step **right** foot to right side
14	Slide **left** foot next to **right** foot
15	Step **right** foot to right side
16	Touch **left** foot next to **right** foot
17-18	Military turn to the right
	17 Step **left** foot forward
	18 Pivot on **both** feet ½ turn right
19	Step **left** foot forward
20	Hold
21-22	Military turn to the left
	21 Step **right** foot forward
	22 Pivot on **both** feet ½ turn left
23	Step **right** foot forward
24	Hold

25-26	Military turn to the right
	25 Step **left** foot forward
	26 Pivot on **both** feet ½ turn right
27	Step **left** foot forward
28	Hold

Latin-Steps

29	Latin-step **right** foot diagonally forward
30	Latin-step **left** foot in place
31	Latin-step **right** foot in place
32	Hold

33	Latin-step **left** foot diagonally forward
34	Latin-step **right** foot in place
35	Latin-step **left** foot in place
36	Hold

37	Latin-step **right** foot diagonally forward
38	Latin-step **left** foot in place
39	Latin-step **right** foot in place
40	Hold

Side Steps and Rocks

41	Step **left** foot across **right** foot
42	Step **right** foot to right side
43	Rock to left side on **left** foot

44	Step **right** foot across **left** foot
45	Step **left** foot to left side
46	Rock to right side on **right** foot

47	Step **left** foot across **right** foot
48	Step **right** foot to right side

Turn and Stomps

49	Pivot on **right** foot ¼ turn left
50	Kick **left** foot forward
51	Step **left** foot next to **right** foot
52	Touch **right** foot next to **left** foot

Strolls

53-56	Right stroll with left slide-up
	53 Step **right** foot diagonally forward
	54 Slide **left** foot to lock behind **right** foot
	55 Step **right** foot diagonally forward
	56 Slide-up **left** foot next to **right** foot

57-60	Left stroll with right slide-up
	57 Step **left** foot diagonally forward
	58 Slide **right** foot to lock behind **left** foot
	59 Step **left** foot diagonally forward
	60 Slide-up **right** foot next to **left** foot

Walk Forward and Heels

61	Step **right** foot diagonally forward
62	Slide **left** foot next to **right** foot
&	Raise heels
63	Lower heels
&	Raise heels
64	Lower heels

Repeat Pattern

Rhythm Line:

```
secs     .....1.....2.....3.....4.....5.....6.....7.....8.....9....10
120bpm   1   2   3   4   1   2   3   4   1   2   3   4   1   2   3   4   1   2   3   4
foot     R   R   L   R   L   R   L   R   L   B   B   R   R   R   L   R   L   L   B   L   .
Other

secs     ....11....12....13....14....15....16....17....18....19....20
120bpm   1   2   3   4   1   2   3   4   1   2   3   4   1   2   3   4   1   2   3   4
foot     R   B   R   .   L   B   L   .   R   L   R   .   L   R   L   .   R   L   R   .
other

secs     ....21....22....23....24....25....26....27....28....29....30
120bpm   1   2   3   4   1   2   3   4   1   2   3   4   1   2   3   4   1   2   3   4
foot     L   R   L   R   L   R   L   R   R   L   L   R   R   R   L   R   L   L   R   L   R
other

secs     ....31....32....33....34....35....36....37....38....39....40
120bpm   1   2 & 3 & 4   1   2   3   4   1   2   3   4   1   2   3   4   1   2   3   4
foot     R   L B B B B   repeat pattern
other
```

Cues:

kick / back / turn / side
turn / back / turn / together
side / turn / turn / together
right / slide / right / touch

left / turn / left / hold
right / turn / right / hold
left / turn / left / hold
sway right / sway / sway / hold
sway left / sway / sway / hold
sway right / sway / sway / hold

cross / side / rock
cross / side / rock
cross / side

turn / kick / together / touch
right / slide / right / slide

left / slide / left / slide
right / slide - heels - down - and - down

Cajun Mambo Walk

About this dance: This Max Perry line dance has a real Latin feel to it. If you like doing rocks and rock-steps, this dance will probably become a favorite of yours. Try dancing it to fast tempo music (such as "Moving On Up", suggested below). When you do, dance the pattern at half-time. Instead of stepping on beats and half-beats, you will be stepping to the traditional Mambo rhythm of "quick, quick, slow."

The Dance

Difficulty Level: IV

Dance Faces: four directions

Choreographer: Max Perry

Pattern Length: 32 Beats

Suggested Music:

For practicing—"Can't Help It" by Scooter Lee (Track 2 on **Free CD**), "Walkin' Away A Winner" originally recorded by Kathy Mattea (Track 1 on CD included with Book 1).

For dancing – "Let's Walk Away In Love" by Jim Yeomans, "High Test Love" by Scooter Lee, "Moving On Up" by Scooter Lee (Track 5 on **Free CD**)

Beats	Description
	Rocks Forward and Back
1	Rock-step **left** foot forward
&	Rock back on **right** foot
2	Step **left** foot next to **right** foot
3	Rock-step **right** foot back
&	Rock forward on **left** foot
4	Step **right** foot next to **left** foot
	Rocks to the Sides
5	Rock-step **left** foot to left side
&	Rock to right side on **right** foot
6	Step **left** foot next to **right** foot
7	Rock-step **right** foot to right side
&	Rock to left side on **left** foot
8	Step **right** foot next to **left** foot
	Turns and Rocks
9	Step **left** foot forward and pivot ½ turn right
&	Rock-step **right** foot forward
10	Step **left** foot next to **right** foot
11	Step **right** foot forward and pivot ½ turn left
&	Rock-step **left** foot forward
12	Step **right** foot next to **left** foot

13	Step **left** foot forward and pivot $\frac{1}{2}$ turn right
&	Step **right** foot back and pivot $\frac{1}{2}$ turn right
14	Step **left** foot next to **right** foot
15	Rock-step **right** foot back
&	Rock forward on **left** foot
16	Kick **right** foot forward
&	Hitch **right** leg

Side Steps and Heels Swivel Together

17	Step **right** foot to right side
&	Step **left** foot next to **right** foot
18	Step **right** foot to right side
&	Step **left** foot next to **right** foot
19	Step **right** foot to right side (step only slightly to right side)
&	Swivel heels to left
20	Swivel heels to right

21	Step **left** foot to left side
&	Step **right** foot next to **left** foot
22	Step **left** foot to left side
&	Step **right** foot next to **left** foot
23	Step **left** foot to left side (step only slightly to left side)
&	Swivel heels to right
24	Swivel heels to left

Side Steps and Heels Swivel Separately

25	Kick **right** foot forward
&	Step **right** foot to right side (step only slightly to right side)
26	Step **left** foot to left side (feet should be shoulder width apart)
27	Swivel **right** heel to left and swivel **left** heel to right
&	Swivel **right** toe to left and swivel **left** toe to right
28	Swivel **right** heel to center and swivel **left** heel to center

Rocks and Turns

29	Rock-step **right** foot *(turned out)* forward
&	Rock back on **left** foot and pivot $\frac{1}{4}$ turn right
30	Rock-step **right** foot *(turned out)* forward
&	Rock back on **left** foot and pivot $\frac{1}{4}$ turn right
31	Rock-step **right** foot *(turned out)* forward
&	Rock back on **left** foot and pivot $\frac{1}{4}$ turn right
32	Step **right** foot forward

Repeat Pattern

Rhythm Line:

```
secs      ...1...2...3...4...5...6...7...8...9..10..11..12..13..14..15
90bpm     1&2 3&4 1&2 3&4 1&2 3&4 1&2 3&4&1&2&3&4 1&2&3&4 1&2 3&4 1&2
foot      LRL RLR LRL RLR LRL RLR LRL RLRRRLRLRBB LRLRLBB RRL BBB RLR
other
```

```
secs      ..16..17..18..19..20..21..22..23..24..25..26..27..28..29..30
90bpm     &3&4 1 2 3 4 1 2 3 4 1 2 3 4 1 2 3 4 1 2 3 4 1 2 3 4 1 2 3 4
foot      LRLR  repeat pattern
other
```

Cues:

rock - rock - together / rock - rock - together
rock - rock - together / rock - rock - together
turn - rock - together / turn - rock - together
turn - turn - together / rock - rock - kick - hitch

right - and - right - and - right - heels - heels
left - and - left - and - left - heels - heels
kick - side - side / split heels - toes - heels
rock forward - turn - forward - turn - forward - turn - forward

Electric Reel

About this dance: This dance, by Irish choreographers Robert and Regina Padden was choreographed to "The Mason's Apron". They tell us that they were inspired to create this dance after attending a birthday party for a member of the "Lord Of The Dance" show where some of Michael Flatley's team performed. Electric Reel has been very well received. It is the winner Linedancer Magazine's "Dance of the Year '97" award. Along with another of their dances, Shamrock Shake, it scored high in Canadian awards as well.

They would like you to know that the CD, "Dancing to Electric Reels", which contains "The Mason's Apron" and music and step descriptions for some of their other dances, is available from them. The booklet that accompanies the CD also includes a description of arm movements you can try with the Electric Reel footwork. You can reach Robert and Regina by writing to 20 Castlehill Park, Castlebar, County Mayo, Ireland. Their telephone and fax number, in Ireland, is 353-94-26206.

Readers of our series of books will note an interesting change in our presentation of Electric Reel. When we first talked about Electric Reel in *UK Line Dance Favourites* it was very new and few written descriptions were available. We had seen swivets done on beats 17-20 and had seen written descriptions that called for swivets on those beats as well. But Robert and Regina assure us that they choreographed opposing swivels for those beats. With pleasure, we present this revised version.

New Concepts, Steps and Combinations

New Steps

Opposing Swivels
Instructs you to swivel both feet so that they move from their beginning position to one that is either *turned out, turned in,* or back to *parallel.* The direction of the opposing swivels will be specified in the dance description (to left, to right, or to center) and both feet will turn toward the direction specified. However, one foot will turn its heel and the other will turn its toe toward that direction. In opposing swivels, your weight will always be on the ball of one foot and the heel of the other. The movement is identical to a swivel of one heel and a swivel of the other toe done at the same time.

If the feet are in *parallel* position when opposing swivels begin, the foot named in the direction of the movement swivels its toe in that direction and the other foot swivels its heel. This movement will result in a slight movement of your body in the direction specified. For example, starting in *parallel* position, "opposing swivels to right" instructs you to swivel your right toe to the right and your left heel to the right. When you finish this movement, your feet will be *turned out.*

If the feet are in any position other than parallel, the matter of which foot swivels its toe and which foot swivels its heel will be determined by the pattern that moves the body in the direction specified. For example, starting in *turned in* position, "opposing swivels to right" instructs you to swivel your right toe to the right and your left heel to the right. When you finish this movement, your feet will be *turned out*. However, starting in *turned out* position, "opposing swivels to right" instructs you to swivel your right heel to the right and your left toe to the right. When you finish this movement, your feet will be *turned in*.

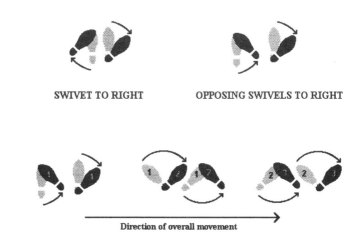

SWIVET TO RIGHT   OPPOSING SWIVELS TO RIGHT

Direction of overall movement

Swivet versus Opposing Swivels and traveling opposing swivels

When the instruction to do opposing swivels *to center* is given, return your feet to parallel position. If the preceeding opposing swivels moved you to the right, return to center by swiveling left, and vice versa.

Opposing swivels are like swivets in that your weight is on the ball of one foot and the heel of another. However, in a swivet your toes always point in the same direction; in opposing swivels, they point in opposite directions (except when you are instructed to do opposing swivels to center).

Other names for opposing swivels are Applejacks, Fancy Feet, and Crazy Feet.

The Dance

Difficulty Level: IV   **Choreographer:** Robert and Regina Padden

Dance Faces: four directions   **Pattern Length:** 32 Beats

Suggested Music:

For practicing – "Can't Help It" by Scooter Lee (Track 2 on **Free CD**), "Talk Some" originally recorded by Billy Ray Cyrus (Track 3 on CD included with Book 1)

For dancing – "The Mason's Apron" by Stockon's Wing, "Cry of the Celts" from the "Lord of the Dance" Album

---

Beats	Description
	Chassés and Heel Switches
1-4	Syncopated right chassé to right side
1	Step **right** foot to right side
2	Hold
&	Step **left** foot next to **right** foot
3	Step **right** foot to right side
&	Step **left** foot next to **right** foot
4	Step **right** foot to right side
5	Touch **left** heel forward
&	Step **left** foot next to **right** foot
6	Touch **right** heel forward
&	Step **right** foot next to **left** foot
7	Touch **left** heel forward
8	Clap
9-12	Syncopated left chassé to left side
9	Step **left** foot to left side
10	Hold
&	Step **right** foot next to **left** foot
11	Step **left** foot to left side
&	Step **right** foot next to **left** foot
12	Step **left** foot to left side
13	Touch **right** heel forward
&	Step **right** foot next to **left** foot
14	Touch **left** heel forward
&	Step **left** foot next to **right** foot
15	Touch **right** heel forward
&	Step **right** foot next to **left** foot
16	Step **left** foot to left side (Step only slightly to left side)

Opposing Swivels With A Hook

17	Opposing swivels to left (feet end *turned out*)
&	Opposing swivels to center (feet end *parallel*)
18	Opposing swivels to right (feet end *turned out*)
&	Opposing swivels to center (feet end *parallel*)
19	Opposing swivels to left (feet end *turned out*)
&	Opposing swivels to center (feet end *parallel*)
20	Opposing swivels to right (feet end *turned out*)
&	Hook **right** leg across **left** leg

Shuffle Forward And Scooting To A Hook

21-22	Right shuffle forward
21	Step **right** foot forward
&	Step **left** foot next to **right** foot
22	Step **right** foot forward
23	Scuff **left** foot forward
&	Hitch **left** leg and scoot **right** foot forward
24	Step **left** foot forward
&	Hook **right** leg across **left** leg

Shuffle Forward And Turn

25-26	Right shuffle forward
25	Step **right** foot forward
&	Step **left** foot next to **right** foot
26	Step **right** foot forward
27	Scuff **left** foot forward
&	Pivot on **right** foot ¾ turn right
28	Step **left** foot back

Coaster Step And Jump

29-30	Right coaster step
29	Step **right** foot back
&	Step **left** foot next to **right** foot
30	Step **right** foot forward
31	Hold
32	Jump forward

Repeat Pattern

Rhythm Line:

```
secs      .....1.....2.....3.....4.....5.....6.....7.....8.....9....10
180 bpm   1 2&3&4 1&2&3 4 1 2&3&4 1&2&3&4 1&2&3&4&1&2 3&4&1&2 3&4 1&2
foot      R .LRLR LLRRL . L .RLRL RRLLRRL BBBBBBBRRLR LBLRRLR LRL RLR
other                   c
                       (clap)

secs      ....11....12....13....14....15....16....17....18....19....10
180 bpm   3 4 1 2 3 4 1 2 3 4 1 2 3 4 1 2 3 4 1 2 3 4 1 2 3 4 1 2 3 4
foot      . B  repeat pattern
```

Cues:

right / hold - chase - right - chase - right
heel - step - heel - step - heel / clap
left / hold - chase - left - chase - left
heel - step - heel - step - heel / step
left - center - right - center - left - center - right - hook
right - and - right / scuff - scoot - step - hook
right - and - right / scuff - turn - back
back - together - forward / hold / jump

A

Across-Ball-Change	See Sailor Step (begin across)
Applejack	See Opposing Swivels and Traveling Opposing Swivels

B

Bend knee Instructs you to bend the knee of the identified leg to a degree that is comfortable for you. Unless otherwise specified in a step description or combination definition, the direction to 'bend knee' should be executed without lifting the heel off the ground. This will result in a subtle lowering of the body to the side of the bending knee. The direction to which the bent knee should point will be specified, as in 'Bend **right** knee forward'.

Body Ripple Describes a movement in which the body undulates like a wave. In a body ripple, the knees, hips, torso, shoulders and head move in sequence forward and back, or side to side. This move is difficult for many dancers and requires practice. A beginner's version of a body ripple might just include moving the hips and shoulders forward and back in opposition to one another.

Body Roll See Body Ripple

Boot Hook Combination Instructs you to make a sequence of four movements, one of which will be a hook, in four beats of music. The four movements are executed by the identified leg, while the other leg supports the weight of the body. On beat one, the heel will touch diagonally forward with foot turned out. On beat two, the foot is hooked in front of the weighted leg. On beat three, the heel is touched diagonally forward with foot turned out. On beat four, the foot steps or touches next to the weighted foot.
For example, 'left boot hook combination' instructs you to: on '1', touch your left heel, with foot turned out, diagonally forward; on '2', hook your left leg in front of your right leg; on '3', touch your left heel, with foot turned out, diagonally forward; on '4', step your left foot next to your right.

Brush Instructs you to move the specified foot by gently dragging the ball of the foot across the floor. Brushes are most often done forward, but the direction will be specified in the dance description. This movement is much like a 'scuff' except that in a 'scuff' the heel comes in contact with the floor (and makes considerable noise) whereas in a 'brush', the ball of the foot is in contact with the floor (and produces much less noise). The brush involves no weight transfer.
For example, 'brush **left** foot forward' instructs you to gently push the ball of the left foot forward across the floor. In 'brush **left** foot forward' the right foot supports your weight during and after the brush.

Bump Gives you an instruction for hip movement independent of foot movement. Bump instructs you to move your hips, once, on the designated musical beat. The hip that moves out (right or left) and the direction of the bump (e.g. forward, backward) will be specified in the dance description. In a bump, your weight is supported by both feet. Bumps generally are easier to execute if the knees are bent slightly.
For example, 'bump **right** hip to the right' instructs you to move your right hip to the right on the beat of music. The expression 'bump **both** hips forward' is sometimes called a 'pelvic thrust'.

Butterfly See Heel Split

Buttermilk   See Heel Split

C

Cha-Cha   Instructs you to take three small steps to two beats of music. The foot which leads the combination, as well as the direction (right, left, forward, back, in place, etc.), will be specified in the dance description.

For example, "right cha-cha forward" instructs you to: On "1", step forward on your right foot; On "&", step forward on your left foot; On "2", step forward on your right foot.

A cha-cha is much like a shuffle: both have three steps to a two beat, syncopated rhythm. However, in a cha-cha forward or back the three steps are all the same size, whereas, in a shuffle forward or back, the second step is shorter than the first and third. Because there is no travelling in a "shuffle in place" or "cha-cha in place", the "in place" versions of these combinations look identical.

Charleston Kick   Instructs you to make four movements to four beats of music. The foot that begins (leads) the combination is specified. On beat one, the lead foot steps forward. On beat two, the following foot kicks forward. On beat three, the following foot steps back, and, on beat four, the lead foot touches back. (On occasion, a movement other than a touch will be specified for beat four.)

For example, 'right Charleston kick' instructs you to: on '1', step your right foot forward; on '2', kick your left foot forward; on '3', step back on your left foot; on '4', touch your right toe back.

For a very advanced 'Charleston' look, swivel your heels alternately out and in to a syncopated rhythm. (We have never seen this done on a country-western dance floor.)

Charleston Swivel   Instructs you to swivel your heels alternately in and out to a syncopated rhythm (e.g., &, 1, &, 2, etc.) Keep your weight over the balls of your feet when you do this movement. When you swivel your heels "in", your toes will point away from each other and both feet will be turned out. When you swivel your heels "out", your toes will point toward each other and both feet will be turned in. Charleston swivels often accompany other steps and are used for extra styling.

Chassé   Instructs you to make a series of movements in which a step is taken on the lead foot and then the following foot quickly replaces the lead foot as the lead foot steps again. The foot that leads the combination and the direction of the chassé will be specified in the dance description. The number of beats involved in the chassé also will be specified and steps will be taken on each beat and half-beat in the series.

For example, "beats 1-3, left chassé to left side" instructs you to step your left foot to the left side, step your right foot next to your left foot, step your left foot to the left side, step your right foot next to your left foot, and step your left foot to the left side, to a rhythm of "one-and-two-and-three".

Chassés often create the look of the following foot "chasing" the leading foot. To effect this illusion, chassés are best done on the balls of the feet and on "&", the following foot should step very close to the leading foot. Shuffles are very much like three-step chassés and sometimes those names are used interchangeably.

Chug   Instructs you to bend the knee of the leg specified and lift the leg slightly from the floor. This move is very much like a 'hitch'. The difference is one of degree. While in a hitch the thigh is nearly parallel to the floor, a chug is a much smaller move. In a chug, the foot is lifted only a few inches from the floor. For example, 'chug **left** leg' instructs you to bend your left knee as you lift your left foot slightly off the floor.

Clap   Instructs you to clap your hands together, once, on the designated musical beat.

Coaster Step   Instructs you to make three back and forward steps in two beats of music. The foot that leads the sequence will be identified in the dance description. On beat one, the lead foot steps back. On '&', the following foot steps next to the lead foot. On beat three, the lead foot steps forward. Because of the quick change of direction involved, the first two steps should be taken on the balls of the feet. This movement produces a look of the feet backing away from the body.

For example, 'right coaster step' instructs you to: on '1', step back on the ball of your right foot, on '&', step the ball of your left foot next to your right, and on '2', step forward on your right foot.

Crazy Feet   See Opposing Swivels and Traveling Opposing Swivels

Cuban-   "Cuban-" is used as a prefix with a variety of steps and instructs you to prepare for a step by bending the knee, and lifting the heel of the leg that will move and straightening the knee and pushing out the hip of the weighted leg. The act of bending the knee of the moving leg and straightening the knee of the other leg results in the hip of the moving leg being lower than the hip of the other leg. A Cuban-step is completed by straightening the knee of the moving leg, pushing its hip out, and bending the knee of the other leg. When you take a cuban-step, bend your knee, step your toe to the indicated location, then lower your heel as you allow your knee to straighten, pushing your hip out.

For example, "Cuban-step left foot forward" instructs you to straighten your right knee, pushing its hip out, bend your left knee, step forward with the ball of your left foot, then lower your left heel as you allow your left knee to straighten, pushing its hip out, and your right knee to bend.

A Cuban-step is different from a Latin-step. In a Latin-step, the hip of the *moving* foot sways out at the beginning of the step. In a Cuban-step, the hip of the *non-moving* foot sways out at the beginning of the step. Both Cuban and Latin motion add hip movement styling to the steps you take. Many dancers find Cuban motion difficult at first, and it is a style that requires practice.

D

Draw   Instructs you to slide the identified foot for a designated number of beats. The action is continuous, but slow. This move produces a look of the foot being pulled from one position to the next. At the conclusion of a draw, most or all of the body weight is supported by the drawn foot. A draw is similar in movement to a slide: they differ only in that a slide is completed in one beat of music. Note that a draw is different from a draw-up. In a draw, the sliding foot bears weight; in a draw-up, it does not.

For example, 'beats 1-3 Draw **left** foot next to **right** foot' specifies a three beat draw of the left foot. On beat one, you would begin to slide your left foot toward your right, and you would continue this motion through beat two. On beat three, the draw is completed with most or all of your weight transferred to your left foot.

Draw-up   Instructs you to slide the identified foot for a designated number of beats. The action is continuous, but slow. This move produces a look of the foot being pulled from one position to the next. When a draw-up Is completed, the drawn foot is touching the floor but bears no weight. A draw-up is similar in movement to a slide-up: they differ only in that a slide-up is completed in one beat of music. Note that a draw is different from a draw-up. In a draw, the sliding foot bears weight; in a draw-up, it does not.

For example, 'beats 1-3 Draw-up **left** foot next to **right** foot' specifies a three beat draw-up of the left foot. On beat one, you would begin to slide your left foot toward your right, and you would continue this motion through beat two. On beat three, the draw is completed with the left foot touching the floor next to the right foot.

E

Electric Kick   Instructs you to make four movements in two beats of music. The foot which "kicks" will be identified in the dance description while the other foot "supports" the weight during the kick. On the half beat before "1", the support foot steps back or diagonally back, as indicated in the step description. On "1", the heel of the kicking foot touches forward or diagonally forward. On "&", the kicking foot steps home. On "2", the support foot touches or steps next to the kicking foot depending on the action required next.

For example, "left electric kick" instructs you to: on "&" step (diagonally) back on your right foot, on "1" touch your left heel (diagonally) forward, on "&" step your left foot home, and on "2" touch your right foot next to your left foot.

Most dancers find the electric kick very difficult to do at first. As with all dance steps, it gets easier with practice. Practice it very slowly and mechanically at first. Start by practicing small movements, and then try separating your feet more and more as you gain familiarity with the moves. As you become proficient with this combination, your four movements will begin to look like two, and your kicking leg will appear to be "flying" to its heel touch. Electric Kicks are also known as "Romps".

F

Face
Instructs you to change, temporarily, the orientation of your body. Face is used with foot directions to add body styling, but it does not change your reference point or wall. 'Face' is different from 'turn' in that 'face' directs body orientation only for the beat(s) on which it appears. 'Turn', however, results in a permanent change of body orientation and a new reference point or wall.

Fancy Feet
See Opposing Swivels and Traveling Opposing Swivels

Flare
Instructs you to make a low kick, keeping the foot parallel to the floor. While a kick generally brings the foot about six inches off the floor, in a flare the foot is lifted only high enough to avoid touching the floor. The direction of the flare will be specified in the dance description.

Flick
Instructs you to kick the identified foot backward. In a flick, the toe points down.

Grapevine
See Vine

H

Half-beat
Most dance steps are choreographed to match full beats of music. On occasion, steps are choreographed also for half-beats. Moving on half versus full beats makes a big difference in the overall look of a dance. In this book, when a dance requires a movement on a half-beat, that half-beat is labelled with the symbol '&' placed between full beats: '&' should be read as 'and'.

Half-time
Instructs you to take twice as long to perform the designated combination as you would ordinarily take. For example, 'half-time right vine' instructs you to execute a right vine on beats one to six instead of on beats '1', '2', and '3' as the vine would be more customarily done. The step description will tell you either to make the steps of the vine 'slow' steps, or to take the steps of the vine on beats '1', '3' and '5' with 'holds' or other movements specified for the intervening beats.

Hand Movements
Many dances include arm and hand movements as part of the pattern. Hand and arm movements may accompany foot movements or they may be the only activity choreographed for a sequence of beats. Commonly used arm and hand movements are individually defined.

Heel Jack
Instructs you to make four movements in four beats of music. Heel Jacks are half-time (or low voltage!) electric kicks. The foot which 'kicks' will be identified in the dance description while the other foot supports the weight. On '1', the support foot steps diagonally back. On '2', the heel of the kicking foot touches diagonally forward. On '3', the kicking foot steps home. On '4', the support foot touches or steps next to the kicking foot depending on the action required next.

For example, 'left heel jack' instructs you to: on '1', step diagonally back on your right foot, on '2', touch your left heel diagonally forward, on '3', step your left foot home, and on '4', touch your right foot next to your left foot.

Heel Split
Instructs you to move your heels apart and then bring them back together in two beats of music. A heel split will begin from a position in which your feet are to-

gether and your weight is supported by both feet. On beat one, move your heels apart. To execute this move, have your weight on the balls of your feet and move your right heel to the right and your left heel to the left. On beat two, move your heels back together. Heel splits are also called 'butterflies', 'buttermilks', 'pigeon toes', and 'scissors'.

Heel Strut   Instructs you to execute two moves in two beats of music. The foot involved in the strut will be specified in the dance description. On beat one, the heel of the specified foot is touched forward with the toe pointing up. On beat two, the toe of the specified foot is lowered as weight is transferred to that foot. Unlike toe struts, heel struts are always done moving forward. Keep in mind that, similar to toe struts, the touch on beat one may bear some weight, particularly when a turn is involved.
For example, 'left heel strut' instructs you, on '1', to touch your left heel forward and on '2', to lower your left toe to the floor and step down.

Hip Roll   Instructs you to move your hips around your body in a specified number of beats. The direction (clockwise or counter-clockwise), extent of rotation (half-circle or full circle) and the starting position of the hips (e.g. left diagonal back) will be specified in the dance description. The hip roll is a continuous movement over the specified beats of music. The hips begin a hip roll by moving out from under the body in the direction specified and remain out from under the body until they reach the roll's end position. As with a hip bump, hip rolls are generally easier to execute if the weight is supported by both feet and the knees are bent slightly. Unlike the hip bump, which is completed at a single point in time, the hip roll will take more than one beat of music to complete. For example, 'beats 1-4 Full hip roll, counter-clockwise (begin left hip diagonally back)' instructs you to move your hips to the left diagonal back position (if they are not already there), push them to the right, then diagonally forward, and next, keeping the hips pushed out, circle them left and back until they reach their starting position.

Hip Scoop   Instructs you to move your hips in a half circle in a specified number of beats. The starting position of the hips (e.g., left side) will be specified in the dance description. The hip scoop is a continuous movement over the specified beats of music. The hips begin a hip scoop by moving down from their starting position, across the line of the body and up to finish at a position one half circle away from their starting position. In order to execute a hip scoop the knees must alternately straighten and bend. The leg under the the beginning position will be straight while the other knee will be bent when the hip scoop begins. The straight leg bends its knee as the hips move across the line of the body, and the knee of the other leg straightens as the hip scoop is completed.
For example, "beats 1-4 Hip scoop (begin left hip to left side)" instructs you to move your hips to the left side position (if they are not already there) by straightening your left knee and bending your right knee, bend the knee of your left leg, push your hips in a straight line across your body, and straighten the knee of your right leg.
A hip scoop is very much like a half hip roll. However, in hip rolls the hips move around the body on a horizontal plane (or plane parallel to the floor) but in a hip scoop, the hips move across the line of the body on a vertical plane (or a plane perpendicular to the floor).

Hitch   Instructs you to bend your knee and raise your leg. During a hitch, the thigh of the hitching leg should be almost parallel to the floor. The feet are almost always parallel to each other although, on occasion, a hitch across or to the side may be specified.

Hitch-hike   Instructs you to bend the designated arm at the elbow and move the hand over the shoulder of that arm. The hand is held with the fingers folded and the thumb perpendicular to the palm.

Hold   This one is easy. 'Hold' instructs you to maintain your position, or do nothing, for the designated beats of music.

Home   Describes a position in which your feet are directly under your body and are parallel to one another. For example, when you are instructed to move your right foot 'home', you are to return it to a comfortable standing position under your right hip. When used in a combination, home also refers to your location just before the combination began. ('Home' is sometimes used to refer to your initial starting position on the dance floor, but that definition will not be used in this book.)

Hook   Instructs you to bend your knee, raise your leg, and cross it in front of or behind the weighted leg. The leg to be hooked and whether it crosses in front of or behind the weighted leg will be specified in the step description. The hooked leg crosses the weighted leg slightly below knee level with the shin nearly parallel to the floor. The foot of the hooked leg should be turned out. This movement is done in one beat of music. On occasion, a step description will instruct you to hook your leg to the side. In a hook to the side, the hooked leg will angle out to the side and the toe will point down.

For example, 'hook **right** leg across **left** leg' instructs you to bend the knee of your right leg, lifting it off the floor, and to cross your right leg in front of your left leg. Your right foot should be turned out.

J

Jazz Box   Instructs you to make three steps, in a specified order, to three beats of music. A jazz box will be described as either right or left, based on the foot that makes the crossing move and leads the jazz box. On beat one, the leading foot steps across the following foot. On beat two, the following foot steps back. On beat three, the leading foot steps to the side (parallel to and shoulder width away from the following foot). Note that you will touch three corners of an imaginary square (or box) as you make these three steps. Jazz boxes are also called 'jazz squares'.

As with vines, a fourth, 'finishing move' for the foot that is free to move after the jazz box is often specified (and, actually, may complete the box). In some dances, rather than having a 'finishing move', the jazz box is preceded by a step (to make up 4 steps). Some jazz box instructions may include turns (giving a funny look to the imaginary box). That is, you will see directions like 'right jazz box with left step' or 'right step with left jazz box ' or 'right jazz box with ¼ turn right'.

For example, 'right jazz box with left step' instructs you to: on '1', step your right foot across your left foot, on '2', step your left foot back, on '3', step your right foot to the right side, and on '4', step your left foot next to your right foot, to a rhythm of 1,2,3,4.

Jump   Instructs you to jump in the specified direction, lifting off from and landing on both feet. Jumps are done to one beat of music.

Jump-   Instructs you to make two jumps and one turn in three beats of music. The direc-
Cross-Turn tion of the turn will be specified in the dance description. On beat '1', the dancer jumps, landing with feet about shoulder width apart. On beat '2', the dancer jumps again, landing with the legs crossed. The leg which is named by the direction of the turn must be crossed behind the other leg. On beat '3', the dancer pivots ½ turn in the direction specified, 'uncrossing' the legs. As with vines and many other three step combinations, a fourth, finishing move is often specified when a jump-cross-turn is used in 4/4 time music.

For example, 'jump-cross-turn to the left' instructs you to: on '1', jump and land with feet apart; on '2', jump and land with left leg crossed behind right leg; and on '3', pivot ½ turn to the left on the balls of both feet.

Some dancers find jump-cross-turns too jarring, especially when several are done in rapid succession. Because of this, an alternative to the jump-cross-turn has been developed. It proceeds as follows: on '1', touch, to the side, the toe of the foot opposite the direction of the turn; on '2', step the foot opposite the direction of the turn across the other foot (leaving weight on both feet); and on '3', pivot half a turn in the direction specified (as in the jump-cross-turn).

For example, (replacing a jump-cross-turn to the left): on '1', touch your right toe to the right side; on '2', step your right foot across your left foot; and on '3', pivot ½ turn to the left on the balls of both feet.

K

Kick
Instructs you to kick the specified foot about halfway between the floor and knee-height. Kicks are most often done forward, but the direction of the kick will be specified in the step instruction. In line dancing, kicks are done with the toes pointing up, as if to shake *something* off the boot.

Kick-Ball-Change
Instructs you to make three steps, in a specified order, to two beats of music. The foot that begins or leads the kick-ball-change will be specified in the dance description. On the first beat of a kick-ball-change, the leading foot is kicked forward (about six inches off the floor). On the half beat, the ball of the leading foot steps next to the following foot. On the second beat, the following foot steps in place. The dancer should note that this third movement is subtle. The following foot has not moved: it has simply stepped in place. An alternative way to think of this third movement is as a transfer of body weight from the leading foot to the following foot.

For example, 'right kick-ball-change' instructs you to kick your right foot forward, step the ball of your right foot next to your left, and step your left foot in place, to a rhythm of 'one-and-two'.

Kick-Ball-Touch
Instructs you to make three steps, in a specified order, to two beats of music. The foot that begins or leads the kick-ball-touch will be specified in the dance description. On the first beat of a kick-ball-touch, the leading foot is kicked forward (about six inches off the floor). On the half-beat, the ball of the leading foot steps next to the following foot. On the second beat, the following foot touches as specified.

For example, 'right kick-ball-touch' instructs you to kick your right foot forward, step the ball of your right foot next to your left, and touch your left foot in place, to a rhythm of 'one-and-two'.

Knee Roll
Instructs you to bend your knee and move it in a circular motion in a specified number of beats. The direction (clockwise or counter-clockwise), extent of rotation (half-circle or full circle) and the starting position of the knee (e.g., left diagonal forward) will be specified. The knee roll is a continuous movement over the specified beats of music. As with a knee swivel, knee rolls are generally easier to execute if the weight of the body is supported primarily on the foot opposite the rolling knee. The knee that rolls pivots on the ball of the foot.

For example, "beats 1-2 Full left knee roll, counter-clockwise (begin forward)" instructs you to push your knee forward (if it is not already there), move it in a circular motion left, then back, and continuing this circular motion, return it to its starting position

Knock knees
Instructs you to, on the designated musical beat, bring your knees together (much as you bring your hands together in a clap.)

L

Latin-
'Latin-' is used as a prefix with a variety of steps and instructs you to sway your hips in the direction of the moving foot. Unlike the bump, which is sharp and pronounced, this sway is a fluid movement of the hips from one location to the next.

For example, 'Latin-step **left** foot to left side' instructs you to step to the left, swaying your left hip to the left as you take the step.

Lean
Instructs you to change, temporarily, the verticality of your body for the beats

specified. Lean is used with foot directions to add body styling. When leaning accompanies hip bumps, the leaning is done from the waist up.

Leap   Instructs you to move the identified foot by lifting off from the other foot and landing on the ball of the identified foot in the specified location. As in a jump, in a leap both feet will be off the floor, if only for a moment.

For example, 'leap **right** foot forward' instructs you to lift off from your left foot and land forward on the ball of your right foot. This move will be more comfortable to execute if you bend, slightly, the knee of your right leg.

Lindy   Instructs you to make a sideways shuffle and two rocks in four beats of music. The direction of movement will be specified in the dance description.

For example, 'right Lindy' instructs you to: on '1&2', do a right shuffle to the right side; on '3', rock-step your left foot behind your right foot, as you face diagonally left; and on '4', rock forward on your right foot, still facing diagonally left.

This combination produces a look of pulling away from a starting point and being 'sprung' back to it. The shuffle and the first rock smoothly move in one direction. On the last rock, you will look as though you are being tugged back towards your starting point.

Lock   Indicates a foot position in which one leg is crossed tightly over the other. For example, "Slide **left** leg to lock across **right** foot" indicates that at the end of the slide, the left leg should be crossed over the right leg.

Lower body Instructs you to squat down a distance comfortable for you. If you are directed to lower your body over several contiguous beats, lower only slightly on each beat so that you finish the sequence in a comfortable squat.

Lower foot Instructs you to return one part of the designated foot to the floor. For example, 'lower **left** heel' would most often follow a move that put your left heel in the air and tells you to return that heel to the floor. When lowering a toe or a heel, the move is like a touch, unless you are also told, in parenthesis, to step that foot down. Some dance writers use 'heel drop' to denote 'lower heel'.

Lunge   Instructs you to take a long step in the indicated direction, bending the knee of the stepping leg. When the step is forward, the move is like a fencing lunge.

Lunge-   Instructs you to move your foot to the indicated location, bending the knee of the
stomp   moving leg and bringing it to the floor in a stomp. Move as far in the indicated direction as you are comfortably able to move.

M

Military   Instructs you to make a 180 degree ($\frac{1}{2}$) turn in two beats of music. The direction
Turn   of the turn (right or left) will always be specified. On beat one, the foot opposite the direction of the turn steps forward. On beat two, the body makes a half turn in the direction specified, pivoting on the balls of both feet. A 'military turn' includes only one instruction for a change of foot location: at the close of a military turn the dancer will be standing with one foot in front of the other with weight supported by both feet and either foot is ready to move next.

For example, 'military turn to the left' instructs you to, on beat one, step forward on your right foot and, on beat two, pivot $\frac{1}{2}$ turn left on the balls of both feet. At the close of a 'military turn to the left' the dancer will be standing with feet separated and with the right foot behind the left.

Monterey   Instructs you to make four movements in four beats of music. The direction of the
Turn   turn will be specified in the dance description. On '1', touch the lead foot (the foot in the direction of the turn) to the side. On '2', on the ball of the following foot, pivot $\frac{1}{2}$ turn in the direction specified. Step the lead foot next to the following foot as the turn is completed. On '3', touch the toe of the following foot to the side. On '4', the following foot will be directed to touch or step next to the lead foot.

For example, 'Monterey turn to the right' instructs you to: on '1', touch your right toe to the side; on '2', pivot $\frac{1}{2}$ turn to the right on your left foot, stepping your right foot next to your left as you complete this turn; on '3', touch your left toe to the left side; and on '4', step your left foot next to your right.

O

Opposing Swivels Instructs you to swivel both feet so that they move from their beginning position to one that is either *turned out, turned in,* or back to *parallel.* The direction of the opposing swivels will be specified in the dance description (to left, to right, or to center) and both feet will turn toward the direction specified. However, one foot will turn its heel and the other will turn its toe toward that direction. In opposing swivels, your weight will always be on the ball of one foot and the heel of the other. The movement is identical to a swivel of one heel and a swivel of the other toe done at the same time.

If the feet are in *parallel* position when opposing swivels begin, the foot named in the direction of the movement swivels its toe in that direction and the other foot swivels its heel. This movement will result in a slight movement of your body in the direction specified. For example, starting in *parallel* position, "opposing swivels to right" instructs you to swivel your right toe to the right and your left heel to the right. When you finish this movement, your feet will be *turned out.*

If the feet are in any position other than *parallel,* the matter of which foot swivels its toe and which foot swivels its heel will be determined by the pattern that moves the body in the direction specified. For example, starting in *turned in* position, "opposing swivels to right" instructs you to swivel your right toe to the right and your left heel to the right. When you finish this movement, your feet will be *turned out.* However, starting in *turned out* position, "opposing swivels to right" instructs you to swivel your right heel to the right and your left toe to the right. When you finish this movement, your feet will be *turned in.*

When the instruction to do opposing swivels *to center* is given, return your feet to parallel position. If the preceding opposing swivels moved you to the right, return to center by swiveling left, and vice versa.

Opposing swivels are like swivets in that your weight is on the ball of one foot and the heel of another. However, in a swivet your toes always point in the same direction; in opposing swivels, they point in opposite directions (except when you are instructed to do opposing swivels to center).

Other names for opposing swivels are Applejacks, Fancy Feet, and Crazy Feet.

P

Paddle Turn Instructs you to make a turn while you alternate weight from your 'anchor' foot (the foot in the direction of the turn) to your 'paddle' foot. In a paddle turn you will make a series of small turns in order to complete a $\frac{1}{4}$, $\frac{1}{2}$, $\frac{3}{4}$ or full turn. Each small turn will involve stepping the 'anchor' foot in place but toward the direction of the turn and stepping the 'paddling' foot in the direction of the turn at about shoulder width from the anchor foot. The paddle turn has the look of a boat going around in a circle as it is paddled with one oar. The number of beats it will take to execute the turn, the total amount of the turn and the direction of the paddle turn will be specified in the dance description.

For example, 'beats 1-4 $\frac{1}{4}$ Paddle turn to the left' instructs you to: on '1', step your left foot in place and pointed diagonally left, on '2', step your right foot parallel to your left foot about shoulder width apart (completing a $\frac{1}{8}$ turn to the left), on '3', step your left foot in place and diagonally left, and on '4', step your right foot parallel to your left about shoulder width apart (completing another $\frac{1}{8}$ turn to the left).

Parallel Indicates that one foot is held in essentially the same direction as the other foot. 'Parallel' for you should be your comfortable standing position.

Pigeon Toes See Heel Split

Pivot Instructs you to turn. The amount of the turn will be specified ($\frac{1}{4}$ or 90 degrees, $\frac{1}{2}$ or 180 degrees, etc.) as will the direction of the turn (right or left). Pivots are usually done on the ball of the designated foot (or feet); however, on occasion a pivot is done on the heel of one foot and the ball of the other. Pivots are easier, if you "prepare" your pivoting foot by slightly pointing it in the direction of the turn before you step down to pivot.

For example, "pivot on **left** foot ¼ turn left" instructs you to turn 90 degrees left while your weight is supported by your left foot. You would begin this move by pointing your left foot diagonally left. The move is completed by pivoting the rest of the ¼ turn on the ball of your left foot.

If a pivot is done on both feet, pay attention to the subsequent step because, at the end of the turn, you will need to prepare for that move by supporting your weight on the leg opposite the leg that will move next. Consider, for example, a pivot on both feet in the following sequence of steps:

1 Step **right** foot forward
2 Step **left** foot forward
3 Pivot on **both** feet ¼ turn right
4 Step **left** foot forward

In this sequence, the turn on beat 3 would be executed by supporting the weight of the body over both feet. During this turn the feet maintain their positions on the floor that were indicated last: The right foot maintains its position from beat 1 and the left foot maintains its position from beat 2. However, when the turn is completed, most of the weight of the body should be supported by the right foot so that the left foot can move easily on beat 4.

Place   Instructs you to execute a foot action without changing the foot's location. In these cases you will be told to do the action 'in place'. For example, if you are told to 'step **right** foot in place' you are to put weight on your right foot, wherever it was after your preceding move.

Polka   Instructs you to make a shuffle and one other movement in two and a half beats of music. The direction of the polka (forward, backward, or to the side) and the foot that begins, or leads, the polka will be specified in the dance description. The three shuffle steps take place on beats '1 & 2'. The fourth step, which takes place on the next half beat after beat '2', may be a kick, turn, or hop and will be specified in the dance description. The steps are done to a rhythm of 'one-and--two-and'.

For example, 'right polka forward with ½ turn left' instructs you to: on '1', step forward on your right foot; on '&', step the ball of your left foot next to the heel of your right foot; on '2', step forward on your right foot; and on '&', pivot ½ turn left on the ball of your right foot.

R

Raise body or Rise   Generally instructs you to return your body from a squat position to your normal standing position. If you are directed to raise your body over several contiguous beats, raise only slightly on each beat so that you finish the sequence in your normal standing position. When told to 'rise on ball of a foot', raise your body slightly by stepping the foot with ball/toe on the floor and heel in the air.

Raise foot   Instructs you to move one part of a foot independent of another. For example, 'raise **right** toe' instructs you to lift the toe of your right foot off the floor while leaving the heel in place. When instructed to raise a heel, remember that you will need to bend the knee of that leg slightly in order to execute the move.

Reverse Three-Step turn   Instructs you to make one full turn in three steps to three beats of music. The turn will be labelled 'to right' or 'to left', indicating the direction of travel and the foot that leads the combination. Unlike a three-step turn, however, in a reverse three-step turn the direction of turn is opposite to (reverse) the direction of travel and opposite the foot that leads the combination. In other words, in a 'Reverse three-step turn to right' the first foot to move will be your right foot and you will be moving to the right, but you will make two half turns left. Most often, a reverse three-step turn will proceed as follows. On '1', step your lead foot (turned in) to the side. On '2', pivot on your lead foot ½ turn in the reverse direction and step your following foot to the side as the turn is completed. On '3', pivot on your following foot ½ turn in the reverse direction and step your lead foot to the side as the turn is completed. On occasion, steps '1' and '2' of a reverse three-step turn will be the turning steps with a step to the side being done on step '3'.

For example, a 'reverse three-step turn to left' means: on beat one, step your left foot (turned in) to your left side; on beat two, pivot on your left foot ½ turn right and step your right foot to your right side as the turn is completed; on beat 'three', pivot on your right foot ½ turn right and step your left foot to your left side as the turn is completed.

If the movement of a reverse three-step turn is not directly to the side, the direction of movement will be specified (for example, reverse three-step turn to left moving forward).

When reverse three-step turns are used in 4/4 time music, a fourth finishing move is often specified with the turn.

Rock	Instructs you to move your body in the direction specified, over the foot that is in that location. The instruction, 'rock', refers to movement of the body, and not the feet. If the dancer needs to move the foot in order to execute the body movement, the term 'rock-step' is used. A rock is easier to execute if the knees are bent slightly. For example, 'rock forward on **right** foot' instructs you to move, or lean, your body forward, over your right foot.
Rock-step	Instructs you to step in the direction specified but, unlike a simple 'step', it requires you to lean your body in the direction of the step. If the dancer does not need to move the foot in order to execute the body movement, the term 'rock' is used. A rock-step is easier to execute if the knees are bent slightly. For example, 'rock-step **left** foot back' instructs you to step back on your left foot and lean your body slightly back, over your left foot, as you take this step.
Romp	See Electric Kick
Running Man	Instructs you to make two movements on a beat and half beat. A running man will be identified as "right" or "left" depending upon which foot moves forward or "leads" the combination. The first movement will involve stepping the leading foot forward and the other foot back. This movement is quick and requires practice. It may help to think of it as jumping and landing with your feet apart. The second movement involves sliding the leading foot to its home position and hitching the other leg. As the name implies, a running man produces the look of running although you will not change your location on the dance floor. For example, " right running man" instructs you to: on "1" step your right foot forward and your left foot back and, on "&" slide your right foot home and hitch your left leg.

S

Sailor Step	Instructs you to make three foot movements in two beats of music. The foot to lead (begin) the pattern, and whether it steps across or behind, will be specified. On beat one, the lead foot steps across or behind the following foot. On the half-beat, the following foot steps to the side. On beat two, the lead foot steps to the side (or as specified). When a sailor step is completed, the feet are about shoulder width apart. In a sailor step, the body leans slightly in the direction of the foot to move first. For example, 'right sailor step (begin behind)' instructs you to step your right foot behind your left, step your left foot to the left side and step your right foot to the right side. These movements are done to a count of 'one and two'. Throughout a right sailor step, you would lean slightly to the right. Sailor steps are sometimes called sailor shuffles. Sailor steps that begin across are sometimes called across-ball-changes.

Scoot   Instructs you to make one movement in one beat of music. On a scoot, the weight of your body is supported by the identified foot and you take a small jump or hop in the indicated direction. This movement is subtle: you neither move very far nor come high off the floor.

Scissors   See Heel Split

Scuff   Instructs you to bring your heel in contact with the floor while you move your foot forward. This will make a noise and that is important in country-western dancing. Scuff sounds are often chosen to accentuate the rhythmic beats in the music to which the dance is done. The scuff involves no weight transfer.

For example, 'scuff **left** foot' instructs you to push or scrape your left heel against the floor. In 'scuff **left** foot' the right foot supports your weight during and after the scuff.

Shimmy   Describes an upper body movement in which the shoulders are alternately moved forward and backward in syncopated rhythm (i.e. on beats and half-beats).

For example, beats 1-4 Shimmy shoulders' tells you to: on '1', move your right shoulder forward (left goes back); on '&', move your left shoulder forward; on '2', move your right shoulder forward; and on '&' move your left shoulder forward, and so on.

Dance descriptions may call for shimmies with or without foot movements. Some individuals, particularly men, inadvertently do hip wiggles instead of shimmies and these hip movements may interfere with foot movements. Thus, alternatives to shimmies, which do not interfere with foot movements, may be offered as 'variations'.

Shuffle   Instructs you to make three steps, in a specified order, to two beats of music. The direction of the shuffle (forward, backward, or to the side) and the foot that begins, or leads, the shuffle, will be specified in the dance description. On the first beat of music in a shuffle, the leading foot steps in the direction specified. On the half-beat, the following foot steps next to leading foot. On the second beat of music, the leading foot again steps in the specified direction. In a shuffle, feet are gently dragged or barely lifted from position to position.

For example, 'right shuffle forward' instructs you to step forward on your right foot, step your left foot next to your right foot, and step forward on your right foot, to a rhythm of 'one-and-two'.

A shuffle is different from a cha-cha. Like a shuffle, the cha-cha includes three steps to two beats of music, however, in a shuffle forward or back, the second step does not move beyond the lead foot while in a cha-cha the three steps are equally long. Sometimes a shuffle is called a triple step.

Side Jack   Instructs you to make four movements in two beats of music. The foot which leads the move will be identified in the dance description. On the half-beat before '1', the leading foot steps to the side. On '1', the following foot steps to the side. On '&', the leading foot steps home. On '2', the following foot steps home or as specified..

For example, 'Side Jack (begin right)' instructs you to: on '&', step your right foot to the right side, on '1', step your left foot to the left side, on '&', step your right foot home, and on '2', step your left foot home.

Skate   Instructs you to move the identified foot by bending the knee of that leg and sliding the foot from a position under the center of the body to the specified location, at which the leg is straightened. When a skate is completed, all or most of the weight is on the skating foot. A skate is usually easier to execute on the ball of the foot.

For example, 'skate **left** foot to left side' instructs you to move your left foot home (if it is not already there), bend your left knee, and slide your left foot to the left side. You would 'unbend' or straighten your leg (to a normal standing position) as your foot reaches the left side.

Slap   Instructs you to slap your foot (or other identified body part). The instruction will identify the slapping hand and the body part. The left hand always slaps the left side of the designated parts and the right hand slaps the right side.

Slide   Instructs you to move the designated foot while keeping it lightly in contact with the floor. This move produces a look of the foot being pulled from one position to the next. When a slide is completed, all or most of the weight is on the sliding foot. Note that a slide is different from a slide-up. In a slide, the sliding foot bears weight; in a slide-up, it does not.

For example, 'slide **right** foot next to **left** foot' instructs you to move your right foot from its last position to a position next to your left foot, keeping your right foot lightly in contact with the floor. As you finish the move, put all or most of your weight on the right foot.

Slide-up   Instructs you to move the designated foot while keeping it lightly in contact with the floor. This move produces a look of the foot being pulled from one position to the next. When a slide-up is completed, the sliding foot is touching the floor but bears no weight. Note that a slide is different from a slide-up. In a slide, the sliding foot bears weight; in a slide-up, it does not.

For example, 'slide-up **right** foot next to **left** foot' instructs you to move your right foot from its last position to a position next to your left foot, while keeping your right foot lightly in contact with the floor.

Sliding Toe Strut   Instructs you to execute a toe strut using a slide-up, instead of a touch, for the first movement. For example, 'Right sliding toe strut forward' instructs you to, on beat '1' slide-up your right toe forward and on beat '2', lower your right heel, thereby stepping your right foot down. Keep in mind that, similar to toe struts, the slide-up on beat '1' may bear some weight, particularly when a turn is involved.

Slow   Instructs you to perform the designated step over two beats of music rather than one. For example, 'slow touch **right** heel forward' instructs you to use two beats of music to touch your right heel to the floor. Initially, the slow move may feel clumsy and seem difficult to do.

Most steps are choreographed to match one beat of music. Although not used in this book, a step done to one beat of music is often called a 'quick' step. It is in contrast to the name 'quick' that steps done to two beats of music are called 'slow'. Steps done on half-beats of music are often called 'syncopated'.

Spiral   Instructs you to make a three step movement to three beats of music. Spirals also involve facing specific directions on each step. A spiral will be described as either a right spiral or left spiral, indicating the foot that moves first. On the first beat, the designated foot will step across the other as you face diagonally in the direction of movement. On the second beat, the other foot steps to the side (this is usually a small step) and you face diagonally in the other direction. On the third beat, facing the same direction as on the second beat, the foot that was first to move steps in place.

For example, "left spiral" instructs you to: 1.) step your left foot across your right foot as you face diagonally right, 2.) step your right foot to the right side and face diagonally left, 3.) step your left foot in place and continue to face diagonally left. Spirals often appear in a series, alternating left and right (or right and left). In such a series of movements it is easy to see the s-shaped motion underlying the name.

Spirals are different from twinkles in that in a spiral, the three steps are taken in different locations on the floor but in a twinkle all three steps are taken at the same point on the floor. Both a spiral and a twinkle involve a change in the orientation of your body, but in spirals the change is always small and temporary while in twinkles the change is more variable.

Step   Instructs you to position your foot at the identified location and to transfer all or most of your weight to that foot. The amount of weight transferred usually depends on the sequence of steps.

For example, 'step **right** foot forward' instructs you to position your right foot ahead of your left (as though you were walking forward), with your weight supported on your right foot, leaving your left foot ready to move next.

Stomp   Instructs you to bring the identified foot down with force and with a weight transfer to the stomping foot. This will make a noise and, as with scuffs, stomp sounds are often used to accentuate the beats of the music. A 'stomp' differs from a 'stomp-up' in that in a 'stomp' the stomping foot bears weight, but in a 'stomp-up', it does not.

For example, 'stomp **right** foot next to **left** foot' instructs you to bring your right foot down with force next to your left. Your right foot supports all or most of your weight after the stomp.

Stomp-up   Instructs you to bring the identified foot down with force, but without a weight transfer to the stomping foot. This will make a noise and, as with scuffs, stomp sounds are often used to accentuate the beats of the music. A 'stomp' differs from a 'stomp-up' in that in a 'stomp' the stomping foot bears weight, but in a 'stomp-up', it does not.

For example, 'stomp-up **right** foot next to **left** foot' instructs you to bring your right foot down with force next to your left. Your left foot supports your weight during and after the stomp.

Straighten knee   Instructs you to return a leg that has been bent to its normal standing position.

Stroll   Instructs you to make three steps diagonally forward to three beats of music. A stroll will be described as either a right stroll or left stroll, indicating the direction of movement and the foot that leads the move. On the first beat, the leading foot steps diagonally forward. On the second beat, the other foot slides to a position where it is locked behind the leading foot. On the third beat, the leading foot moves diagonally forward.

For example, 'right stroll' instructs you to: on '1', step your right foot diagonally forward, on '2', slide your left foot to lock behind your right foot, and on '3', step your right foot diagonally forward.

As with vines, when strolls are used in 4/4 time music, a fourth, 'finishing move' for the foot that is free to move after the stroll is often specified with the stroll.

Sugar Foot   Instructs you to make a heel and toe touch of a designated foot to two beats of music. For these two beats, the weight is supported by the other foot. In a sugar foot, sometimes the heel touches first and sometimes the toe touches first: the order will be specified in the dance description. The heel and toe touches are both done next to the weighted foot. On the heel touches, the foot is turned out. On the toe touches, the foot is turned in.

For example, "Right toe-heel sugar foot" instructs you to, on "1", touch your right toe next to your left foot (right foot turned in), and on "2", touch your right heel next to your left foot (right foot turned out).

Sway   Gives you an instruction for hip movement independent of foot movement. Sway instructs you to move your hips, one time, on the designated musical beat. The hip that moves out (right or left) and the direction of the sway (e.g., forward, backward) will be specified in the dance description. In a sway, your weight is supported by both feet. Sways generally are easier to execute if the knees are bent slightly. Unlike the bump, which is sharp and pronounced, a sway is a fluid movement of the hips from one location to the next.

Swing   Instructs you to lift the identified foot off the floor and move it in a smooth, fluid motion in an arc. The amount of movement (¼ or ½ circle), the direction of movement (clockwise or counterclockwise), the beginning position, and the beats in which the movement must be completed, will be specified in the dance description. Unless otherwise directed, lift your foot about six inches off the floor.

For example, 'Right ¼ swing clockwise (begin forward)' instructs you to put your right foot forward, about six inches off the floor, and, leaving your leg in the air and extended, move your leg clockwise in a quarter circle, to the right side position.

A swing is like a *rondé*, except in a *rondé* the foot is on the floor. A swing is also known as a *rond de jambe en l'air*.

Swivel heels Instructs you to turn one or both heels in the direction specified (i.e. left, right or center). Movement is executed by supporting the weight on the balls of the swiveling feet and turning the heels approximately 45 degrees in the direction indicated. While your feet move in this step, your body continues to face forward. Note that a 'swivel' is different from a 'twist' in which your body would be allowed to move with your feet. Note also, 'swivel heels' (in which your heels are turned) is different from 'swivel toes' (in which your toes are turned.)

For example, 'swivel heels to left' instructs you to put your body weight over the balls of both feet and turn your heels to the left. Note that when you complete this move, your toes will be pointed to the right. 'Swivel heels to center' instructs you to return your heels to their starting position under your body.

Swivel knee Instructs you to bend the identified knee and turn it in the direction specified (i.e. left, right or center). Movement is executed by supporting the weight primarily on the foot opposite the swiveling knee. The knee that moves turns about 45 degrees in the direction indicated and the leg pivots on the ball of the foot.

For example, 'Swivel **left** knee to left side' instructs you to support your weight on the right foot, raise your left heel and turn your leg to the left. 'Swivel **left** knee to center' instructs you to support your weight on the right foot, raise your left heel and turn your leg so that your feet are in parallel position.

Swivel toes Instructs you to turn one or both toes in the direction specified (i.e. left, right or center). Movement is executed by supporting the weight on the heels of both feet and turning the toes approximately 45 degrees in the direction indicated. While your feet move in this step, your body continues to face forward. Note that a 'swivel' is different from a 'twist' in which your body would be allowed to move with your feet. Note, also, that toe swivels differ from heel swivels in which you move your heels while supporting your weight on your toes.

For example, 'swivel toes to left' instructs you to put your body weight over the heels of both feet and turn your toes to the left. Note that when you complete this move, your toes will be pointed to the left. 'Swivel toes to center' instructs you to return your toes to their starting position under your body.

Swivet Instructs you to swivel both feet, on the heel of one and ball of the other. Both feet turn approximately 45 degrees in the direction specified and then back to center in two beats of music. The direction of the swivet identifies the direction your toes will point on the first movement. The foot named in the direction of the swivet swivels its toe and the other foot swivels its heel. While swiveling, your weight will be on the heel of one foot and the ball of the other. At the completion of a swivet, both feet will be centered under your body and flat on the floor.

For example, 'swivet to right' instructs you to: on '1', swivel your right toe to the right and your left heel to the left; and on '2', swivel your right toe to center and your left heel to center.

Syncopated pattern Indicates a set of steps that deviate from the standard step pattern for a particular type of dance or combination.

T

Tap Instructs you to move a particular part of your foot to the identified location without a weight transfer. In contrast to a touch, however, your foot will make only momentary contact with the floor. In a touch, your foot will stay in contact with the floor until the next step description. In a tap, raise your foot from the floor immediately after it makes contact with the floor. Directions to tap specify the part of the foot that should be used to execute the move. Frequently, when an instruction to tap is given, the toe or heel is moving in isolation. Please note that some dance writers use touch and tap synonymously. We do not. In our books, they are given different, specific definitions.

For example, 'tap **left** heel in place (toe remains on floor from beat 5)' instructs you to bring your left heel to the floor, without moving your toe, and immediately lift your heel up from the floor.

Three-Step Turn
Instructs you to make one full turn in three steps to three beats of music. The turn will be labelled right or left, indicating the direction of the turn and the foot that leads the combination. Most often, a three-step turn will proceed as follows. On '1', step your lead foot to the side and pivot ½ turn in the indicated direction. On '2', step your following foot to the side and pivot another ½ turn in the indicated direction. On '3', step your lead foot to the side. On occasion, step '1' of a three-step turn will be the step to the side, with the foot turned out, with the half turns being done on steps '2' and '3'.

For example, a 'three-step turn to left' means: on beat '1', step your left foot to your left side and pivot ½ turn left; on beat '2', step your right foot to your right side and pivot ½ turn left; on beat '3', step your left foot to your left.

If the movement of a three-step turn is not directly to the side, the direction of movement will be specified (for example, three-step turn to left moving forward). Although we do not use this label, three-step turns are sometimes called 'rolling vines'. Three-step turns are often done as variations in place of vines or step-slide-step patterns. When three-step turns are used in 4/4 time music, a fourth finishing move is often specified with the turn.

Toe Fan
Instructs you to make two swivel movements of the identified foot in two beats of music. On '1', the toe swivels away from the stationary foot. On '2', the toe swivels to center.

For example, 'right toe fan' instructs you, on '1', to swivel your right toe to the right, and on '2', to swivel your right toe to center.

Toe Split
Instructs you to move your toes apart and then bring them back together in two beats of music. A toe split will begin from a position in which your feet are together and your weight is supported by both feet. On beat one, move your toes apart. To execute this move, have your weight on the heels of your feet and move your right toe to the right and your left toe to the left. On beat two, move your toes back together.

Toe Strut
Instructs you to execute two movements of one foot in two beats of music. The strutting foot, and the direction of the strut (e.g. forward or backward) will be specified in the dance description. On beat '1', the toe is touched in the direction of travel. On beat '2', the heel is lowered and weight is transferred to that foot.

For example, 'left toe strut forward' instructs you on beat one to touch your left toe forward. On beat two, lower your left heel to the floor and step down on your left foot.

It is important to note that although 'touch' is used to describe the movement on the first beat, in a toe strut this touch may bear some weight. This is especially true if the toe strut is involved in a turn.

Touch
Instructs you to position your foot at the identified location without a weight transfer. Many dancers execute a touch by touching only with the toe of the boot.

For example, 'touch **right** foot next to **left** foot' instructs you to bring your right foot next to your left and lightly touch the floor, leaving your right foot ready to move next.

Traveling Opposing Swivels
Instructs you to do a series of opposing swivels on successive beats and half-beats. The number of beats used by the combination will be specified in the dance description as will the direction of movement. The series of opposing swivels will move your body in the direction specified and the positions of your feet will alternate between *turned out* and *turn in*. The series of opposing swivels

will most likely end by returning your feel to *parallel* position. Other names for traveling opposing swivels are Applejacks, Fancy Feet, and Crazy Feet.

Triple Step   See Shuffle; Also used to refer to any three step pattern done to a rhythm of one-and-two.

Turn   Indicates that the orientation of your body (direction or wall that you face) will change. There are different kinds of turns (pivot, military turn, etc.) and each will be defined as needed.

Instructions to turn will specify a direction and amount of turn. Sometimes dancers become confused with the direction specified for a turn. To turn left means to turn counterclockwise. One way to ensure that you are turning in the prescribed direction is to think of your shoulders. In a turn to the *left*, you will turn toward your left shoulder. Your *left shoulder will move backwards*, while your right shoulder moves forward. Similarly, in a turn to the *right*, you will turn toward your right shoulder. Your *right shoulder will move backwards*, while your left shoulder moves forward. The amount of turn may be given as fractions of a full circle ($\frac{1}{8}$, $\frac{1}{4}$, $\frac{1}{2}$, etc.) or in degrees (90 degrees, 180 degrees, etc.).

Turned In   Indicates that the toe of one foot points diagonally toward the other foot. When the right foot is 'turned in', its toe points diagonally left. When the left foot is 'turned in', its toe points diagonally right.

Turned Out   Indicates that the toe of one foot points diagonally away from the other. When the right foot is 'turned out' its toe points diagonally right. When the left foot is 'turned out' its toe points diagonally left.

Twinkle   Instructs you to make a three step movement to three beats of music. A twinkle will involve taking all three steps at the same point on the floor and making a specified degree of turn. The foot that leads the twinkle, the location at which you step, and the degree of turn involved in the twinkle will be specified in the dance description. On beat one, step to the identified location with your lead foot, on beat two, step your following foot very close to your lead foot, and on beat three, step your lead foot in place. You will be instructed to make some degree of turn in the twinkle and most often this turn will take place on the first beat.

For example, "beats 1-3, Left twinkle across, $\frac{1}{8}$ turn left" instructs you to: on beat 1, step your left foot across your right foot and pivot $\frac{1}{8}$ turn left, on beat 2, step your right foot very close to your left foot, and on beat three step your left foot in place.

Twinkles are different from spirals in that in a twinkle, all three steps are taken at the same point on the floor but in a spiral the three steps are in different locations. Both a twinkle and spiral involve a change in the orientation of your body, but in spirals the change is always small and temporary while in twinkles the change is more variable.

Twist   Instructs you to turn your body without lifting your feet from the floor. The direction of the twist will be specified. Generally, twists are rather small moves and 'twist right' or 'twist left' instructs you to move about 45 degrees in the specified directions. Occasionally, a bigger movement will be required. In these cases, the dance description will contain more precise information, such as 'twist $\frac{1}{4}$ turn right'. Often, after a series of twists, 'twist center' will instruct you to return your body to a forward facing position. Twists are easier to execute if the knees are bent slightly and the weight is over the balls of the feet, not the heels.

For example, 'twist left' instructs you to turn your body diagonally left by supporting your weight on the balls of your feet and moving your heels to the right.

V

Vaudeville   Instructs you to make four movements to two beats of music. The foot that be-
Kick   gins (leads) the combination is specified. On beat "1", the lead foot steps across the following foot. On "&", the following foot steps back (or as specified). On "2", the following heel touches forward or diagonally forward, and, on "&", the lead

foot steps home. To complete the vaudevillian look, try leaning slightly back as you touch your heel forward.

For example, "Right Vaudeville kick" instructs you to: On "1", step your right foot across your left foot; On "&", step your left foot back; On "2", touch your right heel forward; On "&", step your right foot home.

Vine
Instructs you to make a three step sideways movement to three beats of music. A vine will be described as either a right vine or left vine, indicating the direction of movement and the foot that moves first. On the first beat, the designated foot will move to the side. On the second beat, the other foot is crossed behind the first before it steps down. On the third beat, the foot that was first to move, moves again to the side.

For example, 'right vine' instructs you to step your right foot to the right, step your left foot behind your right and, and finally, step your right foot to the right.

When vines are used in 4/4 time music, a fourth, 'finishing move' for the foot that is free to move after the vine is often specified with the vine. For example, you will see directions like 'right vine with left scuff' or 'left vine with right touch'.

If the movement of a vine is not directly to the side, the direction of movement will be specified (for example, left vine diagonally back).

Vines are also referred to as 'grapevines'. Other dance descriptions may use 'vine' or 'grapevine' to describe combinations other than the one described above. That is, combinations that begin with a step other than the side step, or combinations that include more than one cross step are called vines. To avoid confusion, we use other labels to refer to these less common vines (see, for example, 'weave').

W

Waltz Rhythm
Waltzes are done to music played in 3/4 rhythm. Waltz music is counted 1-2-3, 1-2-3 with a stress on the "1". In country-western dancing, waltz dance steps are traditionally counted in two groups of three beats (1-2-3, 4-5-6). With some exceptions, your feet will alternate left - right - left, right - left - right, making it easy to remember which foot moves next: The one different from the one you just moved! In dancing a waltz, it is important to remember that these dances are distinguished not only by the type of music to which the dance is done, but by the style with which the steps are taken. Waltzing is characterized by a subtle accent or emphasis placed on the step to the first beat of each three beat sequence. The accent involves a "fall" on the first beat, followed by a "rise" on beats 2 and 3. In line dancing, the look of falling and rising is achieved by making the first step in each three step unit relatively long, while the second and third steps in each three step unit are relatively short, and/or taken on the toes of the feet.

Weave
Instructs you to make a series of movements in which steps across and behind alternate with steps to the side. The number of beats involved in the weave will be specified in the dance description and each step will be done to one beat of music. The direction of the weave (e.g. 'to left', and 'diagonally right') will be specified. A weave will be identified by its initial step(s): across, behind, side then across, or side then behind.

For example, 'beats 1- 4 Weave to right (begin across)' tells you to: on '1', step your left foot across your right, on '2', step your right foot to the right side, on '3', step your left foot behind your right, and on '4', again step your right foot to the right side.

Doing a weave may feel very much like doing a vine. In fact, a weave is a special type of vine. It is different from vines in that the crossing steps are alternately in front of and behind the other foot and weaves may be longer than three steps.

Weighted leg
Refers to the leg supporting the weight of the body.

MORE BOOKS & CDS FOR DANCING FEET!

COUNTRY & WESTERN LINE DANCING FOR COWGIRLS & COWBOYS:
Step-by-Step Instructions

TOP VALUE BOOK & CD PACKAGE!

Also by the winning team of Judy Dygdon & Tony Conger, this has been the number 1 best-selling line dance package in the UK since we launched it in 1996. Packed with 53 dances to the same high quality as UK LINE DANCE FAVOURITES and supplied with a FREE CD – the same CD referred to throughout this book.

Just £12.95 for the complete package: that's 24 pence per dance plus the pleasure of a top-quality CD of authentic C&W music!

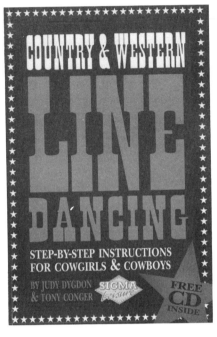

COUNTRY & WESTERN LINE DANCING FOR COWGIRLS & COWBOYS: THE ALBUM!

The dances in UK LINE DANCE FAVOURITES are all keyed to tracks on this CD – first produced for our top-selling book & CD package. The tracks are all tested and approved by the authors for learning both their old and new dances. It comes complete with a booklet of easy-to-learn line dances, so it's a great gift for your friends who aren't yet line dancing!

SPECIAL READER OFFER:

Store price is £7.95

Purchasers of this book can order the CD directly from Sigma Leisure for just £6.95!

In The Name Of Love Video, The ChildLine EP (STKV1) £12.99

An instructional video that accompanies the six track EP of the same name, it includes instruction for all six songs on the EP. The video inlay has printed dances for all six songs. Choreography is taught by Max Perry, one of the worlds leading line dance choreographers.
DANCES; In The Name Of Love, Ribbon Of Highway, The Last Time Slide, You Bad Thang, Christmas Card, Sexy Little Christmas Thang

The Ultimate Line Dance Reference Video (STKV2) £12.99

Tired of being on the outside looking in? Let International Instructor Jo Thompson take you step by step visually through the 49 most used line dance steps in the world. You will no longer feel intimidated on the dance floor. If you want to line dance, then you have to have the basics. You'll feel great on the dance floor!

Moving On Up Video (STKV3) £12.99

Instruction to 7 songs/dances from the latest Scooter Lee album. Features instruction by Max Perry, Joanne Brady & Charlotte Skeeters. Video inlay also includes dance notations.
DANCES; Locomotion 2000, Moving On Up, Make You Mine, OeeOeeO, Here Lately, Ribbon Of Highway, Dizzy

World Line Dance Classics Video (STKV4) £12.99

The ideal beginners video, 7 basic dances that every new dancer should know. Expertly taught by Lisa Kruse, 4 time International Line Dance Champion with 8 consecutive Grand Championships. The definitive beginners video!!!!
Dances; Tush Push, Crusin', Cowgirl's Twist, Louisiana Hot Sauce, Cowboy Strut, Waltz Across Texas, Honky Tonk Twist

The World Classic Partner Video (STKV5) £12.99

Partner dances are Line Dances that people can do alone or with another person. They are not gendered, so many times two girls will do a partner crusin' or waltz. Now that you know the Line Dance, grab a partner and do the partner version to 7 of the most popular dances in the World!
Partner dances must have a partner. That is why they are called partners. They were created by line dancers who had best friends or husbands or boy/girl friends. They got bored and said, lets do something different and dance together.
DANCES; Tush Push, West Coast Shuffle, Waltz Across Texas, Crusin', Last Time Slide, Ribbon Of Highway, Dizzy

The Best Of The Honky Tonk Twist & Scooter Lee's New Album Video (STKV6) £12.99

This video contains easy step-by-step instruction to tracks from Scooter's first two CD's. Instruction by Max Perry, Jo Thompson & Joanne Brady.
DANCES; The Honky Tonk Twist, Be-Bop-A-Lula, Louisiana Hot Sauce, Take It Away, Midnight Waltz, Heartbreak Hotel, Last Time Slide, Baby Once I Get You, Scooter Shuffle, Scooter's Couple Shuffle

High Test Love Video (STKV7) £12.99

Instruction to 8 songs/dances from Scooter's most loved albums, featuring instruction by Max Perry, Joanne Brady & Charlotte Skeeters.
DANCES; High Test Love, Merry Go Round, Scooch & Honey Hush, Twistin' The Night Away, Rompin' Stompin', Shadows Cha Cha, Country Rock & Roll Waltz, Lone Star Cha Cha, Bonus Dance West Coast Shuffle (Be Bop A Lula)

The Ultimate West Coast Swing Reference Video (STKV8) £12.99

West Coast Swing is considered one of the "Coolest" and "Sexiest" dances known to man (and woman) and no one does it better than the World Swing Champions themselves, Robert Royston and Laureen Baldovi who on this video take you step by step through basics to intermediate. Let the masters help you master the West Coast Swing!

The Ultimate Two-Step Reference Video (SKTV9) £12.99

Robert Royston & Laureen Baldovi, also Four Time World Champion Couple Dancers, guide you through basic, easy to follow, step by step instruction that will have you mastering the Two-Step in no time and leave you ready to try couple dancing!

THE CD'S

High Test Love (STKCD1) £14.99

A CD considered by many as Scooters best album.
Comes complete with 20 page full colour booklet
with lyrics and line dance notations.
*Songs; Rompin' Stompin', High Test Love, Shadows In The
Night, What Kind Of Fool, It's A Merry Go Round, Twistin'
The Night Away, Honey Hush, Rock & Roll Waltz, You
Know Where I Am, If You Only Knew*

In The Name Of Love (STKCD2) £6.99

Six track EP, booklet contains lyrics and line dance
notations for all six songs.
*Songs: In The Name Of Love, Ribbon Of Highway, Last
Time Uh Huh, You Bad Thang, A Christmas Card, Sexy
Little Christmas Thang*

Scooter Lee's New Album (SBDCD2) £9.99

Scooter's first album and available at mid-price.
*Songs; Don't Walk Away With My Heart, Last Time Uh-
Huh, Heartbreak Hotel-A Tribute, Can't Help It, No
Options Here, Baby Once I Get You, Losing My Mind, The
Way Things Are, Daniels Boys, Commit Me For Hangin'
On, Last Time Uh-Huh (Dance Mix), Baby Once I Get You (Dance Mix)*

The Honky Tonk Twist....And Then Some (SBDCD3) £9.99

Available at mid-price and containing 14 tracks,
three of which are special dance mixes.
*Songs; Honky Tonk Twist, Be-Bop-A-Lula, Old Friend,
Traces, I'll Two-Step Alone, He's My Little Jalapeno, Well-
Oiled Lovin' Machine, Deal With It, Take It From Me,
Where's Hank Williams (When You Need Him?), I Love The Nightlife, Honky Tonk
Twist (Dance Mix), Old Friend (Competition Mix), I Love The Nightlife (Dance Mix)*

Moving On Up (STKCD3) £14.99

Scooter's latest album which contains the huge
dance hits Dizzy and Locomotion as well as some
classic country songs. The booklet contains lyrics
and dance notations to all tracks.
*Songs; Locomotion, Moving On Up, I Wanna Make You
Mine, Blue Eyes, This Love Of Ours, OeeOeeO, Livewire,
Here Lately, Ribbon Of Highway, Let's Break Up Tomorrow, Dizzy*

LEARN TO DANCE: MODERN JIVE

Sigma is developing an exciting range of dance books and CDs. This new book & CD package is the only complete guide to Modern Jive – the fast and stylish partner dance that's also known as French-style Jive. It's a blend of jitterbug and rock 'n' roll that you can dance to music from fifties swing to today's chart hits!

In this book there are over 50 moves and 12 complete routines to make you the star of the dance floor! The authors are Robert Austin and Claire Hilliard, who run the highly successful leJIVE organisation in the UK.

Price for complete book and practice CD: £10.95, POST FREE – or through booksellers

START TO DANCE: FRENCH JIVE

This fabulous 12-track CD has been specially produced and engineered for jive dancing. It includes brand-new recordings of music from the gently-swinging "My Baby Just Cares For Me" to "Rhythm Is A Dancer" and a techno version of "Just Can't Get Enough" – something for everybody! It's the ideal party album, with a bonus: a booklet from the well-respected Le Roc organisation to teach you the basics of French Jive!

In-store price: £9.95

SPECIAL READER OFFER: £7.95

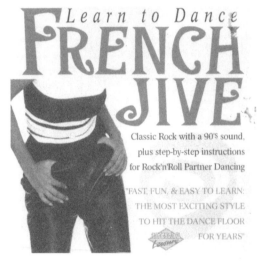

ALL PRICES INCLUSIVE OF POSTAGE – ABSOLUTELY NO EXTRAS!

We welcome VISA & MASTERCARD. Orders to:

Sigma Leisure, 1 South Oak Lane, Wilmslow, Cheshire, SK9 6AR. Tel: 01625-531035; Fax: 01625-536800

Our complete on-line catalogue is on the Internet:

http://www.sigmapress.co.uk